THE PARTY OF EROS

The Party of Eros

RADICAL SOCIAL THOUGHT
AND THE REALM OF FREEDOM

by Richard King

THE UNIVERSITY OF NORTH CAROLINA PRESS
CHAPEL HILL

Manufactured in the United States of America
ISBN 0-8078-1187-4
Library of Congress Catalog Card Number 73-174785

To TERRY WALTER O'HARA
1941-1965

CONTENTS

THE PARTY OF EROS

INTRODUCTION

The student of American intellectual history is plagued by the relationship of America to European thought. If one focuses exclusively on American thought, then a study tends toward the parochial. Conversely, if one treats American thought as an inferior derivative of European sources, one misses the unique features of the American experience and thus tries to fit themes of our intellectual development into theoretical structures formulated in significantly different historical and cultural contexts.

This study by no means escapes this dilemma. Its focus is on the way the thought of Sigmund Freud, no friend of America, has been used by three radical social theorists in the quarter century since the end of World War II. The temptation is thus to focus upon Freud and not the American thinkers who made use of his insights. Yet common sense and even a slight knowledge of the way ideas are transformed by diffusion through space and time reveals that there are many Freuds and many ways his teachings can be applied to social analysis, an area of concern in which Freud was only tangentially interested. The problem, however, does not end there. A minor, more submerged theme of this study is the fate of orthodox Marxist theory in postwar America and the effort to formulate a radical social theory, adequate to deal with unprecedented social and cultural developments, upon the ruins of the Marxist ideology which many considered to be morally and intellectually otiose by the middle 1940s.

There is finally American thought itself. It can be argued quite convincingly that American thought goes astray when it depends too closely upon European intellectual systems of whatever variety. Particularly since World War II one could maintain that, far from being a satellite caught in the orbit of European thought and experience, America has finally assumed the role which Gertrude Stein once attributed to her of being the oldest modern western nation. The possibility of general affluence, the emergence of a society given shape by bureaucratic and technological structures, the development of a far-reaching and all pervasive communication nexus, the political and cultural importance of youth have all become givens which Europeans are just now beginning to see emerging on the continent. Thus the most pertinent social theory concerned with advanced industrial societies should be detectable in the American rather than the European context. Indeed, another theme is that in the first quarter of the century, American social thinkers—Lester Ward, Thorstein Veblen, Randolph Bourne, John Dewey—were handling problems that would emerge with much more urgency after World War II and thus set the terms for much of the analysis that we will be examining here.

Several recent studies have touched upon the theme of radical Freudianism and, though I deal with them at greater length in the main body of this work, a word or two about each of them is in order. The first and most important of these studies is Philip Rieff's imaginatively conceived *The Triumph of the Therapeutic* (1966). In a sense my study is an application of some of Rieff's ideas to the particular context of American social and cultural thought. Paul Robinson's *The Freudian Left* (1969) appeared when I was nearly finished with the first draft of my study.[1] Though Robinson deals with Wilhelm Reich and Herbert Marcuse specifically (along with Geza Roheim), he takes them to be European thinkers primarily and does not concern himself with their place in or influence upon American thought. I do disagree with Robinson's rather uncritical discussion of Marcuse, but *The Freudian Left* is thorough and often incisive and thus of much use. *The Making of a Counter Culture* (1969) by Theodore Roszak appeared shortly after Robinson's work. Roszak devotes much attention to Paul Goodman as well as to Marcuse and Norman Brown as intellectual gurus of today's cultural dissidents. His chapter on Brown and Marcuse is often quite good, but his treatment of Goodman remains generally on the surface. In general, Roszak slights the development of each man's thought; and the implication is that the main values and themes of the counter culture have emerged almost ex nihilo within the last decade.

Readers will inevitably wonder about the omission of certain thinkers. I have chosen not to deal with Erich Fromm because he is, quite simply, not a sexual radical. As Goodman and Marcuse make clear, and as Fromm would admit, he abandoned Freud's libido theory quite early and generally plays down the importance of sexuality in individual and social analysis. A stronger case could be made for the inclusion of Norman Mailer, since he was profoundly influenced by Wilhelm Reich, the real "father" of the effort to combine doctrines of sexual and social liberation. Whatever Mailer's strengths as a participant-observer of sexuality in our society, and I think they are considerable, he is not a systematic thinker, but primarily a novelist and imaginative writer and thus does not receive much attention here.

I was not interested in writing a history of psychoanalytic thought in post-World War II America and for that reason have not dealt with Erik Erikson, psychohistorians Robert Jay Lifton and Kenneth Kenniston, or the so-called "Third Force" psychology represented by Abraham Maslow and Henry Murray. (I do deal with Gestalt therapy, but only in reference to the development of Paul Goodman's thought.) Each of these approaches quite obviously "takes off" from Freud, but in doing so lacks the sexual and/or the radical component which is my central concern.

My main interest is in ideas. For that reason I have avoided as much as possible a "psychoanalysis" of the thinkers in question. Such a study would possibly be fruitful; Marcuse and Brown, for instance, came relatively late and rather surprisingly to Freud from intellectual backgrounds having little to do with psychoanalytic interpretations of social and cultural reality. Nor have I gone into great detail concerning the sociological context within which these men formed their ideas or which proved receptive to their work. A major weakness of intellectual history is that it tends to degenerate into a catalogue of names and ideas linked by a vague something called "influence." Where tracing influences should be suggestive, it is too often exhaustive. Everything is discussed except the ideas themselves, their elaboration, and their validity. Thus much of my study is taken up with the development of certain ideas by certain thinkers. I have tried to be critical without nit-picking; and I have hopefully avoided excessive influence-mongering.

One might also wonder about the absence of any sort of theoretical discussion of race or black radicalism. As far as I know, few social critics have dealt with such problems as racism or racial identity on a theoretical level.[2] A white psychiatrist, Joel Kovel, has written an interesting study, *White Racism* (1970), which makes extensive and systematic use of Freud, Brown, and Marcuse. In the last chapter of *Soul on Ice* (1967) Eldridge Cleaver sketched out, in a prototheoretical way, the structure of sexual and social relationships in American society. And Harold Cruse has noted the debilitating effect that orthodox Marxist ideology has worked upon black radicalism and radical theory generally in twentieth-century America. Other than these studies, which touch upon the relationship of race to social and sexual theory, most students of American race relations have remained contented to apply psychosocial concepts at an individual or group level. Otherwise they have tended to use psychoanalytic terminology (such as paranoia) as a "screen" for moral judgments. All of these efforts are important, but it would seem that the answer to the questions that the black movement has raised about the nature of western culture and society, its value patterns, its crucial institutions, e.g., the family, would profit from an examination of thinkers such as Wilhelm Reich, Goodman, Marcuse, and Brown, though none of them deals with race to any significant degree.

To a certain degree the opposite is true of the radical ideology of Women's Liberation. Kate Millett's *Sexual Politics* exhaustively catalogued the male bias in Freud's thought and in general psychoanalyzed western society and culture to death. Millett also noted the importance of Wilhelm Reich as an alternative to Freud. (The irony here is that Reich personally was guilty of the most blatant sexual double standard and abhorred all deviations from genital sexuality.) As we shall see, Goodman's thought is very decidedly male-oriented, despite or because of his bisexuality. For Marcuse and Brown, men and women become Man in general, while sexual identity and differentiation receive little mention.

In summary, then, I do not deal with the problems of racial and sexual identity because Goodman, Marcuse, and Brown do not. To criticize them on these grounds has a certain validity, but seems to me beside the point. It is not the task of social theory to deal with each particular social and cultural problem. What social thought loses in specificity, it gains in generality by delineating the structures of existing social and cultural reality and then projecting a more desirable alternative. If, for example, there is a general connection between domination as cultural value and our sexual "organization," as Marcuse and Brown would have it, then the assumption is that such is true for male and female, black and white.

These previous remarks should also make clear that I am by no means discussing radical social theory as a whole, but rather a particular facet of postwar radical ideology. In fact, as the last chapter indicates, the implications of much of what Goodman, Marcuse, and Brown say are nonpolitical in the usual sense of the word. Because of a concern with fundamental values and attitudes implicit in western society, their thought has lent itself to what is often called cultural radicalism. In contrast with political and social radicalism, cultural radicalism is concerned with transforming consciousness, with changing the way we see and understand our reality, beyond any specific concern with such matters as elections or the ownership of the means of production. It is the argument of the cultural radicals that for external changes to be lasting, values and attitudes must also (or first) be changed.

Although it has become fashionable to advocate as well as

analyze, I must confess my ambivalence toward sexual radicalism and its offshoot, the ideology of the counter culture. My misgivings arise from the apparent tendency of Wilhelm Reich and Marcuse, and to a lesser extent, Goodman and Brown, to make public all private aspects of existence; to metaphorically see the bedroom as the battleground for change; in short, as Reich put it, to politicize sex. I suppose such a concern reflects my adherence to the classical liberal idea that it is not the duty of the state to promote the personal happiness of its citizens, but rather to minimize their unhappiness. Expressed another way, we are treading on dangerous ground when happiness becomes a public concern. Behind the concern with the transformation of basic values and attitudes lurks, as well, the doctrine of positive freedom, by which one may be forced to be "free" against his own conscious wishes. What we have with thinkers such as Marcuse, particularly, is an identification of freedom with happiness. Thus in our time the idea of positive freedom has become one with what we might call the idea of positive happiness. The further assumption is that there are some—an intellectual-political elite—who know the true content of freedom and happiness. Thus the old political question reappears: who rules the rulers?

And yet if there is anything that Marx and Freud and their epigones have taught us, it is that our inner selves are formed by external forces and that the dichotomy between public and private is largely a myth. I would nevertheless argue that individual autonomy is a useful fiction; but more, that individuals are more than the sum of the forces impinging upon them; and that one vital task of radical social theory is to extend the realm of choice, not hand it over to benevolent elites, and zealously guard the private and the personal realm, rather than speaking of its illusory nature. It is perhaps for these reasons that I find Paul Goodman a much more appealing thinker than Wilhelm Reich, Marcuse, or Brown.

My feelings about the ideology of the counter culture are much less divided. My suspicion is that a new "culture" or "consciousness" is not consciously created, but rather emerges imperceptibly over time. Thus I object most strongly to the impulse at large in the counter culture to promiscuously create a new religion, out of nothing or out of everything. It remains basically a narcissistic enterprise. One must, I suppose, grant that "its heart is in the right place," that much of what the counter culture objects to deserves attack, and that some of its impulses are good. Yet this seems to me insufficient grounds for joining up, since as the hoary old cliché has it: "The road to Hell is paved with good intentions."

1. THE FRAMEWORK OF AMERICAN SOCIAL THOUGHT

The End of Ideology

By the 1950s many observers felt that radical social thought and ideological politics, save for some atavistic rumblings from the Right, were things of the past. As early as 1948 Richard Hofstadter pointed to a historical consensus in American thought and politics when he wrote: "The sanctity of private property, the right of the individual to dispose of and invest it, the value of opportunity, and the natural evolution of self interest and self assertion . . . have been staple tenets of the central faith in American political ideologies."[1] As if to drive the point home Hofstadter noted in his *Age of Reform* (1955) that Franklin Roosevelt had been no radical at all, but rather the pragmatist par excellence, working to preserve by modification America's received economic and political structures. Moreover Hofstadter observed that the New Deal as an intellectual movement "for all its ferment of practical change produced a very slight literature of social criticism. . . . [It] produced no comparable body of political writing that would survive the day's headlines."[2]

Others echoed Hofstadter's "consensus" theme. To explain the historical paucity of interesting and systematic thinking about society and politics in America, Louis Hartz's *The Liberal Tradition in America* (1955) focused on two factors—America's lack of a feudal past and hence a society stratified on class lines, and the hegemony of the Lockean tradition of social contract and political individualism. And although addressing himself to two "conservative" thinkers, Morton White reenforced the Hofstadter-Hartz line when he wrote in the new preface (1957) to his *Social Thought in America*: "It seems to me a sad commentary on the social thought of today that two of the most popular social thinkers on the American scene (Walter Lippmann and Reinhold Niebuhr) can produce nothing more original or natural than the doctrines of original sin and natural law as answers to the pressing problems of the age."[3] For White, Hofstadter, Hartz, and others, such as David Potter in his *People of Plenty* (1954) and Lionel Trilling in *The Liberal Imagination* (1950), the flabbiness of liberal social thought, the irrelevance of conservative thought, and the nonexistence of a radical ideological tradition ill-served America's attempts to deal imaginatively or wisely with domestic and international problems in the post-World War II world.

Not all consensualists were of this unhappy, or at least worried, turn of mind. In 1953 Daniel Boorstin published his *The Genius of American Politics* which was followed in 1958 by *The Americans: The Colonial Experience*. Boorstin focused in Turnerian fashion on the influence of the American environment on men and ideas in the New World. The central message which he emphasized repeatedly was that American experience had rendered European theory, i.e., ideology and utopian dreams, irrelevant to the formation of the American polity and character. By implication Boorstin was saying that Americans had been misled whenever they attempted to adopt European intellectual systems to American reality; indeed they had gone astray whenever systematic thinking had been attempted at all. Thus, although doubts might have arisen in the reader's mind (what then was the relevance of the colonial experience to contemporary reality? Was common sense and a hardy no-nonsense approach still efficacious?), Boorstin clearly celebrated his consensus theme with few if any qualifications.

The best known of consensualists, however, was Daniel Bell, the author of the controversial essay "The End of Ideology in the

West." Like Boorstin, Bell was a veteran of thirties' radical-Marxist battles, and also, like Boorstin, was just as happy to see ideology go. Focusing his essay on the postwar American scene rather than the broad sweep of American history, yet taking into account intellectual developments in Western Europe as well as America, Bell departed from the traditional concept of ideology as formulated by Marx. According to the Marxist notion, an ideology was an intellectual construct used, consciously or unconsciously, to mask an individual or group's "real" interests. But Bell, drawing upon Karl Mannheim, saw ideology as "an all inclusive system of comprehensive reality . . . a set of beliefs, infused with passion, [which] seeks to transform the whole of a way of life. . . . Ideology, in this sense, . . . is a secular religion."[4] Thus consigned to the category of religion and superstition, ideology could be written off as the opiate of the intellectuals. Bell's essay was complicated by the fact that he was both describing a historical situation in which ideologies seemed dead and "old passions spent"[5] and making a normative judgment in calling for an end to ideology, "the end of rhetoric, and rhetoricians, or revolution."[6]

Though others have analyzed Bell's essay at some length,[7] a further comment or two is in order. Bell's descriptive claim concerning the end of ideology was valid, if one identified ideology, as Bell did, with left-wing revolutionary doctrines coming out of the Marxist tradition. Clearly most European and American intellectuals had cast aside traditional Marxism as a world view and a guide to action. On the other hand, Bell's judgment as to the desirability of the end of ideology was acceptable only if one agreed with Bell that ideology, as a secular religion aiming to transform "the whole way of life," was necessarily "rhetorical" and led inevitably to "degrading means in the name of some Utopian or revolutionary end."[8] That ideology and the latter undesirable traits were identical was not at all self-evident.

Bell correctly observed, as Dwight Macdonald had earlier in "The Root Is Man," that the old labels—left and right, radical and conservative—were devoid of content and that new problems were at hand with which older, received ideologies found it hard to deal. His analysis fell short, however, because he could only think according to the traditional Marxist categories—or in terms of the new "consensus . . . the acceptance of the Welfare State; the desirability of decentralized power; a system of mixed economy, and of political pluralism."[9]

Indeed in retrospect this was the failure of most of the above-mentioned observers. Lurking behind the consensus "school" of analysis was the concern with the relevance of Marxist ideology to American reality. No intellectual or ideological alternatives seemed to exist besides a discredited Marxism, a general celebration of American life, or the new and slightly critical consensus liberalism. In so closely identifying Marxism with radical social theory, these men blinded themselves to other theoretical possibilities. With Marxist ideology thus disposed of, critical thinking about American society as a whole seemed passé—or positively dangerous.

In reality Marxism as a total ideology has never influenced American social thought very deeply. As T. B. Bottomore has noted, the Americans who wrote first-rate studies of Marx and Marxism during the thirties—Sidney Hook and Edmund Wilson— made no attempt to relate their studies to American social reality in the Depression decade.[10] To understand why Marxism has never taken root in American soil as well as to identify certain continuing themes and concerns of twentieth-century American social thought, it is necessary to examine briefly the social thought of the Progressive period. Having done this, we can better understand the post-World War II attempt to forge a radical social theory which, abandoning Marx and encompassing Freud as well as some of the older themes of American social thought, would be pertinent to the realities of advanced industrial society.

Two Strands of Progressive Social Thought

Central to the Marxist view is a theory of class conflict in which the industrial proletariat serves as the embodiment of the contradictions inherent in an industrial, capitalist society. Underlying the Marxist position is the further assumption that revolutionary possibility emerges only in an industrial society which, though divided along class lines, is ethnically and racially homogeneous. By way of contrast the nineteenth-century American liberal-radical tradition focused on the farmers rather than the nascent working class as the group from which social and economic change would arise. When America began its industrialization in a thoroughgoing way, the working class that emerged was in no sense a homogeneous body. It was made up of a hodgepodge of "native" Americans and recent immigrants who, literally as well as figuratively, could scarcely communicate with one another. Thus the development of a class-conscious working class was all but impossible. Furthermore with the migration of Negroes from the South into northern urban-industrial areas, the situation became even more complicated. Though "native" Americans, the blacks were seldom regarded by the white working class, whether of native or foreign origin, as potential allies in a class struggle; indeed the appearance of Negroes on the industrial scene was usually perceived as a threat to the other workers.

To these factors we should also add that of mobility. Some observers have suggested that the very fact of geographical mobility in American society has militated against the development of class consciousness.[11] Socioeconomic mobility has also been of crucial importance. Historians and sociologists have long debated the possibility of upward mobility in American society throughout its development. One would, however, be hard put to deny the pervasive belief Americans have held that they could better their lot. Thus neither farmers nor workers have seen themselves as farmers or workers per se. American farmers have been agrarian capitalists and, violent though labor relations have been in this country, the most powerful institutional embodiments of the workers' interests, the AF of L and the CIO, have rarely if ever challenged the capitalist system on ideological grounds. The upshot of all this is that American radical social thought has lacked a coherent and readily identifiable socio-economic group upon which it could pin its hopes and around which a coherent theory could be erected. Radical social theory is obviously hard to sustain in a vacuum.

At the other end of the spectrum, European "conservative" and "reactionary" ideologies have been less than to the point. As the nineteenth century came to an end in Europe there was a flourish of conservative "kulturpessimismus" which involved a general revolt against modernism. This conservative criticism, which had been growing apace throughout the century, ranged in quality from the writings of Burckhardt and Nietzsche to the protofascist theorizing of artists and philosophers manqués.[12] Behind it lay the core assumption that something had gone terribly wrong with western civilization. Industrialization and urbanization, the irruption of the lower and excluded classes into all aspects of European life, parliamentary politics, all these signaled a time of spiritual crisis. The seamy underside of this conservative ideology often revealed racialism, ultranationalism and anti-Semitism. Biological and medical metaphors of growth and decay, stagnation and rejuvenation, sickness and health pointed to an underlying yearning for purgation and a restored wholeness, an organic unity.

In general the orientation of this mode of thought was backward in time toward the Middle Ages, when European society and culture had been of one piece under the unifying control of the Roman Church and a feudal aristocracy. In this supposedly organic society, each man—from peasant to nobleman, artisan to priest—had a function and knew his place; art and daily life were integrated; and a nexus of hierarchical loyalties and values prevailed over those of the marketplace and the political party.

In America, interestingly enough, a similar cultural reaction made a bid for attention. Under the onslaught of waves of immigrants and forced to come to terms with a new and strange world, segments of the population ranging from New England Brahmins to southern farmers to Progressive intellectuals fell prey to racist and nativist ideologies that reached their peak in the first quarter of this century.[13] In 1907 Henry Adams finished his monument to psychological and historical displacement, *The Education of Henry Adams* (1907), in which he expressed his disdain for arriviste politicians and immigrant groups. And Theodore Roosevelt's politics were part of an attempt to bolster up the flagging will and revivify the fading energy of the Anglo-Saxon race which some thought was heading for extinction.

Yet for American conservatives there was no "Middle Age" to which to return. Writers, such as Henry James and, later, T. S. Eliot and Ezra Pound, found it necessary to leave the country to escape the supposed cultural barrenness, the sway of vulgar opinion, and the cash nexus of American society. They could find little of use in the American experience. Others like Adams could write in *Mont-Saint-Michel and Chartres* (1904) of the glorious unity of twelfth- and thirteenth-century Europe. But Adams's work, for all its compelling power, was the expression of a private vision and, as Adams himself recognized, an impossibility in a world dominated by the dynamo rather than the virgin.

Perhaps the most coherent conservative response to modernity was that of the Vanderbilt Agrarians as expressed in *I'll Take My Stand* (1930). In this volume twelve southern writers and intellectuals cast a glance longingly at the only period and region in which the liberal ideology had not prevailed—the antebellum South. Yet for all the cogency of its criticisms of "progress" and rampant commercialism, *I'll Take My Stand* was shot through with ambiguities. The idea for the volume had grown out of the Agrarians' distaste for the northern "liberal" reaction to the Scopes Trial in 1925. Yet if any society was nonaristocratic and hostile to "culture" it was the yeoman and small-town South. Within the book there was also a crucial ambiguity. Some of the Agrarians counterposed an aristocratic South of gracious planters and cultivated leisure to the modern urban capitalist ethos. Yet others saw the ideal South, and hence ideal society, as one composed primarily of sturdy yeomen, good Jeffersonians to the core. Thus Burke vied with Jefferson and Locke for the dominant role in the agrarian ideology. If one adds to this that the antebellum South, for all its graciousness of style and hostility to moneygrubbing capitalism, was based on chattel slavery, one can see that the effort of the Agrarians was doomed to failure. There were no "American" models which would serve to counteract the facts of modern life.

Hence the dilemma of American conservatism. If it is truly

conservative in the European fashion, it is, by the same token, not American and largely irrelevant. If it is truly American, it can only be the expression of Manchester liberal capitalism mixed with large doses of political federalism and Darwinism, or a defense of the specious and limited southern experience of aristocracy.

Thus when America "came of age" around the turn of the twentieth century, she lacked either a class-conscious proletariat or a past-conscious aristocracy. As a result contemporary social thought was forced to cast about for a social focus and projective models to serve as alternatives to the irrelevant European ideologies or the superannuated American schemes of agrarian populism and conservative Darwinism.

The book furnishing the best overall synthesis of the Progressive Era is Robert Wiebe's *The Search for Order: 1877-1920*. According to Wiebe, this period saw the rise of an urban, professional middle class bent upon ordering and rationalizing the newly emerging industrial, urban society. In the language of sociology, American society was moving from congeries of Gemeinschaften to a national Gesellschaft, directed from above through the national government and informed by a bureaucratic ideology interested in "continuity and regularity, functionality and rationality, administration and management."[14] The central figure in the new order was to become the academically trained expert, the product of an increasingly professionalized and specialized system of higher education.[15] As the "Wisconsin idea" attested, this new expert generally aligned himself with the political reformer. Philosophically the expert was a pragmatist; politically he was a "liberal (in the American sense of the word), progressive, or radical."[16]

Thus from the Progressive Era on, one strand of American social thought, best described as "liberal," has been elitist in nature, though acting in the name of traditional American values. Or, to use Herbert Croly's phrase, it has sought to wed Hamiltonian means with Jeffersonian ends. Government on all levels, but especially the federal level, came to be seen as the fundamental instrument for regularizing and taming American economic and social life. This liberal ideology can best be characterized as an ideology of social control.[17]

According to most students of the period, this new ideology arose in reaction to the conservative Darwinian emphasis on the identification of the natural-biological order with the social-historical order, on competition and unregulated development as productive of the optimal social and economic benefits, on the reification of competition as natural law, and on the minimalization of planning and control by governmental institutions. Rather than directly challenging the Darwinian concept of nature, the new liberalism placed its stress on man as an intelligent being capable of action and initiative rather than a being merely reacting to natural forces, and held out for beneficial effects of cooperation.

It was from Lester Frank Ward that the new ideology received its first systematic formulation. A self-educated man, and fittingly enough a civil servant for forty years, Ward's central theme was that the "intelligent mind, fortified with knowledge, is the only form of the directive force"[18] of society. No passive plaything of biological and social evolution, man should use his intelligence to shape the development of society and should "resist the law of nature" since the dynamics of society is "the antithesis of animal life."[19]

Ward held that the sociopolitical embodiment of human intelligence was a centralized government guided by scientific and statistical data to "influence and direct legislation."[20] This centralized power was furthermore to be above partisan or political considerations and should act purely to the advantage of society as a whole. The supposedly nonideological character of Ward's thought can best be seen in his statement that "reforms are chiefly advocated by those who have no interest in them."[21] In his Sociocracy, which he distinguished from Socialism (class rule), Ward assumed that there would be those who could rise above self-interest to guide the society to obviously needed reforms. Thus government would be "the art that results from the science of society through the legislative application of sociological principles."[22] Profound social and political conflicts were illusory;

through "popular scientific education" the vast majority of people would come to realize and support the needed reforms. No better example exists of the tendency to consider moral and political problems amenable to technical manipulation and solution.

From Ward we can jump to the last and probably greatest social theorist of the Progressive Era, Thorstein Veblen. Though Veblen's work defies any neat pigeonholing, central aspects reenforced and added depth to the emergent liberal ideology of the first third of the century. If Ward's thought expressed the elitism of a newly educated "progressive minded" civil servant, Veblen pointed to the emergence of a managerial class in American capitalism which had interests (or at least Veblen imputed to it interests) divergent from those of the traditional hard-driving entrepreneurs, captains of industry, and financial titans.

Veblen, like Ward and an entire generation of liberal social thinkers, reacted against economic doctrine of natural law. Veblen went beyond most of his contemporaries, however, by also rejecting *homo economicus*, the utilitarian maximizer of pleasure and profit, who stood at the center of both capitalist and Marxist economic dogma. Indeed for Veblen the salient feature of human economic behavior was its irrationality and absurdity. And thus in his writings, particularly in *The Theory of the Leisure Class*, Veblen dissected and exposed not so much the exploitative nature of capitalism as its stupidities, its infelicities, and, most centrally, its wastefulness.

Veblen's thought was informed by the "instinct of workmanship," a drive which Veblen saw as ever-present throughout man's evolution. This propensity to accomplish "some concrete, objective, impersonal end . . . [this] taste for effective work and a distaste for futile effort . . . a sense of merit of serviceability or efficiency and the demerit of futility, waste or incapacity"[23] was the essential civilizing agent in human evolution; it had "brought the life of mankind from the brute to the human plane."[24] As mankind developed through what Veblen called the predatory and pecuniary stages of barbarism, workmanship had become less valued while aggression, economic dominance or "exploit," private property, conspicuous leisure, and consumption came to characterize the economic, social, and cultural ethos.

Veblen's thought looked both backward and forward in time. He posited "an archaic phase of culture in which industry is organized on the ground of workmanship" which was then superseded by "a pecuniary control of industry."[25] On the other hand, he hoped that mankind would eventually arrive at a future stage, through the full development of technology, in which the instinct of workmanship and efficiency would again reign. The key to future social development was "the Discipline of the Machine." In the essay of the same name, Veblen discussed the effect of machines and large-scale mechanization on human beings. Whatever Veblen's doubts (or ours) as to its salutary nature, he felt that the coming dominance of the machine would lead to a "standardization of the workman's intellectual life in terms of mechanical processes . . . regularity of sequence and mechanical precision."[26] With the machine age, all life and work would be demystified and deanthropomorphized in preparation for the next stage of social development.

It was in this essay that Veblen set forth the dichotomy between industry and business, mechanical and pecuniary pursuits. For Veblen the business class was replete with "conventional anthropomorphic" justifications of property and "money values."[27] In contrast Veblen saw a new class of technicians or engineers emerging whose devotion to the machine process led them to uphold the values of production against profit making, and to defend innovative and nonconventional thinking against natural law and conservative modes of thought. The business mentality, as embodied in the growing absentee ownership class, was in fact devoted to the sabotage of the industrial machine in the name of price maintenance and higher profits. Thus Veblen concluded that in the American economy there was a conflict shaping up between the pecuniary goals of the business system and the productive goals of the new industrial class of technicians.

Veblen's most provocative development of this line of thought came in his *Engineers and the Price System* (1921) where he speculated on the possibility of a revolutionary overthrow of the price system, not by the workers, but by the engineers. Ever the skeptic, Veblen almost immediately admitted that his thoughts were extremely speculative since the "technicians, engineers and industrial experts are a harmless and docile sort."[28] Nevertheless he proceeded to sketch out what might take place.

Veblen repeated his earlier characterization of the industrial mentality, but added his explicit approval of it by noting that though "mechanical technology is impersonal and dispassionate, . . . its end is very simply to serve human needs"[29] through the natural sciences and technology. There was no doubt but that the engineers were the vital cogs in the industrial machine without whom a revolution could not be successful in modern industrial societies.

Interesting yet disturbing in Veblen's discussion was his elitist bias. Since the technicians "represented the community at large in its industrial capacity"[30] Veblen apparently trusted that the will of the people would be divined and carried out by a soviet of engineers who oversaw the production, transportation, and distribution of goods. Thus in the new order the producers and consumers would be joined by some unspecified community of interests against those who still held out for "private gain."

A necessary prerequisite for the overthrow of the business system was the emergence of class consciousness among the technicians who had "hitherto been working piecemeal, as scattered individuals under the master's eye."[31] When this consciousness had been attained the engineers would hopefully put into effect a "conscientious withdrawal of efficiency; that is to say a general strike . . ."; publicize their actions and move toward a "solidarity of sentiment with . . . the working force."[32] But as Veblen hastened to add once more in conclusion, there was little need to worry "just yet."

Though in his provocative and prescient analysis Veblen correctly foretold the emergence of a managerial class distinct from the ownership, as well as the managers' acquiescence to the business ethos, he made a serious mistake in linking the instinct of workmanship, the machine mentality, the process of mechanization, and the engineer. In point of fact the latter three could fit quite well into the price system since all three were instrumentalities toward the achievements of ends and were not value-determining in themselves. Veblen assumed that because the instinct of workmanship emerged most clearly with the engineer that it would override the demands of profit-oriented production. Nor did Veblen seem to recognize that the machine process and mechanization in general could become mystifying in themselves, the objects of devotion and the focus of anthropomorphic fantasies.[33] Never a political man Veblen devoted little attention to the political questions concerning the nature of decision making, the gaining and losing of power, and popular participation in his technocratic society. Though isolated insights proved valuable to later radicals, particularly those engaged in critiques of mass consumption, the clear implications of his social thought were elitist and nondemocratic, focusing on the newly emergent engineer-managers as the agents and embodiments of progress and social control. Clearly they, not the workers, were the key to any radical change from the profit-oriented to a production-oriented industrial society.

Nevertheless Veblen's concept of the workmanship instinct was in itself a powerfully critical and radical tool for analyzing any social and economic system. Shorn of its contemporary reference, the concept fell within the tradition of American "functionalist" thought and ethics reaching back as far as Horatio Greenough and Thoreau. Likewise Veblen's emphasis on man as a maker and a doer was in the pragmatic tradition of James and Dewey. More widely considered, the instinct of workmanship brought to mind the concern of the young Karl Marx with the alienation of man from his own labor. For both thinkers, man was defined by his labor and both believed that the society which used this labor for extraneous ends should be changed. Also like Marx, Veblen embraced rather than rejected technology as the way to the desirable society of the future. Finally, the instinct of workmanship and the syndicalism of Veblen's producers anticipated the concern of later American radicals such as Paul Goodman who criticized organized technological society precisely because it did not nurture what Freud described as the essence of mental well-being—the ability to love and work.[34]

Another strand of social thought which emerged during the Progressive period was one concerned with individual "release" and cultural rejuvenation. Though this line of thought held institutional change to be important, it dealt most centrally with the ethos, the quality of life, which characterized industrial and urban America. Rejecting genteel middle-class culture as well as unrestrained capitalism, many American intellectuals turned to the excluded and exploited segments of the society for an answer to its problems as well as their own. Some saw the workers as a source of salvation; others of a more bohemian bent looked to art and the artist. Still others embraced the cause of the immigrant.[35] Yet the most novel development was the focus upon a newly emerging social group—the youth. In focusing upon young people as a distinct social and cultural force, these cultural radicals came to see the school and the educational process as the key to the revitalization of American life. The clearest expression of this general line of thought was found in the Progressive Education movement, which some consider the most enduring and representative reform of the Progressive period.[36]

In turning to the child and youth as the hope for a rejuvenation of American life, these cultural radicals drew upon a well-established tradition in American culture. As Richard Hofstadter has noted, "primitivism . . . has won an extraordinarily wide credence in America."[37] From the eighteenth century on, Americans and often Europeans had seen America as a sort of new Eden peopled by a new man, unsullied by tradition or sophistication. This image of the new Adam dovetailed neatly with the Progressive preoccupation with children, since the image of the new Adam described metaphorically the child's situation.

In a similar fashion popular education had long been regarded by Americans as the key to the ongoing success of the American enterprise. Education has been the means of inculcating children with American values and attitudes, and has thus contributed to socialization as much as it has to the cultivation of the intellect.

Likewise education as a social policy has been a device which the conservative could embrace as the "only alternative to public disorder" as well as one which the middle and lower classes could support as "the door to opportunity, the great equalizer."[38] Thus seen by some as a method of social control and by others as a way of opening up the social structure, and then in the early twentieth century as a rejuvenating cultural force, educational reform has been perhaps the quintessential reform in American history. Progressive education as an intellectual and social movement signaled the realization that not the farm or factory, but the school was to be the one institution through which all Americans had to pass.

No figure illustrates better than Randolph Bourne the interwoven concern with youth, education, and the revitalization of American life and culture. A student of Dewey's at Columbia, Bourne was the "first of the culture heroes of the youth."[39] At the heart of Bourne's thought was a profound antipathy toward the received American tradition of genteel manners, dessicated Protestantism and a blind adherence to conventional values and attitudes. Throughout his writings, particularly those appearing before World War I, ran the demand that youth not only be served but exalted.

For Bourne, "to keep one's reactions warm and true is to have found the secret of perpetual youth and perpetual youth is salvation."[40] Because he and his generation of middle-class youths had grown up in relative affluence, Bourne realized that conventional cultural values were otiose and thus opted for pleasure-seeking and the cultivation of vitality. This new ethic, Bourne noted, was "the result of the absence of repression in our bringing up."[41] Furthermore Bourne thought that the youth of his time was more sensitive to inequalities than his elders, and maintained that "we feel social injustice as our fathers felt personal sin."[42] For Bourne a virtuous life was "a life responsive to its powers and its opportunities, a life not of inhibitions, but of a straining up to the limit of its strengths."[43] Thus the youthful individual did best to listen to the stirrings of his own heart rather than the claims of an insensitive older generation.

Though attracted to political reform and radicalism, Bourne was no doctrinaire socialist. As Lasch notes, Bourne's was "a continuing preoccupation with the personal as opposed to the public."[44] To his homegrown Nietzschean vitalism, Bourne added a Deweyan emphasis on openness to experience and experimentation. True morality was "healthy with intelligence."[45] As one grew older in years he should remain true to the "finer idealism and impersonal aims that formed one's philosophy of youth" and keep alive "the tradition that is vital."[46] This vitality was to be produced by substituting the "experimental ideal" for the "rational ideal"; we should, he said, "test all hypotheses by experience."[47] "Self cultivation becomes almost a duty"[48] and by cultivating one's powers the American ethos might be transformed.

Yet Bourne did not retreat into the quietism implicit in his thought. As a student of Dewey he was also attracted to the burgeoning movement of educational reform in his time. In his book *The Gary Schools* (1916), Bourne saw the goal of the progressive school system to be the construction of "a genuine children's community."[49] Rather than "a preparation for life, it is to be life itself."[50] The school was as much a refuge from the urban environment as it was a preparation for it, since Bourne felt that the home and the street were demoralizing to the student and to be counteracted at all costs. Progressive learning proceeded by doing while seeking to avoid the excessive concentration on either the "cultural" or the "utilitarian." Yet, and here was the contradiction, all school activities were to be "subjected to the Social."[51] Obviously one could question what constituted the social other than the home and the street and beyond that a social order moving in the direction of specialization and compartmentalization.

In fact the school was to be run by the "ingenious application of principles well recognized in business and industry,"[52] precisely those forces which had helped to fragment the social order. It was, according to Bourne, necessary to isolate children in a school "family" away from the community, yet the ultimate goal was to prepare them for life in the new industrial order. And showing his partial allegiance to the social control stream of contemporary social thought, Bourne envisaged the end product of the schools to be "versatile engineers" who displayed "exactness, resourcefulness, inventiveness, pragmatic judgment of a machine by its product, the sense of machinery as a means not an end in itself."[53]

As already pointed out, there was a contradiction in Bourne's conception of the relationship of the school to the community. Likewise there was a contradiction between the goal of producing versatile engineers who would keep the industrial machine humming, and Bourne's aesthetic, vitalistic ethics of self-regulation and self-imposed goals.

Finally Bourne's notion of Progressive Education reflected the ambiguous and transitional nature of his society. From one angle the development of individual needs and capacities within a "community" was desirable in order to work against the growing standardization and impersonality of American society. This was Progressive Education as a liberating ideology. Yet in its need for "versatile engineers" the society transformed Progressive Education into an instrument of socialization and social control. Thus it was the child *vs.* the expert, self-direction *vs.* external imposition, Progressive Education as ideology *vs.* Progressive Education as technique.

Although this brief discussion by no means exhausts Bourne's variety of concerns (particularly as expressed in his war essays), it does indicate the emergence of another line of social and cultural criticism in twentieth-century America. Bourne stands as a representative figure and as one of the first in the tradition of American cultural radicalism. Neither an artist nor a philosopher, Bourne worked at the fringes of politics, art, and social criticism toward uniting them in a thorough critique of American culture. Like many of his contemporaries Bourne felt that politics and culture, the personal and the public, were inextricably bound up with each other, and that health and vitality in one sphere depended upon and in turn influenced these qualities in other areas of life.

One must also recognize that Bourne's efforts expressed a mood in search of ideology, a feeling in search of conceptualization. Bourne expressed both a celebration of life and a sense of cultural crisis. His thought, however, lacked a certain concreteness and specificity and, as a thinker, Bourne lacked an overall, integrative system which would have tied together the problems of youth, education, and the need for cultural rejuvenation and related them to America's newly emerging industrial order.

In his critique of the Deweyan instrumentalists who jumped head over heels into the war effort, Bourne groped toward an ideology different from the sort of liberal social engineering which neglected ends for means, values for techniques, and served inhumane objectives in the name of objectivity. By 1918 he had come to see the dangers of a society run by his "versatile engineers" since, as Veblen later noted, the engineers were a docile lot ready to act at the behest of those who controlled the mechanisms and determined the ends. Thus Bourne and Veblen, in reacting to the war experience and noting the potential power of the engineers and managers, drew opposite conclusions as to what might and should happen in the future. The war experience revealed to Veblen the potential power of the engineers; to Bourne, their fatal weakness.

Bourne's critique of the liberal war supporters was much more biting and cogent than much of his earlier writing, works which had smacked of the YMCA as much as they had of Nietzsche. Bourne's thought was a peculiarly American brew; unsystematic, implicitly anarchistic, vitalistic and hostile to imposed values and structures, focusing on youth and education as keys to reform. Not the class struggle but the generational struggle, a battle of moods not concrete interests, was at the heart of his thought. In this sense Bourne was continuing the tradition begun by the first immigrants from Europe—a revolt against the dead hand of the past. Bourne's thought went beyond this, however, and reflected a split *within* American society rather than *between* America and Europe. He recognized the emergence of youth as a distinctive social force which had definite goals and particular interests in American society.

The figure in whom these two strands of social thought were

uneasily joined was John Dewey. In his philosophy and practice, as thinker and educator, Dewey conceived his main task to be that of the mediator of all the polarities plaguing contemporary American society, education, and thought. Believing that life was a continual process, that education and philosophy must enter into and direct experience, and that there was finally no dichotomy between individual and society, theory and practice, Dewey sought to synthesize the scientific aspect of human study with a close attention to individuality.

John Dewey was America's Karl Marx. In his 11th Thesis on Feuerbach, Marx had written: "The philosophers have only interpreted the world, in various ways; the point, however, is to change it";[54] this as no other dictum describes Dewey's efforts as a philosopher and social theorist. Indeed for Dewey, philosophy became social thought, the systematic application of human intelligence to experience so as to effect certain desired results. To accomplish this task, philosophy had to discontinue its interest in universals and transcendent concerns and come down to earth and the specific problems of man in society. The sharp division between doing and knowing which had been generalized into a complete separation of theory and practice had to be overcome.[55]

For Dewey the paradigm of this union of theory and practice was not, as for Marx, the revolutionary, but the scientist in the laboratory and, even more pertinently, the educational theorist applying his ideas in the Progressive school. "Education," said Dewey, "is the fundamental method of social progress and reform."[56] Thus the child as student, not the worker, became the focus and instrument of change.

In a sense to stress education as a separate and discrete part of Dewey's thought is misleading. It was his fundamental conviction that the school was a part of society and that the good society was one which was never static, but rather continually educational. Scholastic education was a particular aspect of social life in a complex society. "Education" as he wrote in *Democracy and Education,* "is the means of this social continuity of life."[57] Yet conversely "all communication (and hence all genuine social life) is educative."[58] Education should inculcate attitudes of "sympathetic curiosity, unbiased responsiveness and open minded-ness,"[59] those qualities best suited to insure survival in a complex society changing under the pressure of technological and industrial development.

One misleading interpretation of Dewey has it that he was a child worshiper of sorts and an unstinting defender of the child's wishes.[60] This view is not totally correct. It is far more true of educationalists such as G. Stanley Hall. In this matter as in others Dewey sought to strike a middle position. Dewey repeatedly rejected both Rousseauian notions of the child's clear insight into his own needs and desires, and the conventional pedagogy of rote learning, rigid discipline, and passive indoctrination. The child was not to be allowed free rein in the classroom. Rather the teacher was to use the curriculum to give content and direction to the child's own organic needs and natural activities. Learning was neither purely intellectual nor mindlessly practical, just as school was neither a refuge from society nor identical with it.

Finally the thrust of Dewey's educational theory was to enable the child to become an effective adult while making adults more like children. His goals—"sympathetic curiosity, unbiased responsiveness and openness of mind"—were the virtues both of the child and of the scientist.

What happened to Dewey's thought is reminiscent of what happened to Hegel's. One interpretation, which stressed education as supportive of the status quo and a direct preparation for it, would degenerate into the much-maligned ideology of life adjustment so characteristic of public education in the forties and fifties. The other interpretation, stressing experimentation, openness to experience, and individual expression, led to more radical educational experiments in the ensuing years. The needs of society and those of the child which were held in tension by Dewey soon parted company. With the increasing influence of Freud in the twenties and after, the radical wing of Progressive Education became all but indistinguishable from the educational ideology of a man like A. S. Neill and others who added to educational self-direction and self-expression a belief in the healthy effects of untrammeled sexual expression.

Generally these polarities of social control and individual release evident in Progressive thought defined the contours of subsequent twentieth-century American social theory. In theory and practice American liberalism shucked off its agrarian and decentralist biases and moved to embrace the centralized political state, regulation of the economy, and more generally a commitment to a wide ranging rationalization of individual and collective existence.

After its flirtation with Marxist thought in the twenties and thirties, a phenomenon as all-pervasive as it was superficial, radical social theory ran aground. Many former radicals withdrew from public, political concerns. Others for all intents and purposes went over to liberalism and transformed it into a strange brew of native American protest, technocratic elitism, and European social democracy. But there were others, such as many of the intellectuals associated with *Politics*, who found these solutions unsatisfactory. In attempting to redefine radical social theory they were driven to a reevaluation of American and European thought. What united them was a fear of the totalitarian potential of the centralized state, its close connection with a permanent war economy, and the power of large-scale institutions and the mass media to manipulate consciousness. On the positive side they noted the emergence of a society of potential abundance presenting new opportunities for individual fulfillment and making necessary a movement beyond the "Protestant Ethic," the set of social and cultural values common to industrializing societies, whether capitalist or socialist. No longer did the older dualities of capitalism and socialism make much sense for, as T. B. Bottomore observed, "social criticism, which had meant in the latter part of the nineteenth century and up to the 1930's principally a criticism of capitalist society, must now be taken to embrace the critical examination of both capitalism and socialism."[61]

It is to *Politics* and the effort to formulate a new radicalism that we will now turn since it was in that journal that many of the themes of post-World War II radical social thought were first discussed and the "end of ideology" first announced. Also it was in *Politics* that Freud made his appearance as a potential ally for a new type of radicalism.

The Example of Politics

The most interesting effort in the postwar years to formulate a new radical social theory appeared in Dwight Macdonald's journal *Politics* (1944-49). Macdonald's purpose in starting *Politics* was "to create a center of consciousness on the Left," but a Left of the "democratic socialist" not Stalinist vintage.[62] Behind this impulse lay several years of growing disillusionment with orthodox Marxism on Macdonald's part and an ever increasing bitterness over Stalin's betrayal of the socialist ideal. Though the focus here will be on the efforts made by Macdonald and others to lay the groundwork for a new type of radical social thought, the journal's basic impulse was negative, involving primarily an attack on the Soviet Union as a "new form of class society . . . a bureaucratic collectivism" which Macdonald considered the "most dangerous future enemy of Socialism."[63] Second only to Stalin's Russia as an object of withering abuse were American "liblabs" who urged mindless unity in the war effort, gave unstinting support to the USSR, and issued blanket denunciations of the German people. Included under the rubric of "liblab" were journals such as *The New Republic, Nation,* and *PM,* publicists such as Max Lerner and I. F. Stone, and, later, political figures such as Henry Wallace.[64]

For Macdonald there existed an intimate connection between the rhetorical style and the quality of ideas a man held. He took considerable pleasure in exposing the cant of American fellow travelers and the sloppy thinking he detected in their pronouncements. The best and most effective example of Macdonald's aesthetic-political criticism came in his hatchet job on Henry Wallace. Wallace and his "factitious optimism" regarding the possibility of American-Soviet cooperation were for Macdonald symbols of the disintegration in "the American lib-labor movement generally."[65] Thus though disillusioned with the theory and practice of Marxism, postwar liberalism of the Wallace vintage was no temptation for Macdonald.

Politics also focused critical attention on Allied reconstruction plans in postwar Europe. Great Britain's efforts to crush the Greek resistance movement and restore the royal family and a conservative regime in Athens came under heavy fire. In like manner Allied support for conservatives and monarchists in Italy was strenuously attacked. On the other end of the spectrum, *Politics* criticized American acquiescence to the Soviet Union and her minions in postwar Germany. An article in 1948 accused western Stalinists and liberals of aiding German Communists to gain control of communications media to the exclusion of the noncommunist socialists of the revived Social-Democratic party.

Viewed from our own perspective, Macdonald's hope of finding a third way in the postwar international political mess seems quixotic and his evaluation of the USSR as an expansionist power overdrawn. But to his credit, Macdonald realized as early as 1947 how futile his endeavors along this line would probably be. He felt that "the Soviet Union plays in world politics the same role Nazi Germany did in 1936-39."[66] On the other hand, he recognized that American foreign policy as embodied in the Truman Doctrine and the Marshall Plan, while valuable in resisting Soviet expansion, meant support for reactionary regimes. "The Truman Doctrine appears to be more a competitor than an opponent of the Kremlin," Macdonald wrote without explaining the difference between a competitor and an opponent. He then went on to draw the dreary yet basically sound conclusion that "the situation seems desperate . . . on the world scale politics is a desert without hope."[67]

For many readers of *Politics* its tone was too negative and the standards too exacting, indeed utopian. Macdonald in essence admitted the substance without granting the judgment of this criticism when he replied in 1944 that "the task now seems to be one primarily of criticism."[68] Indeed its negativism represented both the strength and the weakness of the journal. After the American Left's involvement with Marxism in the 1930s, it was imperative that one of their own make the reasons for ending the affair quite clear without succumbing to the opposite temptation of joining the growing numbers of what would later be called Cold War liberals.

Yet a thoroughgoing and exhilarating negativism was not enough. By instinct and training men such as Macdonald and others associated with *Politics* were hostile to both the business-oriented American conservatism and New Deal liberal reformism. The intellectual and moral capital of Marxism was exhausted. The problem was to find an intellectually and morally justifiable basis upon which a new radicalism could be built. And it is to this effort, one which continued throughout the existence of *Politics*, that we will now turn.

A basic assumption in the attempt to define a new radicalism was that the Soviet Union had betrayed the socialist faith and could no longer serve as a model for any future radical reconstruction of society. The Moscow Trials, the exile and murder of Trotsky, the existence of forced labor camps, the Nazi-Soviet pact, all made support of Russian Communism an impossibility. Another compelling factor in the disillusionment with Marxism was the apparent failure of Marxist prophecy; Russia had become a bureaucratic collectivism whose economy was "stimulated by dominance of war . . . and whose production was planned by a bureaucratic apparatus."[69] The inescapable conclusion was that the USSR was in reality not a socialist state. Although Macdonald had severely attacked James Burnham's *Managerial Revolution* when it had appeared in 1941, his eventual position resembled very nearly that of Burnham's, even though Macdonald always denied that this "third way" of managerial or bureaucratic planning was inevitable. Macdonald and others were less concerned with the socioeconomic structure of contemporary American reality, since as a capitalist society it was rejected out of hand. In general, however, America was no longer seen as a capitalist economy in the classical sense, but rather was described as being well on its way to becoming a centralized bureaucracy geared for the waging of war.

Given this animus against the growth of the warfare state and the centralization inherent in such a development, it seems almost inevitable that the *Politics* radicals would be attracted to the "other" radical tradition of anarchism and syndicalism. Reacting as well to the horrors of strategic bombing, total war, and the use of atomic weapons, they also moved toward pacifism. And disillusioned with the historical positivism of Marxism, they made an attempt to found a new radicalism on a psychobiological base.

One approach to a reformulation was a backward glance to earlier non-Marxist radicals. The general form which these "Ancestor" profiles took was a short biographical-intellectual sketch of the particular radical in question, followed by excerpts from his work. In a brief note prefacing the first profile, Macdonald hoped the series would "supplement and reshape the Marxist heritage,"[70] and promised future profiles of Diderot, Condorcet, Tom Paine, St. Simon, Fourier, Herzen, Kropotkin, Tolstoy, Daniel DeLeon, and Rosa Luxemburg. Few of these figures were ever discussed in *Politics* and some who were profiled did not appear in the original list.

The natural first choice for the "Ancestors" series was Proudhon. In his profile of Proudhon, J. H. Jackson emphasized the centrality of a federative principle in Proudhon's thought which would serve as a much needed corrective to Marxism, Fabianism, and Social Democracy, all of which "preached centralization."[71] The next Ancestor was a strange face in radical circles—Alexis de Tocqueville.[72] For Sebastian Frank, Tocqueville was relevant to the postwar scene because he had prophesied the emergence of the concentration of power in the "Total State."[73] Tocqueville, Frank noted, had observed that men tended to be exclusively concerned with private affairs in American society. As a result political apathy would become widespread and the commonwealth, by default, the exclusive concern of an ever-growing central government.[74] The growth of centralized power and the emphasis on egalitarianism served as well to vitiate the "pouvoirs secondaire"[75]—guilds, communities, clubs—which served to mediate the direct power and influence of the central government. Without these mediating and "checking" groups, which gave citizens a genuine taste for self-government and political participation, the society would drive toward disaster.

The third in the series (May 1946) was a more familiar figure to anarchist-radicals—Leo Tolstoy. Instead of an extended commentary, Macdonald reprinted two of Tolstoy's essays in which Tolstoy rejected the notion that society could be understood and described by reductionist, scientific methods. Tolstoy also charged science with neglecting the higher priority of helping man solve his problems in favor of "studying everything" as though it were equally important.[76] Science, Tolstoy maintained, "is occupied on the one hand with the justification of the existing order, and on the other hand with playthings."[77] In the other essay Tolstoy questioned the European obsession with activity, especially work, for its own sake; for Tolstoy it was this constant activity which obscured man's real thoughts and desires and foreclosed the possibility of a life based on the ethic of love.[78] In printing these two essays, Macdonald pointed to two problems which would be central in postwar social thought—the role of science in human affairs and the nature and quality of work.

In September of the same year an English intellectual, George Woodcock, contributed a profile of William Godwin. Woodcock noted Godwin's "distrust of political solutions"[79] and thus put his finger on one source of appeal the Anarchist tradition held for postwar radicals, disillusioned with conventional politics of any stripe. That appeal was Anarchism's antipolitical animus, its positive distrust of conventional political institutions such as representative bodies, and its emphasis on "natural," i.e., economic or social, groupings, rather than artificial geographical ones as the basis of political organization. For Godwin: "Beneath the questions like parliamentary representation and methods of taxation . . . there lay the fundamental and concrete reality of personal contacts between men within society."[80] And finally Godwin's interest in education and his feeling that "authority should play no part in the educational processes"[81] sounded much like the ideas on education expressed by Paul Goodman, though the rationales for their respective libertarian theories of education were somewhat different.

In the winter of 1948 Macdonald devoted a profile to Alexander Herzen. Macdonald praised Herzen's critical insight into the

Revolutions of 1848 and valued his sense of the ironic which developed after that date.[82] According to Macdonald, Herzen's response to the events of 1848 had been much more realistic than Marx's: "if Marx was our man in the thirties, Herzen may be our man for the forties."[83]

A final ancestor—Kurt Tucholsky—was presented in the summer, 1948, issue of *Politics*. Tucholsky, a vibrant and central figure in the intellectual life of Weimar Germany, had been a polemicist, social-critic-satirist and writer of verse and fiction. Tucholsky, wrote Hans Sahl, was "the eternal fault finder . . . a brilliant personality—original, witty, full of ideas."[84] It was, however, disturbing that Tucholsky was more interesting as a personality than as a thinker in his own right. And the placing of Tucholsky, whose description resembled no one so much as it did Dwight Macdonald, at the end of the series was symptomatic of the dead end many radicals had reached by 1948.

Nevertheless some of the themes which were to dominate radical thought in *Politics* emerged in the historical profiles: a hostility to political and economic centralization, concern for the preservation, or, more to the point, the restoration of natural associations and voluntary groupings, a suspicion of science in its immoral and antihuman uses, and concern with the nature of work. No doubt the Ancestor series was a fine idea. There was a tradition there to be mined, but somehow a confluence of Macdonald's personal predilections and an increasing pessimism as to the possibility of an ideological "third way" worked to make the series a failure. Nothing was more revealing than that the series began with Proudhon and ended with Tucholsky, one a product of nineteenth-century revolutionary optimism at its peak, the other a figure of a brilliant yet disillusioned sensibility, who committed suicide shortly after the demise of the Weimar Republic.

Besides the Ancestors series there appeared in *Politics* an ongoing theoretical effort to define in a positive way the contours of a new radicalism. Macdonald himself began the effort in September, 1944, by sketching out what he considered the principles around which a new radical theory should form itself.

These were: no one should own more property than he could use or work himself, all other property was to be controlled by those who worked with it; political power should be allocated functionally as in the soviet or worker's council basis; all those in authority—politicians, judges, military officers, industrial and government executives—should be elected and subjected to recall and limited to a maximum continuous term in office; and the only limitation on political activities was to be a veto on overt attempts to overthrow the government by force.[85]

Although sketchy, these tentative guidelines indicated the direction of Macdonald's radicalism. The "program" was interesting for several reasons. First, it did not call for the abolition of private property and by implication, betraying a Proudhonist influence, saw some benefit in the institution. Nor did it call for nationalization of major industries. Again the Anarcho-Syndicalist tradition cropped up with the idea of workers' control of industries and economic rather than geographical units as the basis of political power. Macdonald's program was democratic in the Populist-Progressive tradition in its call for popular election of public officials and went beyond that tradition in calling for the election of industrial management. Conspicuously missing were any references to the "movement" or "logic" of history, indeed to any historical metaphysics at all. Nor was there any discussion of who might put these ideas into practice or how it might be done.

Paul Goodman picked up where Macdonald left off by attacking the neo-Freudians for abandoning Freud's emphasis upon the centrality of sex and thereby implicitly sanctioning a psychology which led to social engineering. Goodman then introduced the thought of Freudian renegade Wilhelm Reich, who had speculated upon the intimate connection between sexual and political repression. For Goodman, Reich's work suggested a new basis for radicalism in the realm of psychology and biology to replace outworn Marxist notions.[86]

Others in *Politics* were concerned with a reevaluation of Marxism. In January, 1946, Helen Costas maintained that the essence of socialism was not any particular institutional arrangements but "a set of moral relationships . . . a struggle for a moral

ideal."[87] Miss Costas also attacked the intellectual, moral, and
political authoritarianism of the western Communist parties and,
as a counterweight, proposed "a maximum of self-activity, suggestions and criticisms from below."[88] Thus socialism was to be a
system of moral imperatives rather than objective and "scientific."

Albert Votaw in his "Toward a Personalist Socialist Philosophy" echoed some of Goodman's themes. Instead of grounding
socialist thought in the logic of history and the class struggle,
Votaw opted for the view that "if Socialist thinking requires an
absolute, it can well be found in what modern psychology has
built in the discoveries of Freud."[89] And Votaw, like Goodman,
favored "the decentralization of productive units" with economic
planning done "by a commission elected democratically on an
industrial basis."[90] Only in this way did Votaw feel that the
individual could be protected against the impersonality of modern economic and social relationships.

The reassessment was continued along much the same lines in
the following two issues of *Politics*, with heavy emphasis falling
on the need to recover the moral impulse behind socialism and
the necessity for a nonauthoritarian, genuinely democratic radical theory and practice. Nicola Chiaromonte pointed out that a
socialism claiming to be based on "science" rather than on "an
experience of Justice" was inadequate for the times.[91] Philip
Spratt also dealt with the ethical problems inherent in Marxism
when he noted that insofar as Marxism was a form of materialism, it had no ethical content; yet insofar as it was a plan for
action, it profoundly needed an ethic. He charged, along with
many critics of Marxism, that Marxist ethics were built on a
historical positivism according to which that which is "progressive" or "in tune with" history is good and that which is not, is
not.[92]

These various positions were by no means in harmony. While
Goodman and Votaw wanted to replace the economic-historical
basis of Marxism with a psychobiological one, it is difficult to see
how this would have been much of an improvement for Chiaromonte or Spratt with their emphasis on the moral. A biological

positivism would have hardly been an adequate substitute for an historical one. Yet neither Chiaromonte nor Spratt defined the basis of "justice." There was obviously an agreement that Marxism, as ideology and practice, was bankrupt; its prophetic pretensions belied by historical developments and its ethical nihilism revealed by the policies of Stalinist Russia. More positively, these thinkers did agree that any future radical theory and practice should be nonauthoritarian and should allow for widespread participation from below. Hence the appeal of the communitarian-anarchist position; the appeal to the nonhistorical, whether biological or moral; and the emphasis on the quality of economic and social relationships.

The culmination of this effort at redefinition was Dwight Macdonald's two-part essay, "The Root Is Man" (April and June 1946). Macdonald's interest in clarity of expression and precision with language served him well in his first section, where he attempted to redefine the ideological terminology of conventional political discourse. He called all those thinkers "Progressives"— whether orthodox Marxists or Liberals—who believed in historical progress and found ethical imperatives in the historical process. The antithesis to the Progressive was the "Radical." The Radical affirmed certain "non-historical absolutes (truth, justice, love)"[93] as the basis for political thought and action. Following from this position the Radical "rejects the concept of Progress" in history and focuses his attention on the individual in the present.[94] The tragic, the ethical, and the nonscientific aspects of existence must be taken into account by any radical ideology.

After this exercise in redefinition, Macdonald proceeded to examine Marxist theory. He pointed out, as so many others had, that contrary to Marx's prediction, the state was manifestly not withering away, but rather aggrandizing power to itself by leaps and bounds.[95] This, Macdonald noted, was at least partly the result of two world wars and meant that the state structure had become "a new method of organizing natural resources—human, cultural, economic—for effective warmaking."[96] This new state was neither socialist, since workers had no effective control over it, nor capitalist, since the free market no longer determined production. Echoing Bourne's prophetic utterance—"War is the health of the State"—Macdonald went on to assert that this condition was no temporary aberration; rather "the preparation and waging of war is now the normal mode of existence of every great nation."[97] This development was completely unaccounted for by Marxist social thought.

Nor was it the case that the warfare state was erected and maintained against the will of the workers. Indeed, Macdonald observed, the workers' condition was often improved by war and national unity was achieved not through a more just economic, social, and political order, but by a semimobilization of all resources against some vague and undefined enemy. In short, and this was the second gaping hole in the Marxist armor, the idea of a proletarian-led revolution or even the "progressive" role of the working class was no longer tenable. Even the revolutions that had occurred had generally failed to follow the "working class pattern";[98] in nonrevolutionary settings unions had "narrowed not broadened their concerns."[99]

The responses to the first installment of Macdonald's essay came mostly from Marxists, and were predictably obtuse. They were best summed up by George P. Elliot's injunction to Macdonald that he "Join the Church."[100] Though rejecting this advice and denying imminent conversion to some sort of transcendent faith, Macdonald did admit in response to his critics that he had become a little "fatigued by the rarified atmosphere of the magazine."[101]

In July, 1946, Macdonald resumed his efforts on a yet more rarified level. The last half of "The Root Is Man" was devoted chiefly to the question of ethics and the possibility of a new radicalism. Reflecting his own abhorrence at the most recent perversion of science and technology—the use of atomic weapons—Macdonald rejected the claim that science could settle ethical questions. He then went on to locate the source of values in the individual when he wrote: "The locus of value choice . . . lies within the individual, not in Marx's history, Dewey's science, or Tolstoy's God."[102] Realizing that this was little more than rhetoric, Macdonald qualified the assertion by stating: "If there is a possibility of scientifically grounding socialism, I think it will be found along the Utopian and anarchist (and today Reichian) lines and not in Marx's historical emphasis."[103] This was as definite as Macdonald chose to be.

Macdonald ended "The Root Is Man" by sketching out the broad outlines of any future radical social theory and guide to action. According to Macdonald the two central problems facing radicalism were "the alienation of man from his own nature"[104] and, a bit less profound though nevertheless crucial, that "the man in the street . . . is quite simply bored with socialism."[105] Given these conditions, Macdonald held that in the future, radical political action should take place on a more modest and personal level, aiming at the satisfaction of "psychological needs."[106] Radicals should stop judging their effectiveness by the number of supporters they gained. The source of radical action must be a community acting together as a whole. Furthermore the new radical must be guided by a commitment to pacifism, a belief that coercion was wrong in principle, a suspicion of future-oriented plans and actions, ethical socialism and a freedom from the fetishism of mass support.[107]

In evaluating "The Root Is Man" one must keep in mind that it was an assertion of principle, a manifesto, and hence its main points were left unproven. As Macdonald himself admitted, such philosophic flights were not exactly his cup of tea, and obviously neither were more mundane matters of hard research such as both Marx and Freud had done to support their generalizations. But this is only to say the obvious—Macdonald was no Marx or Freud, as he would probably have been the first to admit. The essay is best understood as an attempt by a non-Marxist radical to affirm a rather tenuous position, one rendered so by the events of the past decade.

Though again fairly predictable, the responses to the second half of "The Root Is Man" were a cut above the reaction to the first installment. Louis Clair's (Lewis Coser) "Digging at the Roots or Striking at the Branches" charged Macdonald with choosing purity over engagement, individualism over collective action, and accused him of a contempt for the masses which

betrayed "a voluntarism and impatience with history."[108] Aspects
of the charge were obviously true. Macdonald admitted his turn
to individualism. His new radicalism *was* voluntaristic and opposed coercion of others. Yet as Irving Howe noted in his
critique, "The Thirteenth Disciple," there was a contradiction
between Macdonald's opposition to coercion and his advocacy of
sabotage under certain conditions.[109]

Howe also quite correctly criticized Macdonald for claiming
the existence of certain moral absolutes without asserting, much
less demonstrating, their source. This indeed was a major weakness of the essay, though Macdonald did go a bit farther than
Howe admitted by tentatively adopting Goodman's position that
a new radicalism could best be rooted in man's psychobiological
nature. Yet this one really novel point in the theoretical discussions in *Politics*, and the one most in need of elaboration, was no
more than stated by Macdonald.

Though Howe's refusal to "read off the working class as
finished" and his assertion that the revolutionary movement was
still alive was wrong,[110] he was to the point in his charge that
Macdonald's advocacy of psychological community bordered on
the snobbish and implied that corruption could only be avoided
in a "community of intellectuals and other saints."[111] Obviously
Macdonald's idea of community needed much development. As a
"psychological" community, one could see how it might easily fall
prey to an incestuous perpetuation of its own ideas and attitudes
and remain a community of feeling rather than action.

It was also significant and supportive in spirit of Howe's point
that Macdonald failed to discuss at any length such ideas as
workers' control of industries or the nature of political representation or decentralization of political and economic power. Thus
Macdonald's communitarian-anarchism was reduced in reality to
the advocacy of a vague something called community, based less
upon common work or shared geographical space than upon
intellectual and cultural predilections. There was no particularity
of purpose; no specific goals were laid out.

What Macdonald's essay gave witness to on another level was
the emergence of a new intellectual elite—the New York intellec-

tuals. This elite was characterized by a shared radical past, an intense intellectuality, a disillusionment with day-to-day domestic and world politics, and an intense anti-Stalinism.[112] As a sociological phenomenon the elite was to prove fascinating to itself and to others. But what they lacked, as Macdonald and the whole career of *Politics* indicated, was a positive vision or ideology.

At one point in "The Root Is Man," Macdonald wrote that "After the First World War American radicalism lost its mass roots." After the Second War it lost its ideology and was reduced, at least for a time, to impotence. Most surprising in retrospect was the failure of the *Politics'* intellectuals to make use of American thinkers and an American intellectual tradition of anarchism and communitarianism. One explanation might be that, as Macdonald was later to note, the only American who wrote regularly for the journal was Paul Goodman.[113] Of the "Ancestors" series, not one profile dealt with an American thinker: no Emerson, Thoreau or Wendell Phillips, no William James, Dewey or Veblen, and only passing reference to Randolph Bourne. Marxism hung over the journal like the ghost of a deceased and distant but influential relative whose effect lingered on after death. Only the essays of Goodman and, at times, Macdonald gave a hint of things to come.

The Uses of Freud

The period after World War II was a time of intellectual retrenchment among liberal and radical intellectuals in America and Europe. As they surveyed the physical, moral, and intellectual wreckage of the postwar years, the conviction grew that something had gone amiss in the western tradition. The revelation of the systematic extermination of six million Jews, the realization of the totalitarian nature of Stalinist Russia, and America's use of nuclear weapons did much to disabuse many intellectuals of the notions of progress in history and of the perfectibility of man. From the vogue of existentialism to the rise of neoorthodoxy in Christianity, intellectuals were reassessing their views of man and society.

The demise of Marxism as a persuasive radical ideology was paralleled by the rise of Sigmund Freud's theories to prominence among postwar intellectuals. After World War II Freudian terminology became the common coin of the intellectual realm. As one observer wrote in 1948: "For when the political cliques of the '30's lost their passion and died, they never really died, but rose to the bosom of the Father and were strangely transmogrified. Psychoanalysis is the new look, Sartor Resartus, but the body underneath is the same."[114]

As the years passed, this preoccupation with Freud filtered down from the New York cultural pacesetters to less rarified levels. Leaving behind the populist-Marxist rhetoric of the thirties (class struggle, oppression, reactionary, progressive, etc.) and the traditional rhetoric of western religion (sin, guilt, right, wrong, salvation, damnation), advanced intellectual circles and following them the educated middle class latched on to therapeutic terminology and medical metaphors to explain themselves and their society to themselves. The psychoanalytic gospel, according to Freud, Jung, and lesser popularizers, became something of an ersatz religion, encompassing all sorts of heresies and schisms, orthodoxies and standard texts.[115]

Yet if psychoanalytic terminology was widely applied, it was not used in any rigorous or orthodox sense. There were at least two reasons for this. First the psychoanalytic movement itself had seen a growing intellectual and geographical diaspora since the early thirties. As the psychoanalytic movement was forced to disperse under Nazi pressure in Germany and Austria, most psychoanalysts emigrated to either England or America. And once in their adopted homelands the movement's elements grew even farther apart intellectually.[116]

Psychoanalysis underwent not only theoretical and therapeutic modifications, but also began to be applied afresh in nontherapeutic contexts. Long before the diaspora the ranks of psychoanalysis had included those with interests in other than the strictly therapeutic. Taking a cue from Freud himself, students of anthropology and mythology had brought psychoanalytic concepts to bear on their studies. Others like Wilhelm Reich and

Erich Fromm had in the thirties attempted to wed Freud and Marx. In the postwar years American literary critics such as Lionel Trilling, Alfred Kazin, Leslie Fiedler, and Stanley Edgar Hyman made much use of depth psychology to illuminate literary texts, the process of artistic creation, and the relationship of literature to cultural and psychological archetypes. Likewise the years after the war saw the enrichment (or some would say the dilution) of Judaism and Christianity by psychoanalytic insights and the application of depth psychology to such diverse matters as industrial relations and advertising.[117]

The Chastened Progressives / In America young liberal intellectuals such as Arthur Schlesinger, Jr., were attracted to the critical realism of theologian Reinhold Niebuhr. No longer were progressive pieties about the Soviet Union or the overly optimistic social thought of a John Dewey given much credence.[118] Perhaps the most eloquent spokesman for those chastened progressives who made use of Freud was the literary critic Lionel Trilling. In his *The Liberal Imagination* (1950), Trilling mounted a measured yet incisive critique of the American mind, a mind he characterized as almost unalterably liberal. As a man of letters, Trilling expressed his concern with the radical disjunction between the social and political views of America's educated classes and the vision of man embodied in the best of modern literature.[119] His goal was the reconstitution of "the liberal imagination" so as to allow for a degree of complexity and a sense of the tragic to replace a rather mindless optimism about man.

Though Trilling was talking more of a liberal mood than a coherent set of ideas, he went so far as to define liberalism: "a ready if mild suspiciousness of the profit motive, a belief in progress, science, social legislation, planning and international co-operation, perhaps especially where Russia was in question."[120] It was Trilling's contention that between these rather nebulous principles and "the deep places of the imagination"[121] there was scarcely any commerce. Sigmund Freud became the hero of Trilling's essay since by exploring "the deep places of the imagination" Freud had given voice to the tragic and the complex in the human situation with which superficial liberalism and social engineering were unable to cope. Freud's was a body of thought in the line of "classic tragic realism," and for that reason, far superior to the "simple humanitarian optimism" which Trilling believed had proved "politically and philosophically inadequate" as well as a "kind of check on the creative faculties."[122]

Central to Trilling's argument was the assumption that culture and politics were intimately related. In a time when "all over the world the political mind lies passive before the action and the event" and there seemed to be a "regression from psychoanalysis ... marked by the most astonishing weakness of mind,"[123] Trilling called for a newer more complex thought that would do justice to the complexities of the postwar political and social reality. But it was not to be Dewey or Marx, but Sigmund Freud who would point the way.

In his extended essay *Freud and the Crisis of Our Culture* (1955), Trilling pointed out that Freud was crucial for modern man in that he spoke against the conformist implications of liberal thought which held that "man can be truly himself and fully human only if he is in accord with his cultural environment."[124] For Trilling, as for Goodman, the biological emphasis in Freud's thought provided the justification for the self's resistance to incorporation into whatever social and cultural structures prevailed. The implication was that man was by definition "alienated"; not only was utopian social engineering impossible, it was positively dangerous.

The general tenor of realism which Trilling so lucidly set forth found echoes, though of a slightly different nature, elsewhere. In a volume entitled *Freud and the 20th Century* (1956), several writers noted Freud's affinities with the neoorthodox as well as the tragic view of man. In his essay "Freud and the Revisionists," Will Herberg scored the naïve "Rousseauism" of men such as Erich Fromm and praised Freud's "biologism" which "serves him well in fostering his stubborn insistence that the trouble lies deep in man and is not simply the result of adverse social conditions."[125] In doing so Herberg came close to claiming Freud for the orthodox tradition because of his "iconoclasm." Likewise Reinhold Niebuhr gave Freud credit for destroying the naïve optimism about man which had lingered on since the Enlightenment and generally found more to praise than blame in Freud's "scientific realist account of human behaviour."[126]

The preceding discussion by no means exhausts this line of thought, but it does demonstrate one use of Freud in the postwar period. For the chastened progressives, whether secularists or men of religion, Freud's pessimism as to the possibility of perfecting man or society was a useful antidote to liberal and radical ideologies. In this view the cardinal sin of modern man lay in his forgetfulness of his limitations and the limitations of social engineering. Freud's death-aggression instinct was seen as the secular variant of the doctrine of original sin or as a modern version of the tragic vision.

The problem was that in the hands of lesser men this position became a set of stultifying and conventional pieties and came close to being a rationale for the political and social status quo. It easily led as well to a "wallowing in despair," a mood of self-pity and castigation which ignored the possibility of change in the name of realism. In short, complexity came to be seen as an excuse for inaction and a withdrawal from politics. All utopian schemes and ideological systems were seen as acts of hubris which could only lead to disaster. Unable, and perhaps understandably so, to conceive of a radicalism which was not tainted by dogmatic Marxism or mindless optimism, and mesmerized by the real horrors of the previous decade, this chastened progressivism exhibited much of what David Riesman was to call a "failure of nerve." Historical change and an enthusiasm for experimentation were suspect. Freud had become the great conserver of the western tradition.

At the heart of the position of the chastened progressives was a confusion between the "political" and "cultural." Aside from the validity of the idea of original sin and the attempt to read Freud as a supporter of this view, it was not at all clear what specific or even general political position was thereby entailed. The concept of sin, the tragic, and the death instinct were plainly not categories of political discourse. In fact neither neoorthodoxy nor Freudianism had political content as such. As a result, though Schlesinger, Trilling, and Niebuhr called into question America's "liberal" mind, their politics were of a piece with a John Dewey.[127] On the other hand, Will Herberg moved steadily rightward in the postwar years. And in the realm of foreign policy, the two high priests of neoorthodoxy, Niebuhr and Swiss theologian Karl Barth, parted company on the dangers of communism, with Barth taking the "softer" position. In other words, these men advanced cultural-philosophical arguments against political ideologies and action. Ultimately there was a connection, but in setting the terms of the debate the way they did and confusing the levels of argument, they contributed to, as well as expressed, the stagnation of social and political thought in postwar America.

The Liberal Left / In a series of four essays, three of which were written in 1946 and one in 1950, David Riesman attempted a critique of Freud which was to serve two purposes: to place Freud and his work in the context of late nineteenth-century European society and culture, and to provide a critique of the new pessimism which had claimed Freud for the side of original sin and religion in general.

Riesman's essays focused on the themes of work and play, authority and liberty, heroism and weakness, religion and science in Freud's thought. His method was that of the sociology of knowledge plus a measured psychoanalysis of Freud himself. To Riesman, Freud expressed attitudes in many respects characteristic of the Victorian ethos and an economy of scarcity. Riesman found Freud, for example, "a believer in the theory of elites"[128] in politics and, in his condescending attitude toward the masses, women, children, and artists, the quintessential late nineteenth-century bourgeois gentleman. And yet, Riesman noted, Freud was also a profound democrat in his conception of the relationship between normality and neurosis; each man was subject to psychological disturbances, no matter what his status. Additionally Freud was one of the first to pay serious attention to the child and childhood, the neurotic, the sexually disturbed, and thus to attempt to alleviate human distress. In short Freud "was ambivalent; he provides the texts for the partialities of incorporation, and for contradictory life paths and social policies."[129]

Riesman was particularly insightful in his comments about Freud's popularity among hard-nosed intellectuals and theologians. Though Freud's pessimism and realism were nonconformist in Freud's time Riesman remarked that "it is pessimism which has now become complacent."[130] Freud's own lack of sentimentality and his stoic heroism were particularly appealing to "the current vogue of the tough guy"[131] and Freud's use by an avant-garde "increasingly sympathetic toward religion" particularly misguided. While the neoorthodox intellectuals claimed that Freud "dethroned claims of rationalism and positivism and upheld those of the dark irrational forces in man,"[132] Riesman pointed out that Freud's therapeutic goal had been based on a thoroughgoing Enlightenment hope in the capacity of reason to understand and control those same forces. Likewise Riesman maintained that Freud considered anxiety, one of the favorite concepts of the neoorthodox, a sign of "weakness and sexual inadequacy" rather than "of potential grace."[133] Freud's pessimism allowed for no transcendent source of aid, and to claim Freud for original sin was "at best an analogy."[134] Indeed for Riesman Freud had actually failed to take religion seriously enough and, in questioning all religious and ethical acts, had contributed to "a new kind of hypocrisy, in which we have to cover up anything decent in ourselves and call it tough."[135]

Though Riesman presented no alternative of his own to the "religious" interpretation of Freud, he did call for "a revival of the tradition of utopian thinking" in what he aptly named a "time of disenchantment."[136] In an essay devoted to a discussion of the Goodman brothers' *Communitas*, Riesman scored the "self-styled realists" for their fear of projective plans and their underestimation of the possibilities for alternative social and political arrangements. In a time when "the Jeremiahs share a widespread, and in that sense comforting defeatism,"[137] what was needed were more men possessing a "nerve of failure," a willingness to stand alone, without support from the zeitgeist, and not run with the pack. In this sense Freud was for Riesman "one of the great intellectual heroes of all time."[138] Freud's teachings needed much modification and should be selectively used; indeed the content was more of intellectual interest than personal meaning. Yet Freud the man and thinker stood out as an example of intellectual daring and persistence, one who had dared go against the grain.

Riesman's efforts were clearly to the point in speaking out against a growing antiutopian and narrowly drawn realism. Yet his treatment of Freud was itself disturbing. In saying that Freud's teachings were dated and/or offered something for everybody, Riesman in effect took Freud's work less seriously than the more orthodox Freudians and chastened progressives. In doing this he tended to relegate Freud to intellectual history, safely removed from any contemporary relevance. It was finally Freud, the man, not Freud, the thinker, who was to be emulated.

The Radical Freudians / But there was still another use made of Freud in social and cultural criticism in the postwar years. This was that of the radical Freudians—Paul Goodman, Herbert Marcuse, and Norman Brown. Although thinkers of widely disparate backgrounds and traditions, they had much in common. Each of one degree or another sought to combine a concern for instinctual and erotic liberation with political and social radicalism, cultural with political concerns.

In terms of the psychoanalytic tradition they are a strange breed. Goodman, Marcuse, and Brown share with orthodox Freudians a belief in the centrality of sexuality in human existence, yet reject or radically modify Freud's concept of the death-aggression instinct and Freud's personal and cultural conservatism. They manifestly have little sympathy with the Freud of the chastened progressives. Their concern with political and social forces suggests common ground with revisionists such as Erich Fromm. Yet they fundamentally and explicitly reject the revisionists' demotion of the sexual to a back bench in the parliament of human instincts. Nor are they much concerned with ego psychology or the preoccupation with personal identity. They come closest to the tradition of Wilhelm Reich and his attempt to unite political and sexual radicalism.

2. *FREUD AND REICH*

To understand the relationship between the radical Freudians and the writings of Freud himself, it is necessary not only to be familiar with certain aspects of Freud's own work, but also to examine the theoretical efforts of the Austrian psychoanalyst turned social radical and finally cosmic religionist, Wilhelm Reich.

Reich was a Freudian heretic, one of the more outspoken schismatics, who had, as early as 1933, been excluded from the International Psychoanalytic Movement.[1] Yet Reich's heresy was not that of the neo-Freudians who had come to emphasize social and cultural forces in the development of the individual personality at the expense of Freud's instinct theory.[2] Like the neo-Freudians, Reich rejected Freud's notion of the death-aggression instinct, but clung fast to the original libido theory. Indeed it would not be far off the mark to say that Reich was more Freudian than Freud, in that he went back to the early Freudian instinct theory and refused to accept the master's later teaching regarding the death instinct and the inevitable repressive nature of all cultural and social structures.

Interestingly enough the core of Reich's thought—that neurosis and hence human unhappiness can be traced back to sexual repression—represented quite accurately the manner in which Freud was first "read" and has continued to be interpreted by the popular mind in America.[3] Reich, in truth, did feel that sex was everything and that without sexual liberation a genuinely healthy and just society was an impossibility. It was Reich's contention that Freud failed to carry his own argument far enough by examining, and then trying to change, the society which demanded sexual repression from its members. In other words, Reich held that Freud's teachings had revolutionary implications and that the logical step from individual therapy to social change and even revolution had to be made.

Freud's Instinct Theory

At the heart of the theoretical conflict between Freud and Reich was the matter of man's instinctual makeup and its relationship to the society and culture in which man found himself.[4]

At the outset it must be stressed that Freud never arrived at a final definition of instinct. Nonetheless he maintained that the concept of instinct was still useful as a working tool in his investigations. In his *Three Contributions to a Theory of Sexuality* (1905), Freud advanced a tentative definition of instinct which put stress on the biological source of instinctual energy. In this work Freud wrote that an instinct was "the psychic representation of a continually flowing inner somatic source of stimulation . . . one of the concepts marking the limits between the psychic and the physical."[5] Like the unconscious, this inner somatic source manifested itself in the psychic apparatus, yet was never observable as such. Indeed as he used the term Freud referred to the "psychic representation" rather than the somatic source. The goal of instinctual impulses, the lessening of tension, was the core of Freud's concept of pleasure.

Though in his early writings Freud had posited two basic sets of instincts, "the self-preservative or ego instincts and the sexual instincts,"[6] his stress, theoretically and therapeutically, fell on the sexual instincts and the repression of sexuality as the cause of individual neuroses. In "Three Contributions," he asserted that "this contribution (of sexual instincts) supplies the only constant and most important source of energy in neuroses."[7] Also important in Freud's early discussion were the twin phenomena of sadism and masochism. Freud was later to incorporate these two phenomena into the death instinct, but, in "Three Contributions," he held that sadism was merely an "aggressive component of the sexual instinct."[8] Though less certain as to the source of masochism, Freud tended to the view that it was a secondary phenomenon and resulted from a transformation of sadism.[9]

In "On Narcissism: An Introduction" (1914), Freud took a first crucial step in modifying his instinct theory. In this essay Freud moved to the position that the ego instincts were charged with a heavy libidinal component, and inferred from this that narcissism (self-love yet an ego instinct) was a primary phenomenon.[10] Freud came to this conclusion by observing that the infant initially perceives everything in his world as part of his own self. As a result, the first pleasure he experiences is self-pleasure. Thus the libido, the energy supplying the sexual instincts, is at first directed toward the infant himself. As the infant grows he soon learns to differentiate himself from the world and the external objects of pleasure, e.g., his mother's breasts, from self-pleasure. The upshot of this insight was that narcissism, the original ego instinct, was likewise a function of the sexual instincts. Thus Freud at this point came close to a monistic rather than a dualistic theory of the instincts. The problem which he could not resolve was that though "the hypothesis of separate ego-instincts and sexual instincts . . . is essentially supported upon the facts of biology" this dualism was not supported psychologically.[11]

As a cultivated European, Freud was profoundly shaken by the experience of World War I. In his essay "Thoughts for the Times on War and Death" (1915), Freud expressed a sense of alienation from a Europe which had been plunged into civil war after some one hundred years of relative peace. This sense of standing "helpless in a world that has grown strange"[12] arose from the spectacle of supposedly civilized men reverting to primitive barbarism, and was accompanied by the realization that in Europe there were "many more cultural hypocrites than truly civilized men."[13] Freud also voiced the opinion that one finally had to grant that man's nature was made up of "instinctual impulses" which were neither good nor bad in themselves. As a scientist he was obliged to describe mental phenomena dispassionately. Yet his own sense of values demanded that he judge the results of the imperfect internalization of civilized values and the failure of the erotic instincts to keep the egoistic ones in check. Thus in this essay Freud reverted to his older instinctual dualism. One senses from the essay that Freud felt his original dualistic theory to be inadequate as a tool for explaining the violence and aggression that the war had loosed. Clearly the toll exacted in lives was the result of something more deep-seated, much more ominous, than the instinct of self-preservation.

In the aftermath of the war Freud was led to modify his instinct theory. At the sixth International Psychoanalytic Congress (1920), Freud read a paper entitled "Supplements to the Theory of Dreams" which grew out of his work with war neurotics in the Vienna General Hospital. In the paper Freud moved beyond his earlier view that the goal of dreaming was simply wish fulfillment, according to the pleasure principle, and pointed to a self-punishing component in some dreams. This view he was to develop into his concept of repetition compulsion and ultimately the idea of the death instinct.[14]

With the publication of *Beyond the Pleasure Principle* (1920), Freud returned to a doggedly dualistic theory of instincts by positing a death instinct, Thanatos, which worked against the life instincts or Eros. Eros, for Freud, included the sexual instincts, most of the egoistic or self-preservative impulses, and those drives and forces which enhanced and unified life. Thanatos, on the contrary, included the tendency to self-punishment in the individual as well as those impulses which denied life and disrupted civilized existence. As mentioned before, this new instinctual dualism was grounded in Freud's observation that many of the traumatized soldiers in their dreams attempted to relive and master the battle situation which had occasioned their illness. Thus Freud hypothesized that perhaps there was some innate tendency in the psychobiological makeup of man "which overrides the pleasure principle," was "independent of it," and seemed "to be more primitive."[15]

Freud then proceeded in an admittedly speculative manner to expand on his earlier definition of instinct. He now maintained that the instincts seemed to aim for a restoration of "an earlier state of things"[16] and were thus not only conservative but decidedly reactionary. This reactionary impulse, it seemed to Freud, was "an urge inherent in organic life" in general.[17] As for the life instincts, Freud advanced the idea that these were also conservative in that they expressed the wish of an organism not so much to live as to "die only in its own fashion."[18] The force of Eros was in effect, however, a check on the tendency toward a regression to an earlier state.

The crucial, though perhaps illogical, jump Freud then made in *Beyond the Pleasure Principle* was to link this regressive tendency of organisms with the inevitable death of all organisms, and thus to equate this regressive instinct with what he called the death instinct. Or expressed another way, since the aim of the instincts, according to his older definition, was to diminish tension, and since this was also his definition of pleasure, the ultimate pleasure was complete stasis or death.

One senses from the text that Freud was greatly relieved to have once more established a dualistic instinct theory and in doing so to have countered those critics who had said that "psychoanalysis explains everything by sexuality."[19] Freud tentatively revised his explanations of sadism and masochism as well. He speculated that the individual expression of the death instinct was a masochistic urge, and that masochism thus became a primary phenomenon. In turn this implied that rather than being an aggressive component of the ego instincts, sadism was "a death instinct which, under the influence of the narcissistic libido, has been forced away from the ego and has consequently only emerged in relation to the object."[20] Aggression directed outward was an instinctual but a secondary phenomenon. *Beyond the Pleasure Principle* ended on the somber note that "the pleasure principle seems actively to serve the death instinct."[21]

Freud developed his ideas further in *The Ego and the Id* (1923). It was, however, in *Civilization and Its Discontents* (1930) that Freud extensively developed the implications of the conflict within man and between man and culture; his conclusion was that culture (or civilization) of necessity had to restrain man's instinctual strivings, if both man and civilization were to survive.

From a common-sense standpoint it is self-evident why man's aggressive instincts should be curbed, but it is less than self-evident why sexual renunciation and repression must be imposed on human beings. For Freud, culture demanded that the instincts in general should be curbed in the name of "Beauty, cleanliness and order."[22] The essence of a civilization, indeed its defining characteristic, was the development of man's intellectual and aesthetic capabilities based upon an organized and orderly mode of living. It would be quite valid to argue that the defining characteristics he set down as essential for culture expressed his ethnocentricity and illustrated the extent to which Freud was a prisoner of his times. At any rate, Freud's presupposition was that man was a closed energy system and thus energy expended in one sphere of activity would take away energy from another, i.e., intellectual efforts will subtract from sexual or aggressive energies.

Freud was involved in something of a tautology. He defined culture as that which "differentiates our lives from those of our animal forebears."[23] The answer to the question "what is man?" was that he was the cultural animal. Culture was defined as that which man has. By definition, then, man sublimates and represses his instinctual energies, and thus the source of culture's highest achievements. Repressed instincts are those pushed back into the unconscious to emerge in dreams or reappear in antisocial forms. Or they are "absorbed . . . so that something appears in place of them which in an individual we call a character trait."[24] Thus for Freud culture implied renunciation or rechanneling of the instincts, specifically a lessening of sexual expression.

Speaking more directly to the last point, Freud noted that the sexual attachment of the male to the female and, to a lesser extent, of the parents to the children conflicted with society's need to "cement men and women together in larger units."[25] Civilized life demanded work and cooperative activity in order to survive. As Freud put it: "Women represent the interests of the family and the sexual life; the work of civilization has become more and more men's business."[26] In short, Eros works against sexuality and demands that the latter be diverted from its original object and used in the cooperative efforts demanded by life within civilization.

Yet even within the family the sexual choices are restricted. The basic expression of this restriction is the incest taboo which lies at the heart of the Oedipus complex; indeed it is central to the development of civilization. Whether explained historically by the primal horde story or functionally by the necessity for the child to give up his mother as a libidinal object in order to become independent—a separate human being—and carry on the work of culture, it is inevitable, according to Freud, that society demands this restriction of sexual expression. Thus the centrality of the incest taboo which Freud felt was "perhaps the most maiming wound ever inflicted throughout the ages on the erotic life of man."[27]

Besides the incest taboo Freud pointed out that the peculiar sexual mores of western civilization further restricted sexual choice to members of the opposite sex and demanded as well monogamous heterosexual marriages. Freud's message thus seemed unequivocal: the demands of civilized existence, on the day-to-day level and in the realm of high cultural achievement, are met at the expense of instinctual gratification. Culture is by definition repressive.

At the same time that culture demands libidinal renunciation, modification, and diversion in the service of Eros, it (culture) was also the embodiment of the life instincts working against the disruptive effects of Thanatos and human aggression. Thus civilization demands a renunciation of aggression, or at least that it be channeled into acceptable forms. For Freud, "The tendency to aggression . . . constitutes the most powerful obstacle to culture."[28]

In addition to the erotic forces which bind men together and work against the disintegrative tendencies of aggression, Freud added another controlling force in the individual psyche—the superego or conscience. Man learns to repress himself in the sense that the energy of the superego is supplied by internalized aggression: "it is sent back where it came from, i.e. directed against the ego."[29] Each time an aggressive act or emotion is repressed, the strength of the superego is augmented. In terms of the individual's development, the aggressive impulses felt toward the father are renounced due to the dread of the loss of love; the father is then incorporated psychologically in the form of the superego. The peculiar product of this formation is a sense of guilt; this results both from the conflict between the sexual desire for the mother and the threat of the father and from the aggressive urge against the father in conflict with the fear of losing his love. To repeat, the energy for the superego is supplied by the aggressive impulses turned back on the ego; the content of the superego is composed of society's rules, customs, laws, etc., constraints which the culture uses to control the individual through the agency not only of the father but also of "educators, teachers, people chosen as ideal models."[30] The development of the sense of guilt is the price of life within civilization. It is the outcome of the conflict between the libidinal demands and the superego as well as of that between the aggressive instincts and the superego. Put more succinctly, it is the result of the "eternal struggle between Eros and the destructive or death instinct."[31]

Thus Freud saw the relationship of the individual to his own instinctual makeup as well as his relationship to culture as exceedingly complicated. The life of the individual and the life of the culture are subsumed under the conflict between Eros and Thanatos. Eros—the unifying and binding, the creative and life enhancing power—works in opposition to its own sexual components. And, analogously, Thanatos—the disruptive and destructive—is checked by the aggressive energies as they find embodiment in the superego. Civilization is the working together of Eros and aggression. The sexual and the aggressive instincts seek to break the bonds of culture. Thus there are dualisms within dualisms. Aspects of the opposing instincts work together against aspects of opposing instincts. Eros and guilt hold things together; sexuality and Thanatos threaten to break things apart. Culture, like the unconscious, knows no logic.

A critique of Freud's instinct theory must obviously address itself to the matter of the death instinct. Freud himself had seemed uncertain about exactly how to take this into account, and had recommended that it be ignored in therapy, at least at first. In *The Ego and the Id* (1923), Freud admitted that "I am only putting forward a hypothesis; I have no proof to offer."[32] By 1930 and the appearance of *Civilization and Its Discontents*, however, the death instinct had assumed a prominent position, if not the major one, in his metapsychological speculations.

One source of confusion, conceptually, was Freud's linking together of what he called the death instinct and man's instinctual aggressiveness. As J. A. C. Brown points out in his book *Freud and the Post-Freudians*: "Freud has confused two entirely separate concepts: the first, that aggression is innate in man . . .; the second, that because all men die and all behaviour is striving, they must also be striving for death . . . because aggression can become directed against the self as demonstrated clinically, therefore aggression and the death instinct are one and the same."[33] In short, to believe that man is instinctually aggressive does not mean that man has a biological urge to die.

Even in the context of *Civilization and Its Discontents*, Freud's death-aggression instinct presented problems. The fact of human aggression, whether instinctually grounded or not, was well-integrated into his discussion of the instinctual repression necessary for the existence of civilization. Freud did not, however, make much use of the death instinct, i.e., primary masochism, as such. One might wonder if and how culture also represses the death instinct. Is it sublimated in the same fashion as sexuality? Other than in the cases of suicide and war does the individual or society manifest a tendency to self-destruction in the same way as the sexual impulses manifest themselves? Freud failed to deal with such questions.

It was, of course, because of the death instinct and its concomitant aggression that Freud was profoundly pessimistic concerning the possibility of a nonrepressive social order in which individuals had escaped the dominance/submission nexus characteristic of human existence. Thus on several occasions Freud expressed skepticism about the Marxist vision of a classless society. He had no particular objection to the confiscation and nationalization of private property and, if Reich is to be believed, expressed tentative interest in and approval of attempts in the early years of the Bolshevist rule to do away with some of the repressive laws and customs governing marriage, abortion, and contraception. Yet Freud remained convinced that none of this, in and of itself, would bring about the end of social divisions and domination, or make possible the abolition of cultural restraints on human instinctual life.

Freud has often been charged with neglecting the influence of social forces in the development of the individual in favor of an emphasis on the role that the instincts—the "constants"—play. The contention is true insofar as the main thrust of Freud's thought, especially in later years, placed the locus of instinctual restriction within rather than outside the individual. Man, for Freud, was no "tabula rasa" upon which the forces of society and culture wrote their demands. Rather culture and society came into continual conflict with the instinctual forces within the individual.

On the other hand, few other thinkers in the western tradition have been so aware of and have made so integral a part of their work the idea that the individual human being is profoundly and rather unhappily formed by the cultural and social matrix into which he finds himself born. For Freud, man and culture were inextricably linked and externally in conflict. Man was neither a passive cipher nor the master of his fate. He was conscious and unhappy.

There was in Freud's thought little differentiation among cultures or within cultures as to the type and amount of repression demanded of an individual. Nor did he discuss at any length the *various* functions that the family, the state, or any type of intermediate sized institution played in the development of the individual or the life of the society. Freud did draw the distinction between primitive and more highly developed societies, yet, in doing so, he merely used the primitive societies as analogies illustrating how and why men in "advanced" societies related to themselves, others, and the "gods." For Freud the great watershed in the history of the race was the killing of the father by the sons. Though civilizations rose and fell, man's basic psychic structures, as well as the social context in which he finds himself, were all prefigured in the primordial conflict, murder, guilt, renunciation of the mother, and establishment of collective rituals. As Philip Rieff has written: "If there are original traumas in group history as well as in the life of the individual, evolution supplies no safe distance from them. . . . His [Freud's] desire was always to find, in emergence, sameness; in the dynamic, the static; in the present, latent pasts."[34] Thus for Freud the past, both in the individual and the group experience, was always threatening to break into the open. Nothing was ever lost or transcended in human or individual history. History, just as the unconscious, knew no past or present. Everything had been preserved and could potentially reemerge.

All the above is a way of saying that Freud, unlike Marx and the tradition of western radicalism emerging from the Enlightenment with its historicist and progressivist bias, saw no possibility for a radically different future for the majority of mankind. In order for Freud to be "of use" to radical theorists one of several strategies had to be adopted. One lay along the lines embraced by the neo-Freudians—drop the instinct theory altogether and consider man a tabula rasa, malleable by social and cultural forces. In other words, elevate social engineering, whether radical or conservative, to a position of prominence. In this view individual needs and values would ultimately be brought into harmony with those of society's, on the latter's terms.

Another possible strategy was to do as Wilhelm Reich did and deny the validity of Freud's death instinct, while retaining the sexual instinct as basic and central. Thus for Reich the root cause of human unhappiness was the repression of sexuality; the best society, one which was structured for instinctual liberation. In this view the natural, i.e., sexual, was equated with the moral; what is, should be allowed "exercise." Nature or the "natural" in this view cannot include aggression as a characteristic of itself. If such were the case, the repression of the natural would also be necessary and hence repressive social structures justified. Reich believed otherwise and devoted most of his intellectual efforts to proving Freud wrong. At stake was the possibility of the emergence of a new man in a radically different culture and society.

Wilhelm Reich: The First Sexual Radical[35]

As it developed in the first quarter of this century, Freud's Vienna circle saw itself, often with justification, as something akin to a beleaguered religious sect. As with religious sects, schisms and schismatics abounded; unanimity was rare and the only unifying principle of the group seems to have been a desire to receive Dr. Freud's approval and cast those from the fold who dared to disagree with the master. Freud, like Jehovah, was a jealous being, and thus intellectual deviations were often interpreted by Freud and others (in typical psychoanalytic style) as psychological aberrations, reflecting the weakness of the deviant's psychic makeup, rather than the keenness of his intellect.

In several conversations recorded in 1952, Wilhelm Reich, a veteran of schismatic skirmishes and even full-scale warfare, attempted a psychoanalysis of Freud in which he focused on the early twenties, when Reich first had come into contact with the master. Wrote Reich: "When I met Freud in 1919 he was a very alive person . . . he was outgoing. He was hopeful. . . . Then around 1924 something happened; . . . Freud began to resign . . . there is little doubt that he was very much dissatisfied genitally."[36] Not only was Freud in a personal bind, Reich maintained, he was also "caught with his pupils and his associations. He couldn't move anymore."[37]

The middle and late twenties were crucial for the development of Reich's ideas and the resulting breach with Freud. Reich was beginning to make public his notion that sexual repression was the fundamental cause of neuroses, something he claimed was an outgrowth of Freud's *Three Contributions to a Theory of Sexuality*. This aspect of Reich's thought was of course at odds with Freud's hypothesis of and elaboration upon the death instinct and the inevitability of repression. Reich was also becoming quite interested in the social aspects of neuroses at this time and in the possibility of moving from individual therapy to collective prevention of sexual disturbances on a mass scale. According to Reich, Freud was initially enthusiastic about the sex hygiene movement that Reich had established in Austria, and looked favorably upon sexual reforms in contemporary Russia.[38] Once, however, Freud learned of Reich's intellectual interest in Marx and Engels, whom he had been reading since 1924, Freud began to look with more disfavor at Reich's efforts to draw "the social consequences of the libido theory."[39] By 1927 a combination of personal, political, and theoretical differences had driven the two men farther apart.

In 1928 Reich became an active member of the Communist party and a year later he opened sex hygiene clinics in Vienna and visited Russia.[40] The intellectual break between Reich and Freud was final with the publication of *Civilization and Its Discontents* in 1930. According to Reich the book "was written specifically in response to one of my lectures (Dec. 12, 1929) in Freud's home. I was the one who was 'unbehaglich in der Kultur.' "[41] In the same year Reich published *The Sexual Revolution*. Thus began Reich's open efforts to make his own way, combining sexual with social radicalism.

Reich's basic assumption in *The Sexual Revolution* was that individual neurosis is the result of sexual repression. Accompanying neurosis was what Reich named "armoring." According to Reich: "In the conflict between instinct and morals, ego and outer world, the organism is forced to armor itself against the instincts as well as the outer world."[42] The armor, maintained Reich, was the expression of fear; yet the more the armor was strengthened and sexuality was repressed, the greater the force of sexual anxiety. Thus the basic elements of Reich's thought were set forth; the individual was caught between instinct and externally imposed moral standards and was forced to "armor" himself from outer and inner forces. Behind the individual armoring process, neurosis, and genital disturbance lay the repressive morality imposed by society through its institutions and the process of socialization.

Following upon this description of the individual's relationship to himself and the outside world, Reich advanced the idea of "character analytic treatment" as the therapeutic means of curing the patient. In such a mode of treatment the prime goal was the release of the energy used to erect and maintain the armor so that "immediate natural contact with his impulses as well as his environment" would be possible.[43] Once this happened (and if a suitable sex partner could be found) the patient could act according to the principle of sexual self-regulation rather than obeying externally imposed morals. Thus Reich assumed that not only was the freeing of the instinctual (sexual) energy vital for individual health, but also that the sexual included within it a principle of self-regulation which, if allowed to operate unimpeded, worked toward the psychological health of the individual.

Reich challenged Freud's notion that "the dichotomy of nature and culture, individual and society, sexuality and sociality"[44] was an inevitable one. In a culture which was nonrepressive such conceptual dichotomies would make no sense. Reich did grant, no doubt with *Civilization and Its Discontents* in mind, that Freud was correct in claiming that in "the patriarchal, authoritarian culture" of Western Europe, the dichotomies were operative. This however, only went to show that Freud, pioneer and genius that he was, remained "a middle-class cultural philosopher"[45] unwilling to draw the revolutionary consequences of his own teachings. Rather Freud plumped for a destructive adjustment of the individual to a reality "determined by an authoritarian society."[46] In such a situation theory and practice, "is" and "ought," nature and history remain alienated from each other.

It was not Reich's belief that a mere change in institutions could be sufficient; needed as well was a cultural revolution in which the guiding principle of individual behavior would be "sex-economic regulation."[47] Nor did Reich deny that sublimation was the basis of cultural achievement; he maintained rather that "the pre-genital impulses," not genital sexuality as such, were to be sublimated.[48]

In searching for the crucial institution through which the individual was made neurotic and unhappy, Reich arrived at the conventional patriarchal family. Unlike Freud, who in *Civilization and Its Discontents* had noted that the family often worked against the demands of the group, Reich saw the family structure as the transmitter of society's repressive values, which were grounded in economic interest. Thus the family was sexually repressive and economically oppressive. Indeed the original significance of the family lay in three areas: the economic, in that the family was the basic economic unit in the early stages of capitalism; the social, in that it offered protection for women and children who had no economic or sexual rights; and most importantly, the political, in that the family was "a factory for authoritarian ideologies and conservative structures."[49] The father in the patriarchal family represented "the authority of the state" in inculcating in the child "pre-genital fixation and genital inhibition."[50] Thus the family "creates the individual who is forever afraid of life and of authority and thus creates again and again the possibility that masses of people can be governed by a handful of powerful individuals."[51] The family is the state in microcosm, and it is primarily because a child is reared in the authoritarian family that he gives passive allegiance to the given values and structures around him.

There is little doubt that much of what Reich had to say about the relationship of the individual to the family and the family to the "external" world was true[52] (though his focus on the authoritarian family as a particularly bourgeois phenomenon is undoubtedly overdone). What Reich desired was a society in which infant sexuality was not taboo and sexual abstinence was not required of the adolescent at precisely the time he reached sexual maturity. For Reich the lifelong, monogamous marriage was also a disaster. Individuals should marry and mate as long as they were sexually attracted to one another; if the desire faded, the marriage should be dissolved. And as a corollary women "should be economically independent in the society and . . . the care and education of children should be removed from the family."[53]

In his *Character Analysis* (1933), Reich discussed in greater detail the nature of character-formation in the individual, and linked individual and social restructuring much closer together. In the preface to the first edition he wrote that although it was clear that "neuroses are the result of patriarchal, authoritarian education with its sexual repression . . . all pre-requisites for a practical program of prevention are absent; they will first have to be created by a basic revolution in the social institutions and ideologies."[54]

Reich went beyond Freud's therapeutic goal of bringing to consciousness the cause of neurosis (an intellectual process) and maintained that if "the patient is to get well and stay well, he must become able to establish a satisfactory genital sex life. . . ."[55] Thus the patient must not merely understand his problem and then sublimate it; he must actually satisfy his sexual needs. In this way theory and therapy would be united and mere verbalization avoided.

Reich also elaborated upon the connection between the individual character structure and social reality by asserting that "the character structure . . . is the crystallization of the sociological process of a given epoch."[56] The character structure was in turn linked up to the instinctual makeup of the individual since character was the outcome of the armoring process. The goal of therapy was thus the creation of "character structures which allow of sexual and social mobility. . . ."[57]

Reich named his ideal-typical character the "genital character." The genital character was one who could achieve genital gratification, a satisfactory orgasm, with his partner rather than remaining fixated on pregenital desires or diverted by sexual fantasies. He was one who could truly sublimate, which for Reich meant the rechanneling of pregenital and infantile impulses. For Reich sublimation and instinctual gratification were not mutually exclusive since "a sound libidinal economy was the pre-requisite of successful and lasting sublimation."[58] Having transcended the Oedipal stage, the sexual choices of the genital character were no longer substitutes for the desired parent of the opposite sex. He no longer identified "with frustrating reality,"[59] i.e., the father and by extension the political leader, but was self-determining and capable of independent action. Nor was the genital character a type incapable of anger and hatred; these states he could "rationally" assume.[60] Underlying Reich's ideal type was the assumption that genital potency, the possibility of achieving the satisfactory orgasm, was the key to a "healthy" personality. Only with the free exercise of genital sexuality was individual rationality possible.

In the final section of the original *Character Analysis*, Reich moved to refute Freud's death instinct by pointing out that the masochist "approaches pleasurable activity like any other person but the fear of punishment interferes. The masochistic self-punishment is not the execution of the dreaded punishment, but a milder substitute punishment—a specific mode of defense against punishment anxiety."[61] The masochist thus inflicts psychic or physical pain upon himself because the pain he causes himself is less than that feared from outside sources and in a sense preempts the external threat. It is indeed pleasurable, but only in the sense that it is "not as bad as."

Most crucial for our purposes is that Reich's psychoanalytic vision and its relation to his desire for revolutionary social change depended upon his denial of Freud's death instinct; or, in more general terms, of any instinctual dualism, since to make a destructive principle an integral part of nature and the natural would mean that the natural, defined by Reich as the genital-sexual and the rational, could no longer serve as the regulative principle of individual and social development. Once one admitted that nature was destructive as well as creative, cruel as well as kind, then the necessity for a repressive culture and society to protect the individual against himself and others would become apparent. The possibility of a union between the "is" and the "ought," nature and culture, the scientific and the moral would be an impossibility. A naturalistic ethic and a revolution based on the logic of nature would be unattainable.

It was in *Die Massenpsychologie des Faschismus* (1934) that Reich developed most explicitly his synthesis of Freud and Marx. In this work Reich was concerned with explaining how and why the National Socialists had been able to gain power in Germany and, closely related to that concern, why the Communist party had failed to attract the German people to its cause.

It was Reich's opinion that the failure of the German Communist party could be attributed to a vulgar Marxism which drew simplistic causal connections between an individual's socioeconomic status and his political ideology and loyalty. This view, according to which all workers, indeed all those oppressed by the capitalist order and in a socially precarious position, would automatically turn to the Communist party was mistaken, Reich noted, because it equated the objective situation in Germany with the subjective reaction by individuals and groups to that objective situation. In short, Marxism needed a psychology. Without a psychology the Communists had failed to understand the feelings of the mass of Germans and had dogmatically clung to an economic analysis.[62] More specifically, because Marxism slighted the psychological dimension, it failed to understand that "irrational thinking and action, i.e. not corresponding to the economic situation, is the result of an earlier socio-economic situation."[63] This was to say that the psychological structure of the individual, formed in early childhood and shaped by social structures and values at that time, had a life of its own. Thus, if the structures of a given society underwent radical and rapid change, the individual psychology of its members would not automatically change along with it. In the case of Germany, broad segments of the population had revolutionary feelings, but reactionary or fascist goals. The petit bourgeoisie, while being threatened with engulfment by the proletariat, identified "up" with the traditional middle class. This class acted in a revolutionary manner against the existing though tottering structures of the Weimar Republic and blamed it for their precarious position. At the same time the insecure classes yearned for a return to authority and stability which would halt their downward plunge into the proletariat. This, for Reich, went far to explain the appeal of the National Socialist's "Blut and Boden" ideology with its harking back to times of stability and an organic political and social order.[64]

Why, Reich asked, did men allow themselves to be enslaved? His answer, not unsurprisingly, was that the fault lay with the traditional authoritarian bourgeois family. "Sex repression begins relatively late with private property," Reich noted, and coincided with "the beginning of class divisions. . . ." All this was insured by "the monogamous marriage and patriarchal family."[65] For economic oppression to be maintained, individuals must be sexually repressed. The end product of the patriarchal family is the "patient citizen."[66] Not only fascism but social democratic reform as well was based on the desire for security and order produced in the authoritarian family.[67]

As a counter to the bourgeois family, Reich held up the working-class family and working-class values. In this, the least convincing part of his analysis, Reich pointed out that instead of identifying with the national leader, the workers identified with their class.[68] Also precisely because of their oppressed state, the working-class family structure was weaker and hence more conducive to the development of nonrepressive sexual values.[69] Workers had an "open and matter of fact" attitude toward sex because of their collective existence.[70] The danger was that the workers would also be attracted by the bourgeois life-style with its promised order and stability. Thus to win the workers the Communist party would also have to "develop and further proletarian culture and work against petit bourgeois ways of life. . . ."[71] A cultural as well as an economic revolution was clearly needed.

After analyzing the role that the church and racial theories played in the Nazi hegemony, Reich concluded by asserting that "the sexual political struggle is a part of the entire battle of the exploited and the oppressed against the exploiters and the oppressors."[72] The key was to educate people to change their sexual attitudes and behavior, if need be through mass meetings at which sexual fears and problems could be voiced and clarified, or even better by beginning with children. "The sexual question," he wrote, "must be politicized."[73]

Reich's efforts to provide Marxism with a psychology were ill-rewarded by the Communist party. In 1934 Reich was expelled from the party and accused of being a counterrevolutionary. Nevertheless, for a time, Reich remained committed to a total revolution in human affairs which would come about by changing both individual men and socioeconomic structures. A change in either area alone was clearly not enough.

As if to drive this latter point home, Reich did an extensive analysis of the experiments in communal living and sexual reform which had been attempted in the Soviet Union but then abandoned by the 1930s. In explaining the failure of these experiments Reich returned to the idea that there was little in Marxist ideology which dealt with a transformation of sexual attitudes and behavior, or more generally a radical change in cultural attitudes. Thus "the power of the proletariat and sexual legislation could do no more than create the external conditions for a changed sexual life."[74] The psychological superstructure, despite external rearrangements, remained the same and had a life of its own. Moreover there were the historically conditioned attitudes of the leaders and people of Russia, her economic problems, and the threat to the Revolution from external aggressors and internal civil war.[75] As Reich saw it, the prime goal of the social revolution—"to place the economy again at the service of the satisfaction of the needs of all who do productive work—"[76] had been defeated. Once again individual needs and desires had been subordinated to external economic and political considerations. Instead of self-regulation, externally imposed restrictions remained the rule. Only the rulers had changed.[77]

In evaluating Reich's early Freudian-Marxist point of view it is important to remember that though Reich's views were heretical to both orthodox Marxists and Freudians, he was still in the "intellectual mainstream." For instance Erich Fromm, who was working along similar lines in trying to unite "historical materialism" with psychoanalysis, had words of praise for Reich's work on the psychosocial role of the family. In his "Über Methode und Aufgabe einer analytischen Sozialpsychologie" (1932), Fromm had also attempted to provide Marxism with a psychological dimension.[78] And Karl Landauer reviewed Reich's *Die Massenpsychologie* and *Character-Analyse* quite favorably in 1934 in the *Zeitschrift für Sozialforschung*, though adding a caveat concerning Reich's overestimation of the importance of genital sexuality.[79] There was nothing particularly unusual about Reich's terminology, nor had he yet begun to write openly about his attempts to link up sexuality and biophysics.

Reich's chief innovation by this point had been the attempt to formulate a social theory which would correlate sexual repression, whose chief instrument was the authoritarian bourgeois family, with political and economic oppression. Also Reich had enriched the whole area of social psychology, with his observation, later picked up by Goodman and Marcuse, that the oppressed and exploited often identify with rather than rebel against oppressive-repressive forces. This observation Reich used to illuminate the willingness of individuals and groups to accept, indeed welcome, external domination out of insecurity and/or a desire to be relieved of the burden of independent thought and action. And his observation that a revolutionary change in social and economic structures did not necessarily lead to a change in values and cultural attitudes, particularly in the area of sexuality, was a valid and valuable one in pointing up the complexities of radical change. At no point did Reich equate sexual with social liberation. Rather, he asserted that one had to accompany the other for either to be meaningful.

As far as specific reforms were concerned, Reich combined utopian with rather commonsensical practical remedies. Reich favored the toleration of infantile masturbation and free adolescent sexuality. As has already been pointed out, he thought that monogamous marriage and the subservience of women to men in the family were responsible for much unhappiness which was reflected in the "sex-negative" manner in which children were raised. Abortion and contraception were also vital in order to free sexuality from reproduction. And as we have noted already, Reich moved from a belief in the efficacy of individual therapy to the view that mass sexual hygiene groups should be formed to deal more widely with sexual problems.

Reich's utopian plans centered around what he called "work democracy" in which the rearing of children was to be removed from the immediate control of the parents.[80] He had hoped that the socialist collectives established in Russia would mean, in some measure, a return to a matriarchal clan structure with which he associated free infant and adult sexuality and sex-affirmative attitudes in general. Yet Reich did not see life in his ideal society as one of mindless copulation and pleasure: "The idea of collective living has nothing to do with the idea of paradise. Struggle and pain and sexual pleasure are parts of life. The essential point is that people should be capable of consciously experiencing pleasure and pain and capable of rationally mastering it. . . . Only genitally healthy people are capable of voluntary work and non-authoritarian self-determination of their lives."[81] Only if individuals were sexually free could they be liberated from their pasts and act in a rational manner; once this was the case they would be capable of productive work rather than remaining drones engaged in externally imposed tasks.

Reich's goal was thus a nonrepressive society based on "sex-affirmative" cultural values. Though it played a comparatively minor role in his thought, sublimation, which Freud had considered the basis of cultural achievement, was also to be operative. In contrast with Freud, however, Reich saw sublimation as the process of rechanneling only pregenital sexual impulses. The natural was expressed by genital sexuality rather than sexuality in general. Unlike later theorists of nonrepressive societies such as Marcuse and Norman Brown, Reich was quite orthodox concerning the sexual life of the healthy individual. He strongly rejected the concept of polymorphous perversity and considered homosexuality to be unnatural and unhealthy.[82]

In terms of the western radical tradition, Reich was moving toward an anarchist position with his emphasis on work democracies and individual self-regulation. Reich's peculiar brand of anarchism was one which had at its core an emphasis on instinctual liberation and an identification of the sexual with the natural.[83] Institutions should rightly be the outgrowth of individual and communal needs for love, sociality, and productive labor.

Yet from another angle Reich's anarchism would have to present serious problems for the anarchist. At least one tradition of anarchism has stressed the importance of federations—small groups based on collective interests and needs—as a counterweight to the coercive power of the state or the society in general. And it is precisely the family which has been, from one point of view, the most effective institution working against external coercion. For instance, even in Freud, the family was at one and the same time the instrument for implanting social and cultural values and also the opponent of the demands of the society. Reich, much more than Freud, underestimated the complex role that the family assumes in the socialization of its members. For Reich the superego, part of the "character," was the unobstructed conduit of social control. He tended to believe that there was a direct cause-effect relationship between the oppressive and repressive values of the society in general and the values imparted within the family.[84] Perhaps mesmerized by the Marxist idea that culture, religion, philosophy, etc. are mere epiphenoma, Reich saw societies and cultures as simple monoliths and underplayed the tension within a culture and a society among sets of values. Thus, though Reich had added a psychological dimension to Marxism, he failed to develop it far enough to explain opposition to as well as acquiescence in external domination.

In a real sense Reich was caught in a vicious circle. Only if the conventional authoritarian family structure were abolished could the individual be self-determining and develop values and behavior harmonious with his own nature. Yet the family structure could safely be abolished only after the social and economic revolution had been carried out by "sick" men, molded by a repressive and oppressive society. If the family were abolished before, then the repressive society would still be in a position of hegemony and would surely inculcate those repressive values upon which its authority was based, only much more directly and effectively. We know for instance from studies of slavery in North America and the experience in the Nazi concentration camps that the most effective way to obtain acquiescence from the oppressed is to destroy the family and other social structures which, though inhibiting individual expression, nevertheless protect him against brute and unmediated coercion. Thus again the paradox—the family coerces, yet provides a source of resistance to greater external coercion.

Perhaps the most significant (and ominous) development in Reich's thought grew out of his attempt to combine traditional revolutionary goals with a revolution in sexual attitudes and

behavior; that is, his elevation of sexuality into the political realm. Given the goal of a complete transformation of values, Reich's desire to politicize sex seems to have been inevitable. Reich finally arrived at a concept of politics which would open all aspects of individual and collective life to manipulation and control, from the most public action such as mounting the barricades in broad daylight to the most private and intimate sexual relations between individuals. At that point it is irrelevant whether the external control is the centralized state or a "clan work democracy." The distinction between public and private, history and psychology, civic duty and private pleasure would be obliterated. All actions become political; the ethos, totalitarian.

The expulsion of Reich from the International Psychoanalytic Association and the Communist party and his exile in Scandinavia after 1933 marked the point at which Reich parted company with the traditional vocabulary and concepts of the Freudian and Marxist traditions. While in Scandinavia Reich began working on what he was to call "orgone therapy" in the hope of establishing a natural scientific basis for the cure to psychosexual problems. The central thread of Reich's later work was generally coincident with that of his earlier work—the establishment in the individual of genital satisfaction, or, as Reich was later to call it, "orgiastic potency." By the early 1940s, however, Reich's vocabulary of concepts had been metamorphosized into a quasi-biophysical system distinct from the earlier more or less conventional psychological and sociological conceptual language. According to the later Reich: "We are all simply a complicated electric machine which has a structure of its own and is in interaction with the energy of the universe."[85] The orgasm, which was to become the key to individual well being, was "a phenomenon of electrical discharge."[86]

The satisfactory orgasm (more than mere ejaculative potential) was also more than just electrical discharge. It was the specific manifestation of the link between individual energy and an all-pervasive source which Reich named "cosmic orgone energy." According to Reich, his discovery of cosmic orgone energy put individual therapy on a firm footing in "objective natural scientific processes" and removed it from the speculative psychological and verbal approach of conventional psychoanalysis.[87] Thus the individual had become mechanized, or the cosmos, like politics earlier, had become sexualized.

Reich called his new science "Orgonomy." It took as its basic unit the orgone—"that energy which, according to definite physical laws, is the basis of the sexual functions."[88] The therapeutic goal of Orgonomy was "the mobilization of the patients' plasmatic currents."[89] Expressed less arcanely, the goal of orgone therapy was to unblock static orgone energy so as to allow it to flow again. Until this was done, the armored individual would remain in a state of psychic and physical contactlessness, cut off from the outside world, his own sexual energies, and ultimately the cosmic life-force.

When this state of psychological and physical armoring, orgasmic impotency, was shared by many individuals, even an entire society, it was called the "emotional plague." No longer was the evil a specific social or economic institution as such. Reich was no more explicit than to say that "It [the plague] made its first appearance with the first suppression of genital love life. . . . It is an epidemic disease, like schizophrenia or cancer, with this important difference: it manifests itself essentially in social living."[90] Thus the plague may come to characterize an entire society or culture. Likewise the plague receives somatic expression in that it "may lead to cardiac disease or cancer." In 1952 Reich expanded on this connection between sexual suppression and physical illness by saying that "cancer . . . is a disease following emotional resignation—a bio-energetic shrinking, a giving up of hope."[91]

In summary, then, the purpose of Reich's later therapeutic efforts was to "restore the biophysical equilibrium by releasing the orgastic potency."[92] The patient was no longer merely talked to and called upon to verbalize his free associations. Because Reich felt that muscular hypertension and body rigidity were symptomatic of the same thing as emotional and sexual armoring, he moved to a mode of therapy in which individual body posture and muscle tone were analyzed and touched directly by the therapist. And finally for "man the machine," the conduit of quantifiable observable cosmic energy, Reich's ultimate therapeutic innovation was itself a machine. This "orgone box," as Reich was to call it, was a container in which the suffering human being was placed in order to have focused upon him the cosmic orgone energy and thus be cured of his ailments.[93]

It is obviously difficult to evaluate Reich's later writings without ridiculing them. The obvious irony in Reich's intellectual development was that the "farther out" he went intellectually, the farther back in time he went. While the physical sciences were abandoning simplistic notions of energy and matter and certainly an explicitly materialistic metaphysics, Reich was formulating a materialistic vitalism reminiscent of Häckel. Another and more serious irony was that in his quest for a cure to the problems of neuroses and sexual disturbances, Reich ended by rendering man quite literally a machine; his one claim to happiness—the orgasm—had become a mere electrical discharge. Indeed with all Reich's emphasis on the orgasm as the key to human happiness, it became hard to see why in his later more pseudoscientific work the individual needed a partner to have the perfect orgasm. If man is a machine and the orgasm is a function of that machine, then there is no reason why another is needed to complete the process satisfactorily. The depersonalization of the person thus led to a depersonalization of the function.

Another way of saying this is to note again that Reich paid less and less attention to the clash of specific values and socioeconomic structures and their effect on individual development. Reich argued as early as 1944 that "politics has definitely played out."[94] Disillusioned with the course of the revolution in Russia and of course horrified by Hitler's Germany, Reich oscillated between grasping for grandiose cosmological certainties and, going to the other extreme, describing human emotions in terms of protoplasmic movements and quantifiable energy units.

In the 1940s and 1950s Reich's writings underwent a definite deterioration toward the abstract, the wooden, and at times the hysterical. Unlike Freud, who had refused to play the role of prophet or consider himself the possessor of any all-curative nostrum for human ills, Reich positively leaped at the chance to become the founder and high priest of a new science-religion.[95] And unlike Freud's prose style, which was almost unbearably rigorous, packed with insights, and impatient of jargon, Reich's style was increasingly characterized by capitalized words and slogans, crude diagrams and charts of electrochemical devices and experiments, and self-invented arcania and simplistic over-generalizations.

At the same time this increasingly sterile jargon was combined with the most rampant megalomania. It is quite clear from the reminiscences of Reich's third wife that Reich was mad by the 1950s. He had begun to drink heavily and had also become extremely paranoic about the threats to his life and work posed by Stalinist agents; conversely he felt that President Eisenhower and the American government knew of his work and approved of it, but could not acknowledge the fact openly.[96] The wilder Reich's ideas became, the more he identified himself with the great intellectual and spiritual martyrs of western culture, from Jesus to Giordano Bruno to Nietzsche, all of whom had suffered and died at the hands of a literally "unfeeling" world, suffering from the emotional plague. Yet the ultimate pathos of Reich's life was that he died, not before the public eye as a great martyr to a dawning faith, but in a federal penitentiary in Pennsylvania. Martyr though he was to his own personal vision, his persecutors denied him the glory of his martyrdom, since it was the Pure Food and Drug Administration which sent him to die in prison.

3. PAUL GOODMAN

In the American context the Reichian tradition of social and sexual radicalism has been carried on, though not without significant modification, by Paul Goodman. Since the middle 1940s Goodman has produced a steady stream of social criticism, psychological theory, fiction, and poetry which has illuminated in a unique way the problems of American society. Among American intellectuals Goodman is somewhat the "tertium quid." As a social critic he has been the chief American spokesman for the non-Marxist tradition of western radicalism. His intellectual ancestors include the utopian socialists and anarchists such as Proudhon, Bakunin, and especially Kropotkin. Historically this tradition has attacked the centralized "hard nosed" socialism of the Marxist and Social Democratic Left as well as monopoly capitalism. It has emphasized the decentralization of economic and political power, "from the bottom up" social and political organization, a deeply rooted suspicion of the state, and the search for community. These concerns, once written off by many as either utopian or reactionary, have come to seem increasingly pertinent for a diagnosis of and prognosis for the ills of postwar American society. It is due primarily to Goodman's efforts that this is the case.

In the context of American social thought, Goodman's chief debts are to the pragmatism of James and Dewey with its stress upon the "open-ended" nature of individual and social development, and the practical implementation of ideas. Goodman's work also betrays the influence of functionalism as manifested in

Thorstein Veblen's work and the aesthetics of early twentieth-century American architecture and city planning. As a pedagogue and educational theorist Goodman has combined a heavy dose of Progressive Education with A. S. Neill's Summerhill experiment. And his efforts in depth psychology and psychotherapy have been shaped by the Gestalt psychologists, Freud and especially Reich.

A contributor to *Politics, Commentary,* and more obscure anarchist periodicals in the late 1940s, then subject to a decade of frustrating neglect in the 1950s, Goodman became an intellectual figure to be conjured with after the publication of *Growing Up Absurd* in 1960. Since then, Goodman has achieved a public visibility and influence, which no "New York intellectual," other than perhaps Norman Mailer, can match.

During the high tide of Goodman's influence and fame, his books were generally and rather monotonously lauded. There were detractors as well, but common to both champions and denigrators of Goodman was a tendency to slight Goodman's ideas and focus rather on Goodman the man, in his various intellectual and personal manifestations.

Three recent treatments of Goodman are exemplary: Norman Mailer's snidely ambiguous comments in *Armies of the Night;* Theodore Roszak's more laudatory treatment of Goodman in *The Making of a Counter Culture;* and finally Lewis Feuer's scathing attack on Goodman in *The Conflict of Generations.* Mailer's approach to Goodman was unflaggingly ad hominem, a characteristic critical approach in New York intellectual circles. A pinch of sociology of knowledge, a dash of psychoanalysis, topped by tidbits of gossip, the critical result was exhilarating, but quite distinctly perishable. Mailer seemed most interested in Goodman's prose style and Goodman's influence as related to his own, rather than anything much that Goodman had written. (In fact, Mailer confessed that he had read little of Goodman.) For Mailer, "encountering Goodman's style . . . was not unrelated to the journeys one undertook in the company of a laundry bag"; he was a "sexalogue"; and reminded one of an "old con" emitting whiffs of "superhygiene . . . medicated Vaseline . . . and the YMCA."[1]

Roszak's generally uncritical discussion of Goodman went a bit more into the details of Goodman's thought than Mailer did. However, Roszak took Goodman to be an artist primarily, and insisted on relating Goodman's work to Eastern modes of thought. Thereby Goodman's debt to Anarchist thought, Freud and Reich, Progressive Education, Veblen, or the Pragmatists was totally obscured.

And finally there was Lewis Feuer's almost libelous treatment of Goodman. Near the end of *The Conflict of Generations,* Feuer delivered himself of an attack on Goodman as a middle-aged alienated intellectual who "seeks in youth the redeemers from his own tragic alienation"; as an " 'absurd' homosexual who projects [his] sense of absurdity upon American youth"; as a purveyor of the "cult of violence"; and as a "psychological imperialist." On this view Goodman had been an outside agitator at Berkeley in 1964, stirring up students against their will and hoodwinking them into destructive actions. (Feuer was on the faculty at Berkeley at the time and an opponent of the FSM.) This was manifestly poor psychology and shoddy sociology on Feuer's part. Moreover Feuer's charge that Goodman encouraged a "cult of violence" was and is patently absurd. After his canard, Feuer went on to assert that a main cause of youth revolts in advanced industrial societies was the lack of "environments with real objective tasks, material challenges to youthful aggressive energies."[2] A moment's reflection reveals that this has been precisely Goodman's indictment of American society and leads to the conclusion that Feuer had read precious little of Goodman's work or that he had learned more from Goodman than he was willing to admit.

It must be admitted that Goodman is himself an inveterate practitioner of the ad hominem critique, and that his own work lends itself quite readily to such an approach. While most thinkers clothe their personal-psychological predilections in general ideas, Goodman tends to do the reverse; his ideas are often fleshed out in the most personal of terms. This becomes particularly clear when Goodman's poetry and fiction are examined, since they serve as an imaginative gloss upon the main themes of his social thought.

Goodman's two novels, *Empire City* and *Making Do*, his poetry as collected in *Hawkweed* and *Homespun of Oatmeal Gray*, his short stories *Adam and His Works*, and his diary of the 1950s, *5 Years*, all reveal a man obsessed with two things—sex and general ideas. This dual concern has been vividly portrayed in an excerpt from Alfred Kazin's autobiographical reminiscences of the 1940s. In his piece Kazin describes "Ricardo" (who is obviously Goodman) as a short, shaggy, and very intense young man who, during the war years, "was interested in everything . . . the nearest thing to an eighteenth century philosophe any of us had ever seen." Kazin recounts how he found Ricardo passionately arguing philosophical questions with a woman whom Kazin was having an affair with and notes that: "No one would ever build up ideas into such an atmosphere of violence as Ricardo did. . . . His sense of his own rightness was like a wall around him." Even then Ricardo-Goodman was intensely concerned with sex, yet in a strange way for "with all his talk of sex as divine energy there was something about Ricardo that was so entirely impersonal and didactic that talking theory straight at Mary [Kazin's lover] flattered her more than falling in love ever did."[3]

Most interesting is Kazin's characterization of Ricardo-Goodman as passionately impersonal. For, it is precisely this intellectualized passion and passionate intellection that one discovers in Goodman's writings. As reflected particularly in his imaginative work, Goodman's personal desires often seem peculiarly intellectual, even programmatic, as if personal encounters were always to serve a higher purpose, as exemplary events on the way toward the realization of the ideal of community, or an instructive example of a pet idea.

In Goodman's poetry one finds these impulses given voice most clearly. The themes characteristically revolve around the exigencies of sexual desire and the frustrations attendant upon changing a "messed-up" social order; or, in terms taken from his poetry, the felt lack and futile search for "Adam" and for "Paradise." Goodman's sexual desire, primarily homosexual, receives expression in a yearning for an "Adam" who is discovered at times embodied in complete strangers, workers, sailors, but most centrally in young people. In his various encounters with the potential "Adam," Goodman's own sense of physical ugliness and age is related dialectically to the fact that he can educate his "Adam" to conform with his vision of primordial perfection and nonalienation from self. In thus uniting himself with "Adam," Goodman himself seeks always to overcome his own sense of alienation from others and, in microcosm, achieve community.

Thus Goodman's homosexuality becomes a metaphoric orientation to self and others in which the sexual and the intellectual are united. Sexual desire seems often to be a mere preliminary for the more crucial sense of closeness, which then offers the pedagogic opportunity. Goodman's sexuality thus is desublimated intellectuality and spirituality.

Along with the search for "Adam," the fitting student for the longing pedagogue, goes Goodman's search for "Paradise," the imaginative expression of his quest for community, and then, in the 1960s, his widening concern with American society as a whole. As Goodman has grown older, a growing note of despair has appeared in his work. With the tragic death of his son in 1967 and an increasing disenchantment with American youth, Goodman's sense of alienation from "Adam" and the futility of the search for "Paradise" become clearer: "I have come to hate, it is appalling / Adam I used to love."[4] And "I say back as if I knew? / And once had such a place, but who / took me away and when was that? / I don't know and it is too late."[5] Life has become a "purgatory."[6]

Goodman's imaginative writing is valuable mainly for the closer glimpse it gives us of Goodman the man, and how his personal and intellectual concerns are fundamentally of one piece. It is my feeling that his fiction and poetry are distinctly inferior to his social criticism. Where the latter often gains from the personal voice and a winning frankness, his imaginative work seems wooden and windy. Goodman has a tin ear for dialogue and his characters seem mere embodiments of his own ideas, pawns in an intellectual game, rather than interesting in their own right. They all sound and think like Paul Goodman. And ironically, for all this training and experience in psychotherapy, Goodman's sense of psychology, as it emerges in his fiction, is monotonous and one-dimensional. In like manner, Goodman's poetry is the most "unpoetical" imaginable. His sense of natural rhythm and cadence is sorely lacking; his diction and tone vacillate between mannered simplicity and empty bombast. In short it is strangely "willed" and curiously flat and thus of little intrinsic interest.[7]

Perhaps Goodman's personal-intellectual quest is best understood in reference to another rather maddeningly egotistical and a physically unappealing figure, Socrates. In *Making Do* Goodman has the main character analyze the vital impulses of his life in the following terms taken from Plato's *Symposium*:

> He said that, as a man grows, he is first attracted to the beautiful bodies he sees; and I had certainly been wondrously attracted to them, though with indifferent success in ever getting to touch them.
> But then, he said, a man begins to fall in love with the virtuous characters of people that behave in those bodies and give them the beauty that shines on their faces. It was true. I had found it to be so.
> And then, he said surprisingly, a man's eros turns to the institutions and the customs of the city, that educate character and nurture physical beauty; and now his lively concern is with these. I should never have believed it when I was younger! But as I grew up, I found that it was true. My crowded days were this love affair with my city, a thorny adventure, but often I was so busy at it that I didn't know whether I was unhappy or happy, and that meant, I suppose, that I was sometimes happy.
> But at last, said Plato, a man begins to have intimations of God in whom the city exists, and he comes to love Him. And presumably God comes across. I had not yet found it so. . . .[8]

With this in mind, let us turn to Goodman's social thought.

In July of 1945, Paul Goodman contributed a lengthy article to *Politics*. The essay "The Political Meaning of Some Recent Revisions of Freud" was an attempt to provide a "psychobiological" basis for a non-Marxist radicalism as well as an attack on neo-Freudian revisionists such as Karen Horney and Erich Fromm. Goodman took Horney and Fromm to task for underplaying "the role of instinctual drives" and advocating the view that "character directly reflects the social pattern."[9] Because they downplayed the centrality of instincts at the expense of social forces, the free personality for the neo-Freudians was "sprung from nowhere . . . without a past . . . without an unconscious and transparent through and through."[10] Along with this Goodman attacked Fromm's attempt to define psychological ill-health as the obedience to "irrational" authority, since, as Goodman pointed out, the distinction between rational and irrational authority is meaningless for, say, a child caught up in the Oedipal situation. Goodman saw lurking behind Fromm's attempts to defend "rational authority" a defense of the desirability of society's being ruled politically by representative institutions and economically by a central planning organ. This position Goodman named "sociolatry," a view in which "individual and social aims are identical."[11]

After this attack on Horney and Fromm, Goodman turned to the ideas of Wilhelm Reich. For Goodman, Reich was absolutely essential as a counterpoint to the Revisionists since Reich "took up the original (with Freud) instinct theory" and held that "the repression of infantile and adolescent sexuality is the direct cause of submissiveness of the people to present political rule of whatever kind."[12] Interesting in Goodman's discussion were two points. First, the individual, insofar as he is an instinctual creature, has an ultimate defense against his needs being made identical with those of society. The instincts are thus both a powerfully conservative force in providing a bulwark against social and cultural pressures and a revolutionary force insofar as they are the source of free action by the individual.[13] Thus the existing society could only bring individual needs and desires into "harmony" with society's by repressing the natural fulfillment of those desires. To do this, however, would be to produce individual and group anxiety since "the energy of anxiety is the energy of repressed sexuality."[14]

In reaction to this article, C. Wright Mills and P. J. Salter wrote to *Politics* accusing Goodman of a "gonad theory of revolution . . . a metaphysics of biology."[15] The criticism could have better been leveled at Reich since Goodman had noted in his original article that Reich's ideas were "excessively naive and Rousseauean" and that eventually the more complex, sophisticated views of Freud would have to be taken into consideration.[16] In a rejoinder to the letter Goodman replied that he was not "asserting that the liberation of instincts will of itself produce a heaven on earth. . . . But . . . the repression of instincts makes good institutions unattainable."[17] In other words, instinctual liberation was a necessary though not sufficient condition for a new society. Nor was Goodman ready to write off all cultural products as repressive. Goodman could have been faulted for being rather vague in his discussion of instinct theory since he failed to point out that Freud's instinct theory was dualistic, while Reich's was monistic, a distinction which had definite implications for any radical social thought.[18]

In the December, 1945, issue of *Politics*, Goodman moved to a discussion of the social structures and institutions which would, in his opinion, best nurture individual freedom. In the essay "Revolution, Sociolatry, and War," Goodman noted that American society was organized primarily for the "smooth functioning of the industrial machine";[19] the result was man's alienation from his natural powers. In opposition to a "great state and corporate structure"[20] Goodman advanced the idea that society should be composed of small communitarian groups devoted to mutual aid. Abjuring future-oriented utopian schemes or the movement of history, Goodman called for an immediate establishment of such face-to-face groups. As an antidote to a society which was increasingly characterized by bigness, anonymity, externally imposed planning and decision making, and mass production, these groups would provide a locus for individual fulfillment through involved, meaningful work, direct political decision making, sexual satisfaction, and avoidance of cooperation with the war machine. Individuals belonging to such groups would be like "sane men in a madhouse."[21]

Goodman frankly recognized the dilemma in which he found himself. If American society was so oppressive, how, short of a violent wrenching away of power, could that society be changed?

Yet if violence were resorted to, those desiring a new type of society would be crushed since they were a small minority. Secondly, because American society did provide most of its people with their basic needs, a communitarian-anarchist program such as Goodman's, which called for more than higher wages and better working hours, would lack the broad-based support needed to take effective action.

Goodman's early essays in *Politics* were prophetic in the sense that he assumed the possibility of general affluence and addressed himself to the set of problems attendant to what was later to be called the "affluent society." (Goodman took this position at a time when many economists, especially radicals, were predicting a depression in the postwar world.) Goodman recognized what was crucial for any new radical social thought; namely, that the old political and economic issues connected with radicalism, such as the nationalization of private property and institutional rearrangements in the conventional sense, were no longer to the point. The socioeconomic system which had emerged from World War II was neither "fish nor fowl," neither capitalist nor socialist. Thus the problems Goodman addressed himself to were in the broadest sense "cultural." Only those who had transcended Marx's "realm of necessity" and entered the "realm of freedom" could begin to see that the critical areas of concern had become the nature and quality of work, sexual satisfaction, and the general quality of life in a mass society. Older forms of social theory, whether Marxist or Liberal or Conservative, simply did not address themselves to such problems in a thoroughgoing way.

Then in his "May Pamphlet," Goodman set forth his ideas on the problem of life in a coercive society. Goodman's basic thesis, obviously drawn from Reich, was that "a coercive society depends upon instinctual repression."[22] As a counterpoise Goodman posited the need for a "natural society" or community which, as he wrote in *Politics*, was to be initiated in the present. Instead of waiting for a large scale reordering of society (and this showed a tactical divergence from traditional radicalism), one must live "in the present society as though it were a natural society."[23]

Goodman's idea of community was based on the belief that

"free natural power is the only source of existence."[24] Only insofar as the individual was allowed to live according to the natural did the community fulfill its true function. Reacting against the postwar "cult of the personal," Goodman focused upon the natural—"those drives and forces, on both the animal and the human level, which at present act themselves out in defiance of the conventions"[25]—that the community should foster. Thus for Goodman the natural was a sociobiological concept, synonymous with the moral and the good and by definition resistant to external coercion.

Goodman did not conceive the community to be a conflict-free situation in which individuals lived in continual harmonious cooperation. It was rather a "moral" space where "the primary experience of birth, infantile anxiety, grief and mourning for death, simple sexuality"[26] would become integral aspects of existence. Such was absolutely vital since to avoid these facets of existence would insure that individuals found relief, even enjoyment, in large-scale conflict having little to do with their own lives. Thus by implication war was, in Goodman's view, "a perverted way of trying to re-establish contact with the primary experiences of human existence."[27]

In these early essays Goodman decisively rejected the traditional anarchist suspicion of politics. He held that "direct initiative . . . is itself a noble and integrating act of everyman."[28] Political action in this sense was "positive and natural. . . . Any measure of political initiation, whatever, that is not routine, that faces initial opposition and must win its way to acceptance, is political."[29] Indeed every meaningful act within the community was political insofar as it contributed to the ongoing success of the community. Likewise any action directed outward against the "smooth functioning of the industrial machine"[30] and the coercive effects of the larger society was political. At the core of Goodman's concept of politics (in a sense all natural existence was political) was the belief that civil liberty was not merely negative freedom from coercion. It was, positively conceived, "the opportunity to initiate a policy, enterprise or idea. . . ."[31]

And only if the community allowed such initiative did it remain a community.

Although Goodman's remarks on community were rather abstract and sketchy, they did adumbrate many of the themes which he would later develop. Community, at this point in Goodman's thought, was grounded upon a set of moral principles and an ethos which provided a vantage point from which to judge the larger society. It was an ideal antitype to the repressive and impersonal society emerging in post-World War II America.

The absence of a class analysis or focus was interesting in Goodman's essays and represented a departure from conventional radicalism. Sharing the feelings of many other postwar observers, Goodman recognized the way in which the proletariat had been incorporated into the existing society and had embraced the "mores of the dominant class."[32] Nor did Goodman look to a vigorous middle class for encouragement. Both classes had been *gleichgeschaltet* and were devoted to the "smooth functioning of the industrial machine." Just who would make up Goodman's community was not at all clear. Whatever the case Goodman's idea of community has less in common with working-class radicalism, whether Marxian or Syndicalist, than it did with the idea of the Greek polis.

Finally what emerged from these essays was a view of man and society at variance with what Goodman called "social engineering." Departing from the view that man was a tabula rasa and hence infinitely malleable, Goodman's concept of the natural derived from an antinomian wing of western radicalism, going back to the Quakers, Rousseau, and a Jewish tradition of community. Its specific content was taken from Wilhelm Reich's heretical Freudianism.

Goodman's first sustained work of social criticism was *Communitas* (1947), a book written with his brother Percival. As David Riesman noted, the book's bracing utopianism came as a welcome antidote to the postwar collapse of optimism. *Communitas* represented a renewal of the functionalist-pragmatic line of social analysis which traced its roots back to Thoreau and had been carried in the twentieth century by Dewey and Veblen. As the Goodmans developed it, the concept of community involved much more than a moral and psychological ambience; it also implied that man's social relationships, the way he looked at the world and the values he held were reflected by his own self-constructed habitat. Building design, the layout of work and leisure areas, the arrangement of living units—all these were Weltanschauungen in concrete and iron.

The Goodman brothers operated according to a "neofunctionalist" principle. Believing with the functionalists that "form follows function," the Goodmans went on to "subject the function itself to a formal critique. Is the function good?" For them that which encouraged—"style, power and grace"—was functional and hence of worth.[33] Running throughout the work were two assumptions and two preferences. First, they pointed out that America had "a surplus technology, a technology of free choice," and second, "an economy of abundance." Because of these two givens, American society could and should experiment with all sorts of economic, social, and political arrangements. Their particular preference was a decentralization of industrial enterprise, which they argued was not only desirable, but possible in a technologically developed society. They also plumped for the necessity of regional planning and a reversal of the trend toward urbanization. Thus the decentralist and regionalist bias emerged as the external prerequisite for the establishment of genuine communities.

The first part of *Communitas* concerned itself with a running critique of various urban planning schemes. The Goodmans criticized Ebenezer Howard's Garden City concept and, by extension, suburban living for separating the spheres of work and leisure. The ideas of Buckminster Fuller and Frank Lloyd Wright were scored for excluding political activity from their projected communities. On the other hand, Goodman focused on TVA as an example of beneficial regional planning and had kind words for "intentional communities" such as the kibbutzim and the Progressive schools.

In the latter part of the book the Goodmans presented three "paradigms" or ideal types by which they suggested the directions modern society might move in. These paradigms were "not plans, they are analyses."[34] Each was an attempt to imagine the advantages and disadvantages, the relationship of values and goals inherent in models based upon various presuppositions.

The first, for which they displayed little affection, was named "the Metropolis as Department Store." The Department Store plan was one in which consumption of mass produced goods became the chief impulse of society. This consumption, which was continually stimulated by envy and emulation, was the dynamic by which the economy maintained itself. Because mass consumption was the organizing principle, the model for this paradigm became a city in which goods were arranged for purchase as in a large department store. The city was to be run by "technologists, merchandisers, and semi-economists";[35] politics in the sense of initiative and participation in decision-making would not exist. Periodically a sort of "Carnival" would be instituted. All perishable goods would be burnt or destroyed; traditional moral and sexual restraints would be lifted; and debts would be canceled. The Department Store model was obviously the Keynesian state of stimulated production and consumption, pushed to its illogical (or logical) extreme. Mindless consumption was the keynote.

The second paradigm was the Goodmans' favorite. It involved a social system in which personal and productive environments were closely related, workers had a voice in all stages of production, and economic units were small and relatively self-sufficient.[36] This model represented "the organization of economic democracy on the basis of productive units or . . . an industrial town meeting"[37] and hence the nexus for a meaningful political community. This regional model called for the reintegration of factory and farm, with small urban centers and regional industries developed around regional resources. The goal was "liberty, responsibility, self-esteem as a workman and initiative."[38] In this setup there was no reason, according to the Goodmans, "why the economy must expand or must not expand."[39]

In their third model, the Goodmans proposed an arrangement by which the economy was divided into two sectors. In the first sector the government automatically provided each citizen with his subsistence needs, a sort of guaranteed income very similar to that proposed in Edward Bellamy's *Looking Backward.* Then the individual was to be free to engage as he wanted in activities in the other sector which provided goods and services to satisfy the desire for luxury, power, convenience, etc. The Goodmans pointed out that an individual might start a small business of his own; or, with his subsistence needs met, he could choose to read or make things. Besides a number of years in a national service corps, the individual would be faced with the problem of what to do with his leisure since no one would force him to do anything.

Though this discussion fails to do justice to *Communitas,* a work full of fertile suggestions and valuable insights and remarkably prescient in many matters, it will serve to indicate the relationship of Goodman's ideas on environmental planning to his earlier (and later) work. It was in *Communitas* that the Goodmans laid out institutional and environmental prerequisites for the emergence of community and a healthy national society to be composed of regional communities. It represented the attempt on Goodman's part to make concrete what he had sketched out earlier—the value of individual and small group initiative as well as the necessity of integrating work, leisure, politics, and ecology.

At this point it would do well to examine more closely Goodman's idea of "community," as it had been developed up to this point, and as he was to elaborate upon it later. In the context of Goodman's writings, community is used, first, to describe the relationship between two or more people united by a bond of similar principles and common goals. Second, Goodman uses the term community to characterize an environment inhabited by people with a sense of community. This relationship of people to environment is a symbiotic one, i.e., there is mutuality between environment and people. Instances of "community as people" would be Goodman's oft-cited example of the scientific cooperation across national and linguistic boundaries and the community of scholars. An example of "community as place and people" would be what Goodman calls "intentional communities" such as a Summerhill school or a kibbutz. A crucial prerequisite for the emergence of community in the fullest sense is the decentralization of power and function.

Several objections can legitimately be raised against Goodman's concept of community. Goodman assumes that community is in itself of positive moral value, although one can imagine a community devoted to evil uses in Goodman's or anybody else's sense of the term. Thus one must ask what the goals of the community are, since they are not implied in the concept of community as such. For example the kibbutzim in Israel are various in constitution and purpose. They are also dependent economically and psychologically upon the larger national community in which they exist. One could thus ask if their being communities means that they are devoted to Goodman's goals.

The second criticism of the concept of community is that it involves a practical tautology. That is, community presupposes—community. Just as one cannot in theological terms will belief and faith, but rather has it "granted," it is probable that community cannot be willed into being. It exists or it does not. To be sure one can attempt to facilitate its emergence through environmental arrangements, decentralization, etc., but its existence finally depends on prior value choices and experience.

This latter objection points in turn to a weakness in Goodman's thought in general: the neglect, in the American context, of class, religious, and especially racial divisions. Strangely enough Goodman slights real or even imaginary conflicts of interest or experience in the society. For example, decentralization and community control in the New York schools foundered upon congeries of social and economic divisions, ethnic and racial animosities, and status conflicts which community control seemed to exacerbate rather than minimize. It was not self-evident to any of the sides involved that a commonality of interests existed. Again the emergence of community failed precisely because of the lack of common goals and interests which are prerequisites for community in the first place. Thus American society with its diversity of individual and group experience and history may render impossible or highly unlikely the emergence of community. Or it may be, conversely, that community is only possible in situations presenting a substantial ethnic and socioeconomic homogeneity.

Related to Goodman's concept of community are two principles that seem to be, if not in contradiction, at least hard to join with one another. These are the principles of "organismic self-regulation," i.e., individual freedom from coercion and externally imposed strictures, and that of "mutual aid." There is nothing in either concept which implies the necessity of the other. If, for example, the imperative of mutual aid is imposed upon a group, then the concept of organismic self-regulation is negated. Just as in the ideology of laissez-faire capitalism which linked individual freedom and the common good by an invisible hand, Goodman's linking of self-regulation and mutual aid is not at all convincing and is as unsatisfactory as the "invisible hand" solution was in capitalist ideology.

There is, finally, a function of community which needs examination—community as "continuous group psychotherapy." Goodman's community demands an openness, honesty, and self-revelation which renders all human intercourse political, since individual existence is so tightly bound to that of the group. Group therapy is in actuality a highly political process, in that conflict within the self and with others and its working through become public phenomena. The self becomes a public entity, one subject to manipulation by self and others. As a result there is the sense that life in the Goodmanian community would be lacking in personal privacy, intimacy with others, and with the self (interiority).[40] Goodman's psychology, in which the individual's history is neglected for his present situation, the unconscious is jettisoned as a theoretical or functional concept, and the individual becomes a conduit for the natural (or for the organismic), fits such a concept of community quite nicely.[41] The individual becomes defined by the present situation and the existence of others. What is "interior" or "within" is not an individual's particular past as a vital part of the self, but the natural, an impersonal force which expresses itself through the organism. As such the natural has no history, it is simply process and force. There is little room for the secret or mysterious. Thus from

Goodman's psychology (and from his fiction) one has individuals who seem rather flat and one-dimensional, always related to and caught up in activities, but rarely alone. There is a lack of depth and complexity, of richness of detail, and variety of interest in his discussion of individual psychology which renders the concept of community a bit stale and antiseptic. Indeed related to this lack of depth and richness is Goodman's rather wooden and ineffective use of history and historical examples in his writings. He neglects the context and detail for the abstracted example.

In making the natural or organismic self-regulation the key concept in his social thought as well as his psychology, Goodman also falls victim to the naturalistic fallacy by which the existing is equated with the desirable. That is, within the natural world one can find the good, a view which flows consistently from Goodman's antidualistic bias, and resembles Reich's biological naturalism. Though there are many objections to the equation of the natural with the good and the healthy, a central one is that the equation begs the question. What indeed is natural? If it is organismic self-regulation, does that include aggression? Goodman's solution is to call "harmful" aggressions mere secondary phenomena, the derivatives of primary beneficial drives. But this judgment depends on a previously made value choice and a prior concept of what man's "nature" is. In other words the natural becomes whatever Goodman decides it should be. Within limits, of course, the natural and organismic self-regulation have meaning and indicate the need for a minimum of instinctual repression in individual and social development. What the natural is, is much more problematic. This leads us to Goodman's psychological theory.

In 1951 Goodman collaborated with Frederick Perls and Ralph Hefferline in the writing of *Gestalt Therapy*. The first part of the volume was a manual of self-therapy. The second half was more heavily theoretical and drew the connections between Gestalt psychology as a type of psychotherapy and the theories of Freud and Reich. Although the book was a group effort, the introduction indicated that Goodman had a large hand in part II. And anyone familiar with Goodman's style and approach to problems, his use of examples as well as his diction, could recognize quite readily Goodman's dominating presence in that portion of the book.

In general, Gestalt therapy is based on an antidualistic approach to human experience. According to the Gestaltist, the individual and his environment, mind and body, inner and outer worlds constitute a unity, rather than being dualistically conceived. The health and growth of the human organism depends on "the formation of complete and comprehensive Gestalten."[42] If these Gestalten are rigid and unchanging (corresponding to fixation in orthodox psychoanalysis) or not definite enough (analogous to repression), then the individual is suffering from a neurosis, which can generally be defined as "avoidance of contact."[43] On theoretical grounds Gestalt therapy rejects the Freudian notion of the unconscious as well as an "historical" approach to the etiology of a disturbance. Rather than historical, e.g., what happened when X was 7 years old caused him to . . . , the approach of Gestalt therapy is a phenomenological one; it is interested in how the individual is in the world and deals with it at present. Its concern is primarily with human awareness and with how one contacts, senses, responds to, and uses his environment, in the broadest sense. Thus its central queries are how, what, where, and not why. Finally the therapeutic aim of Gestalt therapy is "to regain the feel of ourselves,"[44] an "unblocking" of the individual's powers to allow him to "grow" and creatively adjust to his surroundings and create new Gestalten.

In his *Ego, Hunger and Aggression*, Perls used Freud as a foil and acknowledged his indebtedness to Reich though substantially modifying Reich's emphasis upon sex. As with Reich, Perls's central focus was upon breaking down psychic and somatic barriers and regaining "contact." In writing off the unconscious and the libido as crucial and in placing the responsibility for personal disorders squarely upon the individual, Perls approached the moralistic and "consciousness" psychology which Goodman earlier and Marcuse later accused the Revisionists of adopting. However, the Perlsian emphasis fitted well with Goodman's voluntarism and emphasis upon political and social initiative. It was left to Goodman in works subsequent to *Gestalt Therapy* to delineate the institutional context which best supported individual initiative. Thus Goodman added the social dimension to Perls's individualistic approach.

Goodman brought many of his earlier concerns to the explication of Gestalt therapy. Because of the complex and organic relationship between the organism and the environment, "there is no single function of any animal that completes itself without objects and environment."[45] That was to say that all human activity is characterized by intentionality. We do not merely think, we think about something. We do not desire, we desire something. We do not exist, we exist in a society which presents certain possibilities and forecloses others. Secondly, for Goodman, the animal functions of the organism are self-regulating. Human beings, and here entered Goodman's libertarian bias influenced by Reich, function best without external physical or intellectual or moral regulation. Thirdly, growth, which is synonymous with health, depends on the possibility of meeting the problem, i.e., "contacting the environment" and carrying things through to completion. If the situation is not completed or the problem solved (the Gestalt not formed), then two things may result. The organism becomes frustrated and will attempt compulsively to complete the situation later. As a result attention and energy will continually be dissipated and hence contacting and completing ability diminished. Or the frustration, characteristic of what Goodman called "chronic low grade emergency," may lead to an identification with and introjection of the values of the frustrating force, be that frustrating force an individual, an organization, or an entire social arrangement. If the environment frustrates or presents no objects worthy of attention, health is impossible, and neurosis may be the only possible way of coping; indeed it may be creative. Finally it was crucial for Goodman that there be continual contacting and assimilation going on in the organism/environment field. The human organism does not aim for stasis; rather the need for growth through "conflict" with the environment is central.

Upon reflection perhaps the most striking thing about Goodman's ideas was their peculiarly American flavor.[46] His version of Gestalt therapy owed much to pragmatism, with its emphasis on the human organism as a "problem solver," as an active creator and not a passive recipient of reality. Likewise the notion of the open-ended nature of reality, that situations continually present themselves for completion, was decidedly Jamesian. Goodman's rejection of the centrality of the unconscious and the emphasis upon the "here and nowness" of experience likewise betrayed an American disinterest in the past and the expectation that all problems were amenable to solution.[47]

There was as well a powerful Reichian undercurrent in the work, though Goodman modified much of Reich's specific teachings. Taking a cue from the therapeutic method of Reich, Goodman stressed the importance of observing how the patient talks, acts, and moves rather than what he says about himself and his past. Just as the goal of Reichian analysis was the dissolution of the individual armor so as to allow libidinal release and the satisfactory orgasm, so Goodman's central therapeutic purpose lay in freeing the individual to complete his situation and bring "organismic self-regulation" into effect. In both cases it was assumed that the natural, in Reich's case the orgasmic and in Goodman's the organismic, was the ultimate source of health. Thus we could say that Reich's satisfactory orgasm became a particular example of Goodman's belief that "situation-completion" was a prerequisite of individual growth. And like Reich, Goodman held that the mind-body dualism was a false and damaging view and in itself a neurotic way of viewing things.

Goodman, however, objected to Reich's location of man's essence in the biological as a way of overcoming the mind-body dichotomy. For, Goodman noted, in doing this Reich evaluated man's cultural achievements, the conscious efforts of man in "the humane sciences, art, history, etc.,"[48] as the outcome of individual and collective neurosis. According to Goodman, the artist as well as therapist, culture was not a neurotic manifestation, an expression of sublimated energy, or a secondary phenomenon. It was best seen as a particularly valuable instance of the human organism in its effort at problem-solving. The satisfactions from art and culture were full ones and not pale substitutes for sexual fulfillment. Rather than the artist being "extraordinary . . . mysterious or virulently neurotic,"[49] Goodman's view was that creativity was profoundly "normal" in the basic sense. Not sexuality as such, but creativity best characterized man's uniqueness.

And finally Freud. In general, Goodman's attitude toward Freud was one of admiration and respect. For Goodman, Freud had first identified many of the basic human problems, even if they now needed reform and rethinking. As mentioned before, Goodman rejected Freud's causal-genetic approach and the emphasis upon the unconscious as the repository of past experience and present repressed desires. Since Goodman's position focused on man as a shaper and molder of his experience, it appeared to him that the ego and the unconscious in Freud's system functioned too much as a passive respondent to reality, in the case of the former, and a mere repository, in the case of the latter. Furthermore Goodman rejected Freud's hypostatization of reality as a "given" to which the individual must adjust. It was Goodman's view rather that reality was a continually developing and still incomplete "Gestalt" which could only be understood as "someone's" reality. The goal of the therapist was not to cure a sick person, but to aid the creative adjustment of the patient to reality on his own terms. Nor was the therapist an aloof, detached figure with finished truths to be dealt out. Therapy was to be educative as well as therapeutic; like the ideal pedagogue, the therapist's task was to free the patient from his care.

Of particular importance was Goodman's interpretation of Freud's aggression-death instinct. Rejecting a dualistic viewpoint, Goodman wrote that "the aggressive drives are not essentially distinct from the erotic drives"[50] since under the rubric of aggression "annihilating, destroying initiative and anger," which are essential to growth, are grouped with "sado-masochism, conquest and domination and suicide" which are neurotic derivatives.[51] In the society which continually stimulates without permitting complete satisfaction of drives, the aggressive instinct had split into two components. In such a situation what Reich named "primary masochism" came into play; pain was not desired in itself, but rather as a way of releasing blocked drives.[52]

Regarding Freud's Thanatos, Goodman took the position that the repetition-compulsion and the return to the initial trauma indicated not the desire for death of self, but the death of "the more deliberate inhibiting self . . . a wish for a fuller life."[53] At the biological level Goodman thought that Freud constructed a specious causal chain; because we want equilibrium, Goodman noted, does not mean we want it in the same manner as the amoeba. Each organism has a mode of life, a Gestalt, appropriate to its nature.[54] To try to complete one's life became a general category under which one could subsume all attempts at creative adjustment. This Goodman held was growth, not a death wish. Organisms died because the entire environment could not support them and they could not adjust to it. Thus death was not a goal inherent in man's biological constitution.

This rejection of a biological teleology on Goodman's part was the counterpart of his rejection of the historical determinism inherent in the Freudian approach. For Goodman, the human organism was neither inextricably bound up with the past nor driven toward some future telos. The organism exists in a "present" where there is a situation to be completed. Human existence is an ongoing process of challenge, response, and completion. Yet there is no progression in the sense that new interests, drives, or appetites develop. For Goodman an adult did not outgrow childish desires. Drives were constants in human existence and as such were healthy; their satisfaction led to growth. It was the focus of these drives and desires which changed as the individual matured: "It is not the instinct or the desire that is infantile . . . but that the fixed attitudes . . . are old-fashioned, unlikely, ineffectual."[55] One must live in an ever-present present.

It is important to stress the centrality of *Gestalt Therapy* in Goodman's thought. Here with the idea of organismic self-regulation, one finds a theoretical basis for Goodman's libertarian views and, with the idea of the necessity of an adequate environment for healthy development, the underpinnings for Goodman's social and environmental concerns.

By the early 1950s Goodman's essays, reviews, and some poetry and fiction had appeared fairly regularly in anarchist periodicals as well as in *Commentary* and *Partisan Review*, the house organs of the New York intelligentsia. In the middle and late 1950s, however, Goodman was published less and less. Though valuable works of social analysis by C. Wright Mills, David Riesman, and William H. Whyte attracted attention, for a thinker with Goodman's utopian cast of mind, the fifties proved an uncongenial era.[56] Freud, despite the efforts of Fromm and Riesman, had been captured for tragic realism and speculative utopian elements in Freud's thought were played down or forgotten. The leading representative of the radical Freudians, Wilhelm Reich, had abandoned his political and social radicalism for cosmological and pseudoreligious, pseudoscientific speculations. What was worth preserving in the Reichian legacy had been taken over by the Beats, William Burroughs, and Norman Mailer.

These years also saw a mounting attack on American education, which had supposedly been done irreparable damage by the all-pervasive influence of John Dewey. From high intellectual quarters to the bastions of philistinism it was claimed, only to be powerfully reenforced by the launching of Sputnik in 1957, that American education was in need of an overhaul. Educators such as Hyman Rickover and James Bryant Conant called for a more selective and rigorous educational process so that the Russian challenge could be met.

Just as symptomatic of social malaise was the behavior of American youth. Academic liberals and radicals bemoaned the political apathy, the mania for security, and the careerism of their students. Young and old alike read Salinger's *Catcher in the Rye* and watched James Dean in *Rebel without a Cause*. Many young people saw in these works their own story of disconnection from their parents and wider public and political concerns. On down the socioeconomic ladder, the highly visible problems were those of juvenile delinquency and gang warfare. From the motorcycle gangs of *Wild One* to the surly, dangerous high schoolers in *Blackboard Jungle*, it was impressed on the nation's conscience that something, particularly among the young, was amiss. The problem of education and the "teen-age problem" became major preoccupations of the nation.

And there were the Beats (or Beatniks as they came to be called). Through their spokesmen, Jack Kerouac and Allen Ginsberg, they announced that they were opting out of the society and forming what would later be called their own subculture. Combining a Whitmanesque *Wunderlust*, Salingerian wistfulness, and the gang spirit, the Beats turned for sustenance to communal living, drugs, self-chosen poverty, and Eastern mysticism.

Nor was the adult world without its problems or its critics. Both Riesman and Whyte noted that a significant change had taken place in American society and behavior in the past few decades. They pointed to the emergence of a new social type— the other-directed man or the organization man—whose values and actions were determined from without rather than from within. No longer was production, based on the Protestant work ethic, central; rather consumption and distribution became supreme values, the patterns of which were shaped by the mass media and the organization. And though the society was now an "affluent" one, as suggested in *The Affluent Society*, Galbraith also argued that the nation's economic and social priorities were sorely in need of rectification.

Thus the mood at the end of the fifties was a curious mixture of pride in affluence and shame at a certain slackness, a sense that American society no longer had any transcendent purpose. Social criticism was mixed with a defensive celebration of the American scene. Indicative of the situation, perhaps as much as anything else, was the Kennedy campaign of 1960. Although its battle slogans were "the New Frontier" and a call to "get the country moving again," no one was quite sure where the new frontier was or to where the country should move. Supported by liberals, Kennedy's campaign was based in part upon a rather militaristic nationalism which promised to meet the Russian challenge in missiles as well as morale. In short, there was at large in the country a feeling that something was wrong, but no one knew exactly where to seek the remedy.

It was in this context that Paul Goodman's *Growing Up Absurd* appeared in 1960. As Norman Podhoretz tells the story, when he first read *Growing Up Absurd* some thirteen publishers had already rejected Goodman's manuscript. Podhoretz was excited by Goodman's work and arranged to print three excerpts from it in *Commentary*, the editorship of which he had recently assumed. It was Goodman's book that made the "new" *Commentary* and, even more centrally, made Paul Goodman, who in recent years had been considered by some as a "has been."[57]

With *Growing Up Absurd* Goodman shifted his focus. The book, unlike his others, was addressed to a clearly felt set of national problems—the disaffection of youth, juvenile delinquency, the organization man, the Beats—rather than being a specialized anarchist tract or a technical exposition of psychotherapy. Though sharing the disquietude of many other social critics, Goodman's analysis and suggestions for change were radically at odds with those of many of his contemporaries. Most important, Goodman found for the first time a subject and an audience—the youth of America, a group which was emerging in the 1960s as a distinct social and economic force.

Growing Up Absurd was in essence a study of what it meant to grow up in American society. In it Goodman ranged far and wide, from education and vocation to the nature of work and leisure, from the junior executive to the juvenile delinquent; his basic thesis, however, was at one with that of *Gestalt Therapy* and his earlier works: in a society that fails to provide meaningful objects for desire and emulation, and in which there is no community in the moral or physical sense, growing up will be an exercise in socialization to a system alienated from and at odds with human nature. As a result, Goodman pointed out, one becomes a cynical role player, as shown by the organization man; a naïve role player, as with the hipster and juvenile delinquent; or else one opts out of what Goodman called the "organized system" a la the Beats.

Basic in *Growing Up Absurd* was the idea that the processes and values of the "organized system" were based upon a false view of human nature, and that this system resorted to manipulation and bribery to force acquiescence. In terms of Gestalt theory, American society frustrated the natural desires of its youth and prevented them from following through or completing a situation on their own terms. Or in Reichian terms, the process of growing up in America was similar to a frustrated and unsatisfactory orgasm. One was continually being interrupted by a system which would not let one be, and thus was unhappy. Once this happened the identification with and partial introjection of external values took place. One went along with the system and squandered his powers—or one withdrew.

At the heart of the rationale for the operation of the organized system was an old enemy of Goodman's—the idea that human beings are "blank tablets" that can be modified to fit externally imposed needs. According to Goodman, the organized system took individuals to be passive beings who were to be matched with the jobs and tasks demanded by the system. For Goodman, building on the philosophical anthropology he developed in *Gestalt Therapy*, "man is a maker, he must use his productive nature or be miserable."[58] In a society which imposes and manipulates rather than drawing out of the individual his unique talents, those who do not or will not fit in are considered deviants. Society should be fitted to human nature, not the reverse.

Goodman's terminology and analysis were couched in traditional language, and thus all the more effective. He took the Protestant terms—vocation and justification—and recast them in secular terms. For Goodman, one's place in society was justified by real tasks. To have a task and hence to belong in the world was what he meant by vocation.[59] In American society, however, young people were faced with an either/or situation. Either one acquiesced in the system and assumed a role rather than a vocation and identity, or one "dropped out." In either case real tasks and serious vocations were lacking.

The central metaphor of *Growing Up Absurd*, descriptive of

the moral structure of American society, was what Goodman named "The Apparently Closed Room" with a "rat race" at the center.[60] Organization men were in the system, but were cynical; juvenile delinquents were outside, but wanted to join. But the group that Goodman called "the Early Resigned" or the Beats attracted most of his attention. Unlike the celebrators of the Beat movement who saw in it the social and artistic salvation of American society, or those who saw the Beats as "a collection of unrelated incidents of individual pathology . . . to be dealt with either sternly by the cops or benevolently by the psychiatrists,"[61] Goodman cast a sympathetic yet critical eye at the Beats. He rightly saw that as a sociological phenomenon they were "a major pilot study of the use of leisure in an economy of abundance."[62] He also praised their explicit rejection of the organized system and felt that their habits—a liberal sexual ethic, a certain sloppiness, a tendency toward communitarian social groupings—were probably more sensible than those of the middle class, and by no means pathological.[63] In a more critical vein, Goodman noted that the artistic productions of the Beats, due to a lack of discipline and personal standards, represented little more than self-therapy. Nor did he care for their use of drugs or the elements of "hipster" coolness he perceived in their manner. As matters turned out, this would in general be Goodman's judgment of the youth throughout the sixties. His was thus an ambivalent attitude toward the Beats—a sympathy with their freedom and incipient sense of community mixed with a distaste for their know-nothingism. And as the new champion of youth after the appearance of *Growing Up Absurd*, Goodman would launch into the task of "how to educate the young now that I have doughtily rescued them from the dragon of the Organization."[64]

In the final chapter of *Growing Up Absurd* Goodman drew back to a historical perspective. The organized system blocked and frustrated natural human powers, he maintained, because of an "accumulation of missed and compromised revolutions . . . tradition has been broken yet there is no new standard to affirm . . . a missed revolution makes irrelevant the community that persists. And a compromised revolution tends to shatter the community that was without an adequate substitute."[65] Goodman's goal was the establishment of a world "where the community is planned as a whole, with an organic interaction of work, living and play . . . production is primarily for use . . . democracy begins in the town meeting . . . regional variety is encouraged. . . ."[66] Until this was the case American society would be a difficult place in which to grow up.

The immediate impression made by *Growing Up Absurd* was that it was a collection of radical utopian proposals. Yet upon examination Goodman's work was profoundly conservative in the values that informed the critique. In fact, this union of traditional values and radical analysis made up much of the book's freshness and, by implication, supported Goodman's "missed revolution" thesis. For, the idea of missed revolutions was another way of describing a society in social and moral transition, informed by neither fixed standards nor a revolutionary imperative.

At the same time *Growing Up Absurd* raised many more questions than it answered. As in *Communitas* there was a diagnosis and a briefer prognosis but no hint of how the distance between existing reality and projected ideal might be traversed. Though Goodman's discussion of American youth was a sympathetic one, his treatment of them hardly indicated that they might be the cutting edge of social transformation. And it could be asked whether Goodman's image of man as a "maker" was any longer relevant or even viable in a system where mass-produced and shoddily made goods were turned out by men who, if Goodman was right, would never find identity or vocation.

Much of the book's provocativeness was related to its wide-ranging focus. Yet a major structural problem was that Goodman failed to develop, to flesh out, the implications of many of his proposals. Matters were introduced, analyzed, and criticized rather offhandedly, and then dropped. For example, Goodman's contention that a series of aborted revolutions were responsible for the unsatisfactory state of American society was certainly interesting and provocative. But Goodman's elaboration of the idea was a mere listing of the missed revolutions with a capsule description of each. They were not related to each other in a rigorous way. The whole enterprise lacked historical specificity, nor was there any hint that some of the revolutions might have been mutually contradictory. Finally the idea failed to add up to much of anything.

Despite these faults Goodman's book received and deserved much notice and praise. In its way *Growing Up Absurd* was to the generation of the early sixties what *Catcher in the Rye* had been to the youth of the fifties. It had the merit of placing certain problems considered formerly to be personal aberrations or special cases in a wider social context, and it suggested that American society had to be worthy of its youth, if it expected the youth to be worthy of it.

As the 1960s progressed and Goodman's fame grew apace, he turned increasingly to the young people as the focus of his interest, to education as the central fact of their lives, and to the educational system as the key institution in the society. In doing so Goodman became the spokesman, a new Randolph Bourne, for the middle-class college student, yet in a way that young people frequently misunderstood. After the student sit-ins at Berkeley in 1964 Goodman was charged by hostile critics with being a pied piper of the young, leading them astray by and while telling them what they wanted to hear. If one reads Goodman's message carefully, it is more complicated than this. Youth were indeed exploited. Yet they also wasted their time and did not know much of anything; a source of hope, but also of despair.

As already mentioned, Goodman placed himself in the Progressive Education tradition and often quoted Dewey approvingly. Goodman's pedagogy was based upon the idea that "good teaching is that which leads the student to want to learn something more."[67] Education was a way of unblocking and releasing spontaneity and energy for a certain task or problem. In this it resembled closely his therapeutic principles. Also important was Goodman's repeated opinion that for most people at most times a rigid separation of classroom and street, schooling and work, learning and doing was harmful to real education.

According to Goodman one best learned "incidentally." Or one learned in conjunction with "something else"—a job or an apprenticeship under the tutelage of someone who was competent in a given field.

Goodman added to his Deweyan strain an admixture of A. S. Neill's Summerhill philosophy which stressed nonauthoritarian school and community structures, voluntary class attendance, and encouragement of instinctual gratification. Nor was it any accident that Neill's educational projects were strongly shaped by the ideas of Wilhelm Reich, and thus fitted in nicely with prominent aspects of Goodman's thought.[68]

At the opposite end of the spectrum from the Progressivist bias was Goodman's commitment to the western intellectual tradition. He noted with concern that few if any young people felt a link with this tradition; in rejecting the organized school system they had also rejected the western tradition. Yet to force-feed the masses of students with the humanities was a mistake, for they were best learned accidentally and of one's own volition. It was the function of the "community of scholars" to preserve and transmit this tradition. Thus education had a dual function—to prepare the individual for a social and vocational role and to carry on the tradition.[69]

In the context of the early sixties it was to the cold war educators such as James Bryant Conant and Hyman Rickover that Goodman addressed many of his remarks. In his books Conant had set up a conflict between individual and national goals and stressed the latter's determining role in educational policy. As Goodman replied: "It is not an interesting question whether the school system should be harnessed to the national goals rather than devoted to individual development, intellectual virtues, or pure research. Any extensive part of society is inevitably harnessed to the national goals. . . . The question is what are the national goals. . . ?"[70] Needless to say Goodman found the national goals of "keeping up" with the Russians and accelerating the growth rate of the economy less than salutary.

It was to the colleges and universities that Goodman directed most of his attention, since they were fast becoming the direct accomplices of national goals and governmental direction. To his distress he found that "the colleges, like the rest of America, have succumbed to the familiar style of the Organized System, smooth, rationalizing, bold and vacuous."[71] As a result college youth were being bribed by government fellowships and research grants and thus locked into the national system. This was particularly distressing to Goodman since for him the "colleges and universities are the only important face-to-face self-governing communities still active in our modern society."[72] The agent of encroachment upon the community of scholars was of course the administration. Due to the enormous growth of college administrations which had resulted from the growth of universities to meet national demands, the university, as Goodman saw it in 1964, was threatened with being transformed into a learning corporation.

Paradoxically, Goodman took as a counterexample the medieval tradition of the academy in which students and teachers constituted the community and managed matters themselves. For a genuine community of scholars to carry on the tradition, it was necessary that teacher and student be in constant contact and that the man teaching be "a better something else." In other words, students should have real and viable models for emulation and admiration, men who had experience and could impart it. If something along this line was not attempted, then Goodman feared that the gap between adults and youth would widen; adults as teachers would be tied to the organized system and youth would either be left isolated in their own subculture, one which was not adequate for growing up, or they would finally acquiesce to the values of the organized system. For Goodman "the academic problem at present is to unblock the intellect in the young, to prove that it is possible for persons to display intellectual virtues . . . and to use them in the community and the world without futility."[73]

The chief purpose of Goodman's writings on education was, as he put it, "to get people at least to begin to think in another direction."[74] Goodman suggested, for example, that students wait at least two years after high school before entering college. At the

end of *The Community of Scholars* he advanced the proposal
that students secede from the large universities and set up shop
on their own, an idea which was influential in the free university
movement of the middle sixties.[75] Goodman had always stressed
the value of decentralizing public school administration and
involving the community in school affairs, and thus undoubtedly
contributed to the moves for school decentralization in the late
1960s.

Perhaps the best way to characterize Goodman's educational
theory and practice is to call it Socratic. Like Socrates, Goodman's fundamental presupposition was that education proceeds
best in face-to-face contact and often with erotic over- and
undertones. As Goodman noted several times, he considered the
teacher-student relationship to be basically an erotic one. And if
the testimony of his diary and his fiction is accurate, erotic
relationships, especially homosexual ones, were also opportunities
for educating. Just as Socrates had done, the dialogue is to be
carried on in the marketplace or the city street as well as in the
enclosed school. The pedagogue must alternately entice and put
the student down. Criticism shows profound concern for the
youth and this concern makes use of the personal and the erotic
to bring the student to a realization of his own powers, the nature
of the society, and the validity of the tradition. Education is both
an instrument of social change and one of social and cultural
solidarity, insofar as it provides the basic link between generations and the models for youth to emulate. If it is tied into the
organized system and seeks to exploit the students, then the
youth as student has no models, no tradition, and thus no
community. This was the situation as Goodman found it in the
1960s. Education seemed neither to encourage the natural nor
conserve the traditional. With education nearly discredited, the
last hope for genuine community was also fast disappearing and
the youth were faced with the prospect of truly growing up
absurd.

Besides his work in education, Goodman also turned his
attention in the early sixties to national politics. In 1962 he wrote
a long article for *Dissent* in which he very perspicaciously

criticized the Kennedy Administration for displaying much energy without a conception of what it wanted to accomplish. Rather than idealists or even genuine pragmatists, Goodman espied behind the concern for "postures" and "stances" of the Kennedyites traces of Norman Mailer's hipsters.[76] Goodman also assumed the role of an elderly activist and was on hand in Berkeley in the heady days of the 1964 student uprisings. Taken by these early stirrings of youthful radicalism, Goodman saw there a movement which promised "the revival of democracy, the human use of technology and getting rid of war."[77] And later in the decade Goodman lent his time and energies to the anti-Vietnam war movement and the organization of draft resistance.

Goodman's main theoretical work of social criticism in the sixties was his *People or Personnel.* In *People or Personnel* Goodman discussed the relative merits of centralization and decentralization and arrived at a combination which he called "the Mixed System." While never abandoning his fundamental commitment to communitarian social organization, Goodman turned from utopian speculations and attempted to find in American society as it existed the possibilities for the emergence of community. For Goodman the prerequisite for community was decentralization, an external transformation of political, economic, and educational structures.

Goodman stressed that "decentralization is not a lack of order or planning" and that most anarchists were not "anarchists but decentralists."[78] Returning to an old theme, Goodman's thesis was that people, if left to their own devices and allowed to make their own decisions, were psychologically better off and did not need to be coerced or bribed into functioning together. But Goodman granted, in a less doctrinaire manner than formerly, that in some areas centralization was necessary; e.g., for facilitation and execution, once a basic decision was made as in mass production of necessities such as construction materials, domestic machinery, cars; in natural monopolies of water and power supply; and to meet ecological problems requiring widespread cooperation.[79]

In areas involving basic moral and political decisions, in

intellectual and scientific work, decentralization, however, was vital. The goal of the Mixed System would be to "relax this interlocking" of all individual and social activities into one "social machine, running for its own aggrandizement, in which all citizens are personnel."[80]

Once decentralization had been carried out "the best means of creating community is to delegate power."[81] As things stood Goodman saw as a central fact of American society a sense of powerlessness among rich and poor, white and black. In such a situation of constant frustration, of "acting according to someone else's schedule," of "chronic low grade emergency" people either gave up and retreated into their own private concerns or identified with the externally imposed system. The danger was that in responding to this frustration people would want "to get it over with." Frustrated and anxious citizens received vicarious satisfaction from the exercise of power by the national government against those who would not acquiesce.[82] Thus again Goodman went back to his own writings in *Gestalt Therapy* (and ultimately to Reich) and pointed out that individuals or groups were frustrated and anxious insofar as they did not have the means to finish their situation.

The only hope for breaking this impasse lay with the youth movement, the only "libertarian and popular counterforce"[83] in the society. As in *Growing Up Absurd* Goodman continued to express admiration for young people and their commitment and willingness to experiment with sexual and social arrangements. Yet he noted that "the radical young still seem averagely messed up, no better than their parents." They had "no coherent program" and tended to "cool off and hop from issue to issue."[84]

Nevertheless youth were in Goodman's terms America's most exploited social group and hence would have to serve as the cutting edge of social regeneration. Goodman's use of "exploited" in itself pointed up the difference between orthodox radicalism and Goodman's brand. Goodman used the term to refer not to economic deprivation as such, but to the fact that students, like industrial workers in the time of developing capitalism, were the key to the functioning of the organized system and must thus be forced into its service. As educated and skilled "personnel," students became valuable commodities, extensions of their talents and training. As such they were alienated from themselves and their desires and thus prime for revolt.

If Goodman had opened the 1960s with a radical analysis grounded in conservative values, he opened the 1970s with a self-styled conservative tract based upon a radical perspective. Most of Goodman's themes were familiar ones: a distaste for statism and social engineering, a dislike for the meretriciousness of much of the society, an advocacy of decentralization and individual initiative, combined with a concern for the possibility of vocation and meaningful activity. Only Goodman's focus had shifted.

The central theme of *New Reformation* was that individuals in American society had no "world" and hence were alienated from their own powers and from others. By "world," an obvious surrogate for community and taken from the language of Gestalt psychology, Goodman referred to a situation in which one "can act and realize [himself.]"[85] A world is given depth and detail by a sense of tradition and history. This lacking, young people, in particular, repeated the mistakes of the past and their actions failed to add up to anything. A world was fully "there" when discoverable vocations existed through which one used his native powers in a meaningful way. And a world was made possible only when people could connect power and function, could carry through on their needs and wants. The clearest sign that Americans felt powerless was their fascination with power in the abstract: conservatives embraced a nonpolitics of law and order, while students and minorities fell prey to half-baked Leninism and were radicalized by manipulation.

Because of this lack of a "world," young professionals tended toward cynicism in the belief that "there was no knowledge but only a sociology of knowledge."[86] The nation's cities were chaotic and unlivable because there "aren't enough citizens,"[87] inhabitants who feel the city is theirs. Institutional education failed to equip its students with useful skills and many in colleges had no interest in being there. As a result most students were not "authentic"; they had no "world" and latched onto "authentic" heroes such as Che Guevera or Eldridge Cleaver who were inappropriate to their situation. It became clear that with *New Reformation* that Goodman had become disillusioned with the radical student movement, whose hero and mentor he had once been. Now his attention had shifted to the young professional classes who possessed some competence and training and were, as Veblen had recognized earlier, the key to the transformation of a highly technologized order.

Goodman found himself in something of a dilemma at this point. His own brand of anarchism had always been based upon the implicit notion that those who had a "world," a sense of competence and skill, could best control their own lives and thus would constitute a self-regulating community that would contradict the view which held that individuals had to be directed from above. By Goodman's own admission, however, the general ethos of alienation allowed none of this and was foreign to anarchist-communitarian possibility. Alienation, he noted, has been a presupposition historically for avant-garde movements or religious revivals, but seldom for communitarian politics. An anarchism which draws upon "the alienated, the dispossessed, the lumpen, the outcasts and criminals, those who have nothing to lose"[88] is liable to end in dictatorship and authoritarianism. Lacking a sense of individual self and group trust, the seriously alienated were prone to fall back onto the strong man who, by absolute power, could weld the alienated together and end their internal conflicts. Thus the question which Goodman left unanswered was, how are the alienated to gain a sense of competence, and overcome their alienation?

It was perhaps because of this last dilemma, fraught with danger, that Goodman made clear his strategy of coming up with the "small step" to meet a specific social need instead of waiting for the apocalypse or the end of history. His role was to be a therapist-pedagogue for American society, called upon to "improvise dumb-bunny alternatives" to alleviate the "metaphysical emergency of Modern Times: feeling powerless. . . ."[89] Rather than a violent collective change which "would be certainly totalitarian," Goodman's strategy was to "try piecemeal to defend and extend the areas of liberty, locally, on the job, in the mores."[90]

Whatever Goodman's practical proposals, his thesis that western society was on the verge of a "New Reformation" made a certain amount of sense. The established faith was the belief in the saving power of science and technology; its institutionalized expression, the interconnecting nexus of government, academy, and industry. Goodman foresaw no erotic pastoral society or a new tribalism to take its place. Rather technology would have to become a "branch of moral philosophy"[91] in a society in which science and technology took an important, but not dominant place. Thus, in the broadest sense, ecology would become the queen of future sciences.

New Reformation was finally a sad and moving book in which Goodman included a moving remembrance of his son Matty, who had been killed in an accident in 1967. It was in a wider sense a valedictory to his role as champion of youth. As a self-confessed "Erasmian sceptic," with considerable insight and some ambivalence, Goodman called attention to the cracks in the once imposing facade of the church universal of science and technology. On the eve of the reformation, however, no Luther had yet emerged.

In retrospect, it appears that Goodman's works of social analysis have become somewhat repetitious. At his best, Goodman's steady vision has been applied to a variety of problems and he has often arrived at the illuminating insight, the suggestion which would break the spell of intellectual and practical stagnation. At his weakest, Goodman has become rather predictable, yet part of this may be due to the fact that so many of his ideas have become part of standard intellectual discourse. Since *Growing Up Absurd* most of his social thought has appeared in essay form and at times some of the essays have read as though they were tossed off without much thought. One cannot help but feel that Goodman should stop writing essays. His proclivity for the essay, small "thought experiments," reflects a weakness of his as a thinker—the quick and often valuable insight left undeveloped. And for that reason one is never sure how seriously Goodman's proposals are to be taken. The strength of *Communitas, Gestalt Therapy,* and *Growing Up Absurd* lay in their sustained focus and developed line of thought and it is to that type of effort that Goodman needs to return.

It is too early to say just what Goodman's status as a thinker will be. His career up to now reminds us again of one of the enduring ironies of the creative life: that the best and most productive period in the life of a thinker or an artist often falls at that time when he is working in relative isolation and not subject to public scrutiny or acclaim. Once a man gains notoriety, as Goodman has, he becomes locked into a set of positions from which he is not expected to deviate. Goodman has apparently felt the pressure of his public role, since, by his own testimony, he published his diary *5 Years* in part to confound his public image as a "good man," a keeper of society's conscience, by giving quite graphic accounts of his homosexual encounters.

Whatever the final evaluation, Goodman has identified problems and suggested solutions to those problems over the last twenty-five years that his more sophisticated and "realistic" contemporaries have ignored. Finally, perhaps, those who focus upon Goodman, the man, are at least partially correct. It has been Goodman's personal witness to his own ideas, his participation in the common life of the society as though it were a genuine community, and his service as a model for a generation of young people which has made it impossible to imagine the current life of the mind in America without him.

4. HERBERT MARCUSE

Although both Herbert Marcuse and Paul Goodman have been of considerable influence in contemporary radical thought, the distance between them in style and procedure is great. Goodman is always ready with the "practical proposal," the suggestion for doing things differently, while Marcuse is a resolutely theoretical thinker who, until fairly recently, abjured a public role as spokesman for anyone. Goodman, it should be recalled, has involved himself in the public life since the forties, whereas until recently Marcuse's name was known chiefly to students of Hegel and Marx. Writing out of the central European tradition of socialist humanism, a composite of Hegel, Marx, Freud, and German cultural criticism, Marcuse's mode of analysis is a far cry from the personal, often chatty essay-style of a Goodman.

As a result, what Marcuse's thought gains in theoretical rigor and complexity (though at times obscure), it loses in specificity and immediate cogency. Where Goodman has obviously written out of his own experience as a teacher, parent, and citizen and uses experience from these areas to make his points, Marcuse's analysis moves along with a heavy eloquence and sometimes ponderous playfulness above the daily muddle. There is, however, a sophistication and subtlety in Marcuse's work, due probably to the theoretical tradition he adheres to, which is missing in Goodman's often rather scatter-gun approach.

In strictest terms Marcuse's focus of concern, from *Eros and Civilization* on, has not been American society and culture as such. Rather it has been America as the prime example of advanced industrial and technological society, a phenomenon which represents for Marcuse the direction of socioeconomic development in Europe and to a degree in the Soviet Union.

The danger with Marcuse's thought for those uninitiated in the European tradition from which he emerges is that one is either totally "put off" by its heavily theoretical nature and willing to consign it to the junk heap—or else so seduced by what passes as profundity that no critical vantage point can be assumed. Hopefully the following discussion of Marcuse's work will avoid either extreme.

The Thirties

In the 1930s Marcuse's essays and reviews appeared primarily in the *Zeitschrift für Sozialforschung,* the publication of the Institut für Sozialforschung which was located in Frankfurt-am-Main until the early years of the decade and then in Geneva and finally New York where it closed in 1941.[1] A reading of these essays is of more than mere historical interest since many of the themes, which he later developed in the 1950s and 1960s in his works, first received expression then. The ideas of a "critical theory," "negative thinking," "one-dimensionality," the definition of rationality in terms of freedom and happiness rather than domination and control can all be found in these early essays. And though Marcuse made practically no references to the work of Freud or to psychoanalysis generally, he laid the theoretical groundwork which would later prove compatible with Freudian concepts.

Marcuse's earliest work was concerned with combining historical materialism and a phenomenological analysis taken from his one-time mentor, Martin Heidegger. Marcuse's procedure of moving from philosophy to social theory was illustrated in an early essay "Über die philosophischen Grundlagen des wirtschaftswissenschaftlichen Arbeitsbegriff" (1933) in which he analyzed the meaning of labor. Marcuse argued that labor was best understood as "an ontological concept that implies the ground [*Sein*] of human existence [*Dasein*]."[2] Any attempt to understand labor as a biological, psychological, or ethical concept was, according to Marcuse, misleading and only secondarily enlightening. Labor was the fundamental mediating activity between man and the world—"the way of being in the world . . . the Form of his existence"[3]—and as such a presupposition of human existence.

With this established, Marcuse contrasted human and animal existence by noting that "man himself must make his existence"[4] while the animal allows existence to happen and is related to the world passively. Self-production through and by labor is the activity whereby man establishes his existence and seeks to perpetuate himself in the world. Moreover through labor one finds oneself "in the service of the other from himself . . . existence is in itself oriented to this objectively given world [Sachlichkeit]."[5] Human existence is by definition "alienated" from the world, yet "only in proceeding through the externalization and alienation can one gain oneself."[6]

Because man is the being who must act upon external reality, i.e., labor, he thus "places himself in the concrete situation of history . . . and becomes a member of a social group or an economic class or assumes a social status."[7] The act of laboring inserts man into society and history, and it is as a social-historical being that man is to be understood rather than "in the realm of nature, of materiality."[8]

Marcuse proceeded then to distinguish two types of labor—intellectual and material. The former becomes possible "only when existence is free of want [Not]. . . ."[9] For Marcuse the important fact was not that these two modes of labor exist, since they are more or less permanent. Rather it was that "The historical community . . . is constituted by the basic relationship of mastery and servitude (Herrschaft und Knechtschaft),"[10] and thus the modes of labor become embodied in different classes. Those who find themselves in either realm (of mastery or servitude) are severed from one vital aspect of existence and hence denied self-fulfillment: "the two-dimensionality of necessity and freedom within the whole of the existent being has become a two-dimensionality of different existing entities and anchored in socio-economically differentiated ways of life."[11]

Thus the split between intellectual and material, freedom and necessity, culture and toil, theory and practice. Only when the separation is abolished by the abolition of the class society can actual and true labor, "the complete and free realization of the whole human being in his social world," become a possibility.[12] Life in a class society remains one-dimensional.

In several ensuing essays Marcuse returned to these and similar problems, investigating the relationship between social reality and philosophical thought and the extent to which the nature of thought is ideological and hence the reflection of social relationships rather than critical of social reality. At the same time Marcuse attempted to recast traditional themes of western philosophy so that they would no longer be ideological. In "The Concept of Essence" (1936), Marcuse suggested that the philosophical disjunction between existence and essence in western thought reflected an enduring social bifurcation. Theory (or thought), the object of which was the "essential" of Greek thought, or the "self certain ego cogito" of bourgeois thought, was the province of an elevated "class," while biological necessities, "mere existence," were won by an underclass.

As a way out for philosophical consciousness Marcuse reverted to Hegel's historization of essence, but modified it by deidealizing it. For Marcuse, "the difference between essence and appearance is an historical constellation of social relationships" and could be subjected to "the practice of transformation."[13] Thus Marcuse's historical dialectic exploded the static eternal relationship between existence and essence. Their union was to be effected by a "praxis" (an informed action) rather than through pure thought or unthinking action. "Essence" was thus historicized and came to refer to the tendencies in the historical situation which transcend the given situation and point to a better possible reality. Essence became a concept which referred to common needs and desires of all men, realizable within and not beyond history and society.

The question remained unanswered, however, as to what those "essentials" were which constituted the telos of social thought and praxis. In "Philosophy and Critical Theory" (1937), Marcuse moved closer to an answer to this problem as well as a definition of his "method." In the essay he staked out a position somewhere between the original impulse of philosophical materialism—the concern for human happiness—and the procedure of idealism—the critical use of reason in the service of human freedom. Marcuse called his approach "critical theory" and defined it as the attempt "to explain the totality of man and his world in terms of his social being" with the focus being the "concern with human happiness . . . a transformation of the material conditions for existence."[14]

At this point, however, Marcuse brought his "idealist" background into play by pointing out that critical theory must in turn be animated by "Reason . . . a critical tribunal" which "represents the highest potentiality of man and his existence."[15] Social theory was thus to be the intellectual mode of transcending the given reality in that "it spoke against the facts and confronted bad facticity with its better potentialities."[16] In Hegelian fashion reality was pregnant with its own negation and transcendence.

Finally the goal of critical theory and praxis was "the realization of reason" in a rational society where "the subordination of the economy to the individual needs" would prevail.[17] Reason was that human power which pointed toward individual freedom and the satisfaction of needs. The rational became in Marcuse's hands the expression in society and history of the structure of human needs which are to be concretely realized. Thus, insofar as critical theory focused on general human needs rather than on class-linked ones, it was nonideological and genuinely critical. For Marcuse critical theory went beyond idealism in attempting to make concrete what was only abstract in idealism. It was "practically" materialistic in that its concern was with the fulfillment of material and physical needs. Yet it retained the cutting edge of idealism in positing a human power, reason, and a future situation which transcended the given situation.

In "The Affirmative Character of Culture" (1937), Marcuse examined the philosophical and social implications of the western concept of culture. Once again he began with the Greeks and noted their separation of "the useful and necessary from the beautiful and from enjoyment."[18] This ontologically grounded cleavage between the realm of "truth, goodness and beauty" (culture) and "material provisions of life" reflected the social division in Greek society between the leisure class, the guardians of culture, and those who toiled in the realm of necessity and thus were excluded from the felicity and wisdom of the good life.[19]

Making his usual jump to the epoch of bourgeois philosophy, Marcuse pointed out that although the bourgeois concept of culture posited the opposition between the spiritual and the material, the possibility was held out to all men that they could transcend the realm of "social utility and means" (or civilization), though the means for achieving this were lacking since "equality does not extend to the condition for attaining the means."[20] Marcuse thus revealed the ambiguity at the heart of bourgeois thought. It was of critical value in that it called into question "the materialism of bourgeois practice";[21] yet the idealist concept of culture was powerless to affect social reality and acquiesced in its own irrelevance. Because of its passivity before social and economic givens, bourgeois culture came more and more to be a "matter of spiritual values" according to which "the concept of soul comes into ever sharper contradiction to mind. . . ."[22] Culture was deprived of a critical thrust and mind was applied chiefly in the realm of technology and material production. Beauty, sensuality, and enjoyment became consolatory rather than critical. Happiness and freedom were "inner" and thus finally illusory since external reality remains unchanged. In sum, the conventional concept of culture was potentially liberating, but in the service of one class it became a way of undergirding the status quo. Consciousness was continually set over against a bad social reality and was continually overcome by that reality.

It was, however, the essay "On Hedonism" (1938) which foreshadowed most clearly Marcuse's later interest in Freud and the shift in his thought toward "the aesthetic" as the central concept. In this essay Marcuse discussed the inadequacy of previous philosophical attempts to formulate a hedonistic philosophy. He found that happiness and reason were traditionally regarded as opposing values. Or in the case of Epicureanism, where "Reason . . . became the adjudicator of pleasure," neither term—happiness or reason—retained its true meaning.[23] Likewise idealism was inadequate as a source for true hedonism since it posited reason as superior and universal and relegated material needs and wants to the merely "arbitrary and subjective."[24]

Marcuse's solution was to link the concept of happiness—"the fulfillment of all potentialities of the individual"—with freedom and reason.[25] Reason became the guide to freedom which was a prerequisite of happiness. In a society no longer riven by class groupings and interests, the satisfaction of individual wants would be precisely the definition of the "rational," the goal of critical theory informed by reason. In this essay Marcuse discussed the problem of sexuality for the first time. He pointed out that in bourgeois society and ethics, sexuality was sanctioned only to the extent that it contributed to "physical or mental health" or "the production of new labor power."[26] In such a society labor was also separated from enjoyable and spontaneous feeling, just as it was separated from thought. Marcuse contrarily linked pleasure with freedom in that "augmented pleasure . . . would represent . . . increased liberation of the individual for it would demand freedom in the choice of object, in the knowledge and in the realization of his potentialities, and freedom of time and of place."[27]

Thus Marcuse's early social thought represented a theoretical attempt to make clear the inadequacy of human activity, material or intellectual, and the impossibility of happiness that was free and responsible to one's self and to others, in a class society. At the core of his thought lay a fundamental identity between reason, freedom, and happiness. Reason uninformed by the other two concepts became rationalization in the Weberian sense, a means of subordinating the individual to economic and social processes. Happiness without the other two was a mindless satisfaction of wants determined by oppressive reality and accomplished at the expense of others. And freedom without reason and happiness led to mere competition within the existing social framework and was thus achieved at the expense of others. Only a critical theory, which combined these elements and criticized existing facts, and a praxis which aimed at their realization could unite the best feature of bourgeois idealism and historical materialism and in Hegelian fashion transcend them both.

The culmination of Marcuse's attempts to forge a new critical theory of society came in *Reason and Revolution* (1941). In this volume Marcuse was concerned with three lines of argument. With Europe faced by Nazi domination, Marcuse defended Hegel against the charge of being an ideological ancestor of National Socialism. Secondly, Marcuse, in a related gambit, sought to demonstrate the similarities rather than the differences between Hegel and Karl Marx. Thus the Hegel who emerged from the pages of *Reason and Revolution* was the Hegel who had supported the French Revolution and the philosopher whose thought had contained the seeds of a critical social theory. Finally Marcuse sought to defend the tradition of German idealism, again represented most centrally by Hegel, against the onslaughts of eighteenth-century empiricism and its nineteenth-century cousin, positivism. In doing so he implicitly defended continental radicalism against liberalism, which he saw as the political expression of empiricism and positivism. Thus *Reason and Revolution* was an explicit effort to anchor Marcuse's own "critical theory" in the Hegelian-Marxist tradition.

It is not my intention to engage in a lengthy discussion of Marcuse's exposition of Hegel's thought. Nevertheless a few brief remarks are in order. In most general terms Hegel's thought was based on the identity of ontology and logic, being and thought, the movement of history and the development of reason. For Marcuse the crucial element in the Hegelian synthesis was Hegel's emphasis upon the dynamic, fluid nature of reality, a concept encompassing both nature and history. Social and historical structures, philosophical systems, and artistic products were real in the sense that they were phenomenally present and existent, yet also "mere" appearances in the sense that they were not yet coincident with the final development of Reason, a force which worked in and through history toward eventual fulfillment. The existing world was suffused with Reason and negativity, Being and Nonbeing; things were what they were, but not yet what they really could be. Thus all reality was pregnant with possibility.

What Marcuse had done in his earlier essays, it became clear, was to deidealize Hegel's metaphysics. Reality, in Marcuse's view, had to be examined not only for what it was, but also for the potentialities inherent in it for development and change. And this development was in turn to be criticized in the light of and toward the development of a rational ordering of things. For Marcuse Reason and the Rational no longer had metaphysical reference, but instead pointed to the full achievement of individual potentialities (freedom) and the satisfaction of individual wants and needs (happiness) within history.

Marcuse readily admitted that Hegel, in his later writings, had abandoned his dialectical thought and came to stress the "status quo" in his political philosophy. Yet Marcuse emphasized repeatedly that the tools for a critical theory of social reality were inherent in Hegel's thought. For all its authoritarian character, Hegel's concept of the state was, Marcuse pointed out, a *Rechtstaat* for the "establishing of reason and freedom," a goal neither society itself nor "das Volk" was capable of realizing.[28] It was thus a radical mistake to confuse Hegel's *Staatslehre* with the National Socialist's concept of the *Volkstaat*.

The philosophically pernicious force which Hegel (and Marcuse) felt called upon to refute was empiricism and its offspring, positivism. For Marcuse, the Hegelian, the danger of empiricism lay in its "refutation of general ideas," its denial of the universal validity of reason, and reason's "faculty to attain truths."[29] With man as a prisoner of individual and social experience, there was no source of values open to the individual other than Hume's "custom and experience." Human existence became one-dimensional, lacking an "ought" to inform the "is." Thus no general validity could be given to the critique of a given social order; empiricism-positivism remained ideological. The value of the rational-idealistic tradition lay in its preservation of a realm of autonomy over and against the phenomenal world. The high point of the tradition came with Hegel's attempt at a synthesis of reason and experience, the spiritual and the phenomenal, the suprahistorical and the historical. Hegel's incarnationist philosophy was incomprehensible to the common-sense approach of empiricism. In going beyond Kantian idealism, Hegel's thought had signaled a break with idealism's "tendency to introversion" and pointed toward "the realization of reason in and through given social institutions."[30] Thus social theory became the next logical stage in western thought.

From Hegel, Marcuse turned to Marx. Marcuse's analysis of Marx was based on the Marxian notion that Marx's own thought was a reflection of the capitalist society in which Marx found himself. In response to the practical materialism of bourgeoisie society, Marx pointed to the failure of capitalist order to provide either for biological existence or self-fulfillment. As a result immiserization and alienation became its defining characteristics. Bourgeois social thought had been based on the universality of reason and had emphasized individual rights and liberty. Marx conversely focused on the proletariat as the concrete negation of the universality of reason and freedom and emphasized the future attainment of individual happiness. Thus Marcuse saw in Marxism a concern for the universal satisfaction of individual potentialities: "the individual is the goal."[31] Marx had reversed Hegel: "the idea of reason has been superseded by the idea of happiness."[32]

Besides emphasizing the individualistic strain in Marxism, Marcuse also drew a distinction between the Hegelian and Marxist dialectic. For both thinkers the dialectical process pointed to the fact of negativity in human reality. Marcuse noted, however, that for Marx negativity was a sociohistorical rather than ontological fact: "Truth is not a realm apart from historical reality, not a region of eternally valid ideas . . . it transcends the given historical reality, but only insofar as it crosses from one historical stage to another."[33] The truth of individual and social existence can only be envisaged within the historical process and emerges in response to human needs rather than above and beyond them.

Finally Marcuse emphasized the voluntaristic rather than

deterministic elements of Marx's historical materialism. Though the development of capitalist structures, of necessity, led to their own destruction, there was, according to Marcuse, no logical necessity in the subsequent development of socialism. The necessity was rather a moral one incumbent upon a "subjective force, namely the revolutionary class itself."[34] And it was highly indicative of the cast of Marcuse's Marxism that he did not refer to the workers or the proletariat, but to a revolutionary class as the bearers of the future. At the end of the discussion of Marx, Marcuse wrote (in what was undoubtedly a thinly veiled reference to the Soviet Union): "Theory will preserve the truth even if revolutionary practice deviates from its proper path. Practice follows the truth, not vice versa."[35] Consciousness and action were only tenuously joined and if a decision were to be made between them, then the side of revolutionary thought would have to be taken against false practice.

In sum Marcuse's Marxism was of a decidedly voluntaristic nature. In keeping with his distaste for the rigid determinism of empiricism and positivism, Marcuse stressed the subjective, existential aspects of revolutionary consciousness as a guide to action. This voluntaristic, intellectualistic bias in turn reflected an elitism of sorts. With consciousness—critical theory—in effect elevated above praxis, it became apparent that not everyone, least of all the proletariat, possessed this true consciousness. Though the proletariat embodied the negation of bourgeois theory and practice, it remained a passive force.[36] Not mundane measures such as the nationalization of industries were the prerequisite for true socialism; it was rather the abolition of alienated labor as such. Who and what determined the latter was left unknown or known only to those armed with critical consciousness; thus Marcuse's intellectual Leninism.

In pointing to the inadequacy of mere external institutional rearrangements, Marcuse moved the problem of revolutionary thought to an internal realm of a change in consciousness, i.e., from a political to a cultural realm. As a result Marcuse's critical theory edged away from social thought back toward philosophy, from Marx back to Hegel. To change social reality the implication was that individual consciousness—values, attitudes and ideals—first had to be transformed.[37]

As it emerged in his essays and *Reason and Revolution,* Marcuse's version of the course of western thought was also a radically skewed one. Repeatedly, he would begin an essay with a discussion of Greek thought only to jump from there to Idealism, ignoring all that came between. Basic to his own neo-Marxist position was the belief that the content of thought reflects social reality. (Whether this idea is particularly helpful or even more than generally the case is not at issue.) The problem was that Marcuse's implicit assumption of an underlying continuity of concern and theme between the Greeks and nineteenth-century European thought would seem to presuppose a similar continuity in social and economic structures, a position that is hardly tenable and seemingly in contradiction with Marcuse's Marxism.

Specifically Marcuse's reading of empiricism as a philosophy and positivism as social theory was highly tendentious. Though occasionally granting the radical and critical elements in these positions, Marcuse consistently underplayed them while at the same time minimizing the deterministic and conservative elements in Hegel as well as Marx and Marxism. It is not my intention to enter into an extended discussion concerning the young versus the old Marx, Marx versus Engels, historical versus dialectical materialism, etc.; it must be emphasized, however, that a strong case can be made for an extreme deterministic side to Marx's thought. One can clearly prefer Marcuse's Marx without going to the lengths that Marcuse did to discredit empiricism and positivism and downplay deterministic elements in Marx.

Indeed with Marcuse's rejection of the ontological grounding of Reason, there was no reason for seeing him as anything other than a radical social theorist who based his critical theory on empirical and historical givens. In truth Marcuse's critical theory had no more philosophical (as opposed to ideological) status than empiricism and positivism; as he himself stated, his truths were transhistorical and not transcendent. Valuable though Marcuse's critical theory might be as a mode of approach, it was no more than an individual attitude based on certain prior intellectual and ethical choices, lacking any general and universally binding validity. With "God" dead and Reason historicized to a functional, intellectual faculty, all had become empiricists of one sort or another.[38]

Finally Marcuse's thought was vague as to what specifically freedom and happiness entailed. That individual freedom and individual happiness were ultimately reconcilable with social good and general welfare was no more self-evident in Marcuse's thought than in classical liberal thought. As presented they were slogans to which no one could really take exception.

One can see in retrospect that by the early 1940s Marcuse had exhausted the Hegelian and Marxist tradition. From it he had forged a methodology. His task then became one of finding a focus for his critical theory and a content for his key concepts.

From Homo Laborans to Homo Ludens

If *Reason and Revolution* and the early essays constituted a tour de force in their rehabilitation and radicalization of Hegel, then *Eros and Civilization*, published by Marcuse in 1955, was even more groundbreaking in its linking of sexual and political radicalism. There was little in Marcuse's previous work to indicate that he might turn specifically to Freud in the 1950s; indeed though Marx and Freud had supplied the two great critiques of western bourgeois civilization, most Freudians looked with suspicion on Marxism, an attitude that was more than reciprocated by most Marxists. Marcuse had been associated with the *Zeitschrift für Sozialforschung* in the thirties when Erich Fromm had been working out a synthesis of historical materialism and depth psychology. The figure linking Freud and social radicalism, Wilhelm Reich, was reviewed rather favorably by Fromm in the pages of the *Zeitschrift* during the same decade. And considered in the light of Marcuse's central concerns—freedom and happiness as the goals of human thought and action—his turn to Freud was at least comprehensible, though by no means inevitable.

From another vantage point Marcuse's critical adoption of

Freud was yet another example of the search for a new radical theory in postwar western society. Living in a society which was ostensibly "capitalist," yet apparently far from revolution, a society which appeared to be slowly inching into the realm of abundance by virtue of unprecedented technological development, a Marxist of Marcuse's bent might validly have asked what the central concerns of radical theory were to become. Obviously though the conceptual framework of Hegel and Marx was still useful, it needed some modifications, shifts in emphases, and fresh injections from new sources. For this task Freud served well.

The Freud that Marcuse made use of was not the Freud of the "chastened Progressives," of the Revisionists, or of the orthodox therapists. As the subtitle to *Eros and Civilization* indicated, Marcuse was primarily concerned with the later Freud, the philosopher and potentially radical critic of civilization. Though in general terms Marcuse was working along the lines set down earlier by Reich, he went well beyond Reich in the sophistication of his analysis. Where Reich had been rather simpleminded in his advocacy of orgasmic potency as indicative of the nonrepressed individual in the nonrepressive society, Marcuse talked of an erotic view of reality of which sexual freedom, as such, became a mere example. Reich had seen the authoritarian family as the central oppressive and repressive agent in western society; Marcuse ignored the family as such. Where Reich had attempted to give Marxism a social psychology, Marcuse attempted to give it a cultural-philosophical psychology. And finally where Reich the therapist had adamantly rejected Freud's death-aggression instinct, Marcuse the philosopher accepted it, though with radical modifications.

As Marcuse saw it, the central conflict in the Freudian schema was between the pleasure principle and the reality principle. Freud had maintained that when this conflict emerged, the former was forced to adjust to the latter. The main effect of this modification was that sexuality, the paradigm in Freud's thought for pleasure, became primarily genital, the chief justification for which lay in procreation. Thus Freud, and even his radical disciple Reich, had conceived of the role of sexuality in significantly restricted terms.

Marcuse modified the Freudian vocabulary of concepts by asserting that in fact Freud's analysis reflected a specific socio-historical situation in which social domination, empowered by competitive economic performance, characterized social reality. In such a situation the reality principle was perverted into what Marcuse named the " 'performance principle'—the prevailing historical form of the reality principle . . . in a society stratified according to competitive economic performance of its members."[39] The performance principle was in turn dictated by the social fact of "scarcity." In Marcuse's view, however, scarcity was not an immutable fact of all social existence but rather "the consequence of a specific organization of scarcity."[40] And in such a society organized around scarcity, "surplus repression" and "restrictions necessitated by social domination" were facts of life.[41] Thus social reality under the domination of the performance principle demanded repression beyond that necessary for "civilized" existence in the true sense.

It was in turn surplus repression which supplied the energy for alienated labor, activity literally not one's own, but imposed by the structure of domination. Thus according to Marcuse, in opposition to Freud, the "irreconcilable conflict is not between work (reality principle) and Eros (pleasure principle), but between alienated labor (performance principle) and Eros."[42] In a society which had abolished "want," the performance principle, and alienated labor, sexuality would be released from its exclusively genital focus, the particular sexual expression of the performance principle, and revert to its original polymorphous mode of expression. The entire body, along with all aspects of human and social existence, would become eroticized. Thus were the outlines of a new order established around a genuine reality principle informed by Eros.

Central to Marcuse's adaptation of Freud was his discussion of the Eros-Thanatos conflict in human existence. Marcuse's interpretation was a fascinating one since his strategy was to seize upon "the common nature of the instincts . . . the fundamental regressive or 'conservative' tendency in all instinctual life."[43] Eros and Thanatos were thus both to be subsumed under the Nirvana principle, that is, the search for stasis. The emergence of instinctual dualism, Marcuse said, arose from a historically determined divergence of the instincts; the source of tragic conflict lay in the different modes of satisfaction demanded by each. Both, however, contained elements of the other as they manifested themselves; e.g., morality, the preservative of civilization, was powered by the death instinct. But most central in Marcuse's analysis was his assertion that technological progress was the result of "the diversion of primary destructiveness from the ego to the external world."[44] Again life and death were intimately bound up with one another. The problem was that a repressive civilization demanded "continuous sublimation; it thereby weakens Eros, the builder of culture" and threatened to give the death instinct the upper hand.[45] Thus the historically determined tragic conflict within individuals and groups.

Marcuse also expanded on the problem of labor and work in Freud's thought. He pointed out that for Freud "the basic work in civilization is nonlibidinal, is labor; labor is unpleasantness."[46] In essence Marcuse equated the Marxian notion of alienated labor with the Freudian idea of nonlibidinal work. The energy needed for alienated labor is expended at the expense of Eros and thus again civilization's development is threatened with the death instinct's overpowering of the weakened life force. Indeed the thrust of Marcuse's discussion was that Freud was essentially correct. Except for intellectual and artistic "work," labor was characterized by alienation. And though some aggression was sublimated in the technological process, much of it was introjected and guilt increased, since in the technological society no individual, clear object of aggression (such as the father) remained. Or such surplus aggression was directed by the dominant and dominating structure against real, or imaginary, external enemies.

At this point in *Eros and Civilization* Marcuse dealt with the central paradox of life in an "advanced" industrial society: increased satisfaction of material wants and needs was combined with an increasingly pervasive control and administration of all aspects of individual and social existence. Progress, defined as technological advance, was a highly ambiguous development. It had rendered otiose older repressive structures and impera- tives, yet at the same time it dulled the individual's critical faculties. As a result "the individual does not really know what is going on."[47] On the other hand Marcuse put his dialectical mode of thought to good use (and illustrated his own very real ambivalence toward technology) by arguing along the lines of "the worse, the better." That is, the more individuals were alienated from their lives and labor through automation, the less they were actually tied to repressive modes of existence and the better the chance "for the elimination of labor from the world of human potentialities."[48]

All this discussion was obviously based on Marcuse's belief that the abolition of *Ananke* (want and material necessity) was at hand and indeed a fact of modern western society.[49] With this accomplished, the performance principle, surplus repression, alienated labor, and genital sexuality could be left behind. The energy diverted by these older social and psychological struc- tures could then be redirected back into everyday social exist- ence and Thanatos, the source of aggression and death, would come under the domination of Eros. Quantitative changes would eventually lead to a qualitatively different individual and social existence.

To his examination and modification of Freud and social theory, Marcuse added excursions into philosophy and aesthetics. It seemed to be Marcuse's intent to formulate an erotic ontology, a "logos of gratification"[50] which would place at the center of western thought the idea of being as the search for gratification, rather than being as the search for domination of self, others, and nature. For his new ontology Marcuse turned first to Hegel's idea that freedom (and hence reason and happiness) ultimately consisted in a "coming to rest in the transparent knowledge and gratification of being."[51] Similarly Nietzsche with his notion of "the eternal return" and cry of *"Alle Lust will Ewigkeit"* had attempted to make eternal "full concreteness and finiteness" and advocated the "total affirmation of the life instincts."[52] It was finally Freud's great appeal that his theory "partakes of this philosophical dynamic . . . Being is essentially striving for pleasure."[53] Thus Hegel, Nietzsche, and Freud were seen as formulators of a new ontology appropriate to the nonrepressive stage of social development.

In the realm of aesthetics Marcuse's discussion pointed in the same direction. Taking his cue from Schiller's concept of the sensuous and the play impulse, Marcuse's idea was that art represented the "liberation of sensuousness through its reconciliation of reason . . ." and thus was a paradigm of activity in the nonrepressive order.[54] In that order, neither Prometheus nor Faust would serve as the central cultural hero; rather Orpheus and Narcissus, who represented play over work, and nature as "an object of contemplation" rather than as an object of exploitation would assume the role of "culture heroes."

Related to this discussion of work and play was Marcuse's idea of the relationship between sexuality and Eros. In essence Marcuse's view was that the erotic was self-sublimated sexuality. In the nonrepressive society sexuality would not merely be "freer"; it would be transformed through its uninhibited expression. What would occur would be "a spread rather than an explosion of libido."[55] Along with Reich and Goodman, Marcuse's call for liberation rested on the assumption that free instinctual expression was not destructive of a nonrepressive social order. Indeed "non-repressive sublimation" would become the social "cement" holding the nonrepressive society together. Sensuality would no longer work in opposition to reason; reason itself would become sensuous. The distinct boundaries between man and nature, subject and object, approved and "perverse" sexuality would be abolished. The paradigm of this mode of being, Marcuse pointed out, was Freud's concept of primary narcissism, the child at the mother's breast. Yet it was to be achieved not by regression, but by movement to a higher synthesis of sensuality and reason.

But there still existed one barrier to the final realization of a nonrepressive society—the human consciousness of death.

Though "joy wants eternity," the awareness of death as reality and as symbol "introduces a repressive element in all libidinal relations and renders pleasure itself painful."[56] Thus time, engendered by consciousness of death, was the ultimate source of frustration; it was beyond the possibility of social restructuring and gave lie to the possibility for an existence of eternal gratification. The final step could never be made. Marcuse did speculate, however, that not death as a fact, but death as an instinctual goal might be abolished with Eros's supremacy; and "like the other necessities, it [death] can be made rational-painless."[57] Thus even in death or approaching death, the rational, "that which sustains the order of gratification,"[58] would eventually reign.

In the epilogue of *Eros and Civilization*, Marcuse moved from the sublime to the polemical. He attacked neo-Freudianism in general and his former colleague, Erich Fromm, in particular, for abandoning Freud's radical instinct theory for a watered-down psychology which served to support rather than undermine the status quo. In an assault remarkably similar to Goodman's in 1945, Marcuse charged that "a weakening . . . of the theory of sexuality . . . must lead to a weakening of the sociological critique."[59] As a result of the de-emphasis of sexuality, of early childhood experiences, and of the unconscious, Fromm had no vantage point from which he could criticize society. In dropping the instinct theory (just as empiricism had dropped the Rational), Fromm's virtue of productiveness, Marcuse held, was defined by the standards of the repressive society; hence individual cure became, in effect, adjustment. Marcuse did not deny that Fromm's values were valid ones; rather "the context in which they are defined and proclaimed . . . are spurious."[60] Finally Fromm's revisionism tended to make neurosis "an essentially moral problem."[61] Though society was to blame, the individual was also; social and cultural patterns were accepted as given. Hence Marcuse joined Goodman the libertarian and Trilling the chastened progressive in opposing neo-Freudianism and its apparent capitulation to conformity.

Fromm's rejoinder to Marcuse's attack was a skillful one. In his

"The Human Implications of Instinctivistic Radicalism," Fromm proceeded first of all to clarify his own position by separating himself from other revisionists such as Karen Horney and Harry Stack Sullivan. He then made the point that Freud's critique was aimed at civilization in general and not at capitalistic society, as such. The core of Fromm's rebuttal was that because man was both a natural and a social being, guided by instincts but also self-consciousness, he could not be satisfied by instinctual gratification alone. He likewise rejected Marcuse's claim that his own values were ideological and strengthened existing society. Fromm ended by urging a more complex view by which it would still be possible to be productive and capable of love even in a badly flawed social order. Thus to Marcuse's "Great Refusal," Fromm countered with a "yes and a no."[62]

Fromm's most interesting point, however, was that Marcuse's advocacy of "unlimited sexual satisfaction [was] only part of a characteristic trait of twentieth century capitalism, the need for mass consumption." In this view man became "a system of desires and gratifications . . . stimulated and directed by the economic machine."[63] (Ironically this point closely resembled Marcuse's concept of repressive desublimation which emerged in his later works.) In this way Fromm turned the tables on Marcuse and accused him of falling victim to the ideology of consumption.

In Marcuse's reply to Fromm's rejoinder, he pointed out that Fromm had misinterpreted him by saying that he had equated happiness and sexual satisfaction, love and sexual desire.[64] Marcuse did agree that Freud had not offered a critique of capitalist society as such, yet reasserted that Freud's teachings did have "radical critical implications."[65] Finally Marcuse accepted the claim that his "Great Refusal" was a type of "human nihilism in that it is a great refusal to play the game."[66] Already by 1956 Marcuse was beginning to withdraw from the more optimistic claims of *Eros and Civilization* and stress instead the negative.

A critique of *Eros and Civilization* must avoid demanding that Marcuse's use of Freudian concepts be consonant with Freud's own use of them. At one point in *Eros and Civilization* Marcuse spoke of the "symbolic value" of Freud's primal murder myth;

this should be the spirit in which one considers Marcuse's use of Freud which, as he admitted to Fromm, was a tendentious one.

A critique of a work so ostensibly radical must stress the resemblance of the structure and thrust of *Eros and Civilization* to the society which it "critiqued." Just as Marcuse maintained that the concept of the individual had, in advanced societies, dissolved into a generic and social entity, so in *Eros and Civilization*, concrete individuals or their actions were never mentioned. Ironically, Marcuse's work was deficient in psychological detail and analysis. Nor did he couch his analysis in terms of classes or the conflict of socioeconomic groups. The terms "proletariat" and "bourgeoisie," "capitalism" and "socialism" scarcely appeared in the pages of *Eros and Civilization*.

Furthermore labor, which had earlier signified man's basic way of being in the world and that characteristic which distinguished him from nature and the animal world, became almost exclusively alienated labor, an activity hopefully to be transcended. In the context of *Eros and Civilization*, play, sensuous activity, and gratification were the desired human activities. Gratification in stasis, a libidinal yet, withal, essentially passive mode of existence became the telos of technological development. Clearly "homo laborans" had given way to "homo ludens."

Marcuse's examples of nonrepressive existence were taken from literature and myth. Clearly the demand that Marcuse sketch in all the details of life in such a desirable society is an unreasonable one. Still, his utopian meditations would have been more convincing had he given a few hints as to the nature of his new order. What would the fate of the traditional family become? What form would libidinally charged work take? Life in a nonrepressive society would demand a high degree of organization and coordination, according to "rational" authority. Yet one could only wonder if Marcuse's projected utopia would not demand new taboos and restriction as restrictive in their way as those demanded by the performance principle. Indeed lurking behind Marcuse's entire schema was the Platonic idea that an elite was in possession of the "rational" and that recalcitrant individuals might rightly be forced to be "free" and "happy."

Moreover with his absolutistic "Great Refusal" Marcuse revealed what would become more apparent in *One-Dimensional Man*—a radicalism so thoroughgoing as to become a type of quietism. He wrote off sexual reform, "the progressive father," and the like as mere playthings which served to strengthen the existing order rather than undermine it. Likewise it was ironic that in contrast to his earlier work where he had stressed the dialectical relationship between radical theory and praxis as the agent of change, in *Eros and Civilization* the agent of change seemed to be technology. Marcuse's hope was that somehow technology, the instrument of domination, would reduce work time and energy and at some point quantitative changes would "flip-flop" over into a qualitatively different social order. Alienated labor, increasingly subtle domination and administration, remained strangely "external" to individuals. Once the new reality emerged from the dialectical development of technology, the past would somehow be abolished.

Finally Marcuse's caveat concerning death seemed rather gratuitous and irrelevant to his argument. Nor was it clear exactly why the awareness of death introduced a repressive element into human existence.[67] Indeed the consciousness of temporality could as well be considered a way of heightening pleasure rather than rendering all existence fundamentally painful, as Marcuse admitted. Marcuse reversed himself at one point and spoke of "the restoration of remembrance . . . as a vehicle of liberation."[68] Yet most ominous was Marcuse's "solution" to the problem of death—to make it painless and hence no longer an object of dread. In doing this, the individual would be denied even the uniqueness of his own death. Though benevolently administered, death would nevertheless be administered. And in proposing this Marcuse approached the most totalitarian of claims—the right to deny the individual his pain as well as his pleasures.

Despite these strictures, *Eros and Civilization* was a powerful and daring work. In combining polemical skill and high seriousness, it was a landmark attempt in postwar western culture to renew radical theory. In essence it was a philosophical vision of the nature of human existence once the traditional tasks of radicalism had been met. Like all utopian speculations it failed to suggest convincingly how utopia might be achieved, and like most utopian projects it mirrored the faults of the society under examination as much as it criticized them. Just as Marcuse called for a "regression" to polymorphous perversity and primary narcissism, a new erotic pastoral, so his own work was a regression to early nineteenth-century radical Romanticism, only at a higher stage of historical development. The Nirvana principle, under which both Eros and Thanatos were to be subsumed, functioned as an ersatz universal, a quasi-biological counterpart of Hegel's Reason, and as such provided a critical vantage point from which existing social reality could be criticized. But as Marcuse wrote in a different context, the strength of psychoanalysis was drawn from its obsolescence and "what is obsolescent is not also false."[69]

Pessimism and Politics

Since *Eros and Civilization*, Marcuse's theoretical works have swung between a rather bleak pessimism as to the possibility of radical change in advanced industrial societies, and a measured optimism (particularly after the May, 1968, student uprisings in Paris) concerning the development of a genuinely radical alternative to the established order. As he wrote in his introduction to *One-Dimensional Man*, the book "will vacillate throughout between two contradictory hypotheses: (1) that advanced industrial society is capable of containing qualitative change for the foreseeable future; (2) that forces and tendencies exist which may break this containment and explode the society."[70]

One year after the publication of *One-Dimensional Man* Marcuse explored Max Weber's ambivalent relationship to rationality and domination in an essay "Industrialization and Capitalism in the Work of Max Weber" (1965). In a symbolic sense it was Weber who emerged as the chief prophet of advanced industrial society and thus became in retrospect the hero/villain of *One-Dimensional Man*, all this without his name ever being mentioned by Marcuse in the volume.[71] Over and against the rational as that which led to the order of gratification and liberation,

Weber had described rationality as the logos of domination and administration. Or in Marcusian terms, Weber's concept of rationality indicated that in advanced industrial society "irrationality becomes reason."[72] Rationality was the motive force behind a social order characterized by bureaucratic administration and domination, justified by a scientific-technological ideology.

In the context of American social thought, *One-Dimensional Man* was, as Marcuse suggested, a theoretical gloss on the popular and academic social critics of the 1950s—C. Wright Mills, Vance Packard, William H. Whyte, Fred Cook, and, one should add, John Kenneth Galbraith and David Riesman. Taking their investigations of growing governmental and industrial interconnections, their critiques of the role of the media and technology in American society, and their speculations concerning a transformation in value orientation and social character, Marcuse put together, with America as his focus, a radically pessimistic critique of the social and ideological structures inherent in advanced industrial societies. In doing so Marcuse once again made use of a neo-Romantic mode of cultural criticism with its traditionally antiscientific bias, and an accompanying elevation of art and metaphysical speculation to prominence over "conservative" positivism.

The very title *One-Dimensional Man* suggested the basic thrust of Marcuse's critique of contemporary American society and the ideologies which justified it. For Marcuse, like Goodman, the distressing feature of the society lay in its ability to pervade all aspects of individual and social existence. In the existing order, Marcuse pointed out, one "cannot imagine a qualitatively different universe of discourse and action."[73] Thus no conceptual alternatives or critical standpoints found general validity. Indeed, *pace* Daniel Bell, radical ideologies had come to seem undesirable and disruptive of the given order. In like manner, physical privacy and spiritual autonomy had been reduced to a minimum by the all-pervasive effects of "technological Reality"; from the media to the omnipresent bureaucratic machinery, one was never alone.

Marcuse made particularly explicit his abandonment of conventional Marxist notions of the role of proletariat. For Marcuse the working class "no longer appears to be the living contradiction to the established society."[74] In a society where "domination [was] transfigured into administration" the proletariat had become mystified by the ideology of technological progress and pacified by material satisfaction.[75] Like the bourgeoisie it had become thoroughly integrated into the society and constituted a supportive rather than critical element of the society. Thus the social system had in its integration become thoroughly one-dimensional, and internal contradictions were subjectively nonexistent.

Likewise Marcuse found that two vital components of the "Great Refusal"—art and sexuality—were rather easily incorporated into the dominant system. They had become "cogs in a cultural machine . . . entertaining without endangering. . . ."[76] The classics, avant-garde, and dissident cultural movements all became items for mass consumption, embraced by and serving to bolster existing reality. Perhaps most interesting was Marcuse's reexamination of the sexual and the erotic as the foundation for a critical stance over and against the existing order. For this he introduced his concept of "repressive de-sublimation" which described the way in which advanced industrial society allowed a modicum of sexual expression and was ostensibly antipuritanical. Far from undercutting the social and economic order, however, this "sexual freedom" only strengthened it further. He found that business and advertising, the popular cinema and mass media, all made deliberate use of the erotic to further the ends of the economy: "sex is integrated into work and public relations and is thus made more susceptible to [controlled] satisfaction."[77] Reich had been proven wrong. A class society and capitalist economy could do very well without a puritanical attitude toward sexuality. Like Goodman, Marcuse pointed out that the socially induced stimulation of erotic desire, followed by little or no satisfaction, was fully compatible with and indeed fed "the growth of unsublimated as well as sublimated forms of aggressiveness . . . a simultaneous release of repressed sexuality and aggressiveness."[78] Thus neither the realm of culture nor private sexuality escaped the pervasive influence of the bureaucratic-commercial nexus. Both were still under the control of the performance principle. As in Goodman's social "carnival" in the first paradigm in *Communitas*, the periodic release of instinctual energies only bound individuals more closely to existing social and economic existence.

The third section of *One-Dimensional Man* contained an analysis of the language of the *Lebenswelt* of advanced industrial society. Taking examples from advertising, *Time* magazine, and industrial relations studies, Marcuse maintained that the world of discourse created by this language was one in which propositions "are evocative rather than demonstrative,"[79] eliciting ritualized response rather than genuine thought, and empty double-talk instead of dialectical thinking. As a result the possibility of entertaining alternatives, and the critical function of language and thought in general, were diluted or covered over with mystification. All discourse was geared to adjustment rather than questioning. Transcendence or two-dimensionality was foreclosed. According to Marcuse the very language of advanced industrial society had become ideological to fit the world of total administration.

In the central section of *One-Dimensional Man* Marcuse moved to a critique of the formal ideology of the society—science and its handmaiden, linguistic analysis—and followed this with a presentation of his own brand of dialectical or negative thinking. As in his earlier efforts, Marcuse began at the beginning with Greek thought and promptly identified Aristotle's formal logic as the "villain" of the piece. In Aristotle's logic "concepts become instruments of prediction and control" and "material content is neutralized."[80] Thus Aristotle's was a static mode of thought, concerned with the form rather than the content of arguments. It undergirded a mode of thought which focused on what was and not what should be. It was, in short, one-dimensional. By way of contrast Marcuse proposed what he named dialectical or two-dimensional logic. In this way of grasping and conceptualizing the world, "the predicative 'is' implies an 'ought' "[81] and thus simultaneously describes and judges. Rather than reflecting (as with Hegel) an ontological tension between essence and appearance, Marcuse's dialectical logic reflected and referred to a social-historical tension between the way things are and the way they might be, what is given and what is potential: "Reason becomes historical reason . . . a mode of thought which is geared to reduce ignorance, destruction, brutality and oppression."[82]

With this dichotomy between formal and dialectical modes of logic established, Marcuse proceeded to scrutinize the scientific world view, and to revise the rather optimistic attitude toward science and technology which he had set forth in *Eros and Civilization.* In *One-Dimensional Man,* Marcuse advanced the proposition that "pure" science and technology were one in conception, ideological in nature, and inherently repressive in application. Rather than being value free, Marcuse held that from the beginning "Galilean science is, in the formation of concepts, the technic of a specific Lebenswelt."[83] Based upon a "quantification of Nature," the separation of the realms of fact and value, and seeing "nature as potential instrumentality,"[84] natural science was philosophically and historically linked with "a specific technology—namely, technology as a form of social control and domination."[85] Thus science and technology were not neutral schemas to be judged by their application, but in essence repressive. Closely related to the scientific-technological Weltanschauung, furthermore, was a particular way of understanding man and society. Nature quantified and manipulated led, in advanced industrial society, to the real possibility of the quantification and manipulation of the individual and social reality. The logic of domination, Weberian rationality, had triumphed over the logic of historical reason, gratification and freedom.

With science and technology established as ideological, Marcuse took on the philosophy of linguistic analysis. Marcuse objected to linguistic analysis for its "debunking of transcendent concepts."[86] In addition, linguistic philosophy served to justify and clarify science rather than standing in judgment of and criticizing it.[87] Though ostensibly "radical" in its examination of the use of concepts and propositions, linguistic analysis was thoroughly conservative in reality. Metaphysics, emotive language, aesthetics, and ethics were considered philosophical non-sense and consigned to the realm of triviality. They were rendered harmless and hence invalid as judgments upon the scientific world view. Masquerading as "objective," linguistic analysis rendered "the rational rather than the irrational . . . the most effective vehicle of mystification . . . by leaving them [the terms of ordinary language] in the repressive context of the established universe of discourse."[88] Philosophy had become a technique for facilitating rationalization.

What then was to be done and thought? Marcuse's first move was to propose a third way between positivism and outmoded metaphysics. As might be expected, he was sympathetic to the traditional concern of philosophy with universals and held that universals reflected "the unhappy consciousness of a divided world."[89] At the same time they also pointed to "the very qualities of the world with which one is daily confronted."[90] In Marcusian terms universals were substantive generalizations, e.g., beauty as the common characteristic of several things, each of which taken individually fails to match the "ideal." Thus universals could serve as critical as well as descriptive concepts: "the universal concept denotes that which the particular entity is, and is not."[91] As such they were absolutely crucial in any philosophical enterprise that pretended to be genuinely dialecti-cal and not merely ideological.

Though universals were historically conditioned, Marcuse maintained that they could be judged by an objective standard, the standard of rationality. The philosophic universal or any "transcendent project" was to be measured against the existing possibilities at the material and intellectual level of the existing culture, and should preserve the "productive achievement" of the attained civilization. Finally the universal or transcendent project should clearly define and comprehend the "established totality" and provide for "a greater chance for the pacification of existence . . . the free development of human needs and faculties."[92] While Marcuse held that such a critical vantage point was still possible within existing reality, it was his fear that such a "determinate choice" was rapidly disappearing, and with it the chance for critical theory.[93]

Beyond this point Marcuse was wary. He asserted that "dialectical theory . . . cannot offer the remedy," but suggested several areas that deserved particular attention.[94] He spoke of the need for a redefinition of technology which would involve a "liberating mastery" of nature, "a reduction of overdevelopment," birth control, a restoration of privacy, and a redefinition of needs.[95] A political structure would be needed that provided for a "combination of centralized authority and direct democracy," the former to provide for necessary goods and services, the latter to be concerned with the use of surpluses and individual actions.[96] (This obviously had much in common with Goodman's third paradigm in *Communitas*.) Finally the source of and motive force behind social transformation was not clear but would perhaps emerge from the "historical extremes . . . the most advanced consciousness of humanity, and its most exploited force." But he added, "It is nothing but a chance."[97]

As some radical thinkers were quick to point out, *One-Dimensional Man* represented Marcuse's explicit break with orthodox Marxism, if indeed he had ever been very orthodox. Wolfgang Fritz Haug noted that at the core of Marxism as theory and practice was the exposure of contradictions within capitalist society. Yet Marcuse had stressed the elimination of social and intellectual contradictions in advanced industrial society, most obviously in his dismissal of the working class. This, for Haug, was a mistake since it vastly overestimated the stability of the advanced industrial society; "instead of contesting the world with its masters, Marcuse projects a second world. . . ." At best Marcuse's was an abstract and utopian enterprise.[98]

A second line of criticism questioned Marcuse's heavy emphasis upon the positive and negative power of technology. This, according to Haug, represented a definite shift from Marx's concern with the relationship of productive forces, i.e., capital and labor, to an almost exclusive focus on the means of production.[99] In moving in this direction and writing off the working class while stressing the biological needs of men in general,

Claus Offe suggested that Marcuse had failed to equip his radical critique with a specific social focus by which human needs "can be carried through as social interests."[100] That is, as in *Eros and Civilization*, there were no social forces which could be considered "bearers" of radical change. As a result Marcuse's analysis remained abstract.

Finally Marxists as well as less radical leftists scored Marcuse's almost undiluted pessimism concerning the likelihood of a collapse of the capitalist order or the possibility of reform within it.[101] With such a monolithic picture in mind, Marcuse was forced to fall back on individual consciousness, social outcasts, and "third world" forces as sources of change. As a guide to praxis, Marcuse was thus of little help.

Interestingly enough, Marcuse turned his critical theory inside out (or upside down) in *One-Dimensional Man*. Crucial to critical theory up to *One-Dimensional Man* had been a refusal to accept given facts as established and the need to go beyond these to project a more desirable alternative. In *One-Dimensional Man* Marcuse reversed this procedure; instead of extrapolating from the undesirable to the desirable, he extrapolated from the undesirable present to the more undesirable future. The positive side of the dialectic was relatively neglected. The description of advanced industrial society, which Marcuse presented, was less an empirical enterprise than an ideal-typical construct, composed of all the repressive and oppressive tendencies at work in the society. Aspects of technology, freer sexuality, material satisfaction were stressed only to the degree that they strengthened rather than undermined the technological-bureaucratic order. There was no way to prove—or disprove—his assertions and as such the book was suggestive, but hardly compelling.

Perhaps the most provocative of Marcuse's points was his claim that science and technology represented ways of understanding and dealing with the world that were repressive and led to the exploitation and domination of man and nature. That modern science was not presuppositionless had been noted by Alfred North Whitehead in *Science and the Modern World*, several decades before. Whitehead, however, had referred to certain philosophical presuppositions without discussing the social effects that their embodiment in science and technology would mean. The Cartesian notion that material being (*res extensa*) was mathematically describable, i.e., quantifiable and "dead," and Bacon's famous "knowledge is power" dictum would seem to support Marcuse's claim up to a certain point. Marcuse's thesis suffered, however, from a failure of historical perspective; that is, within the context of the time, the rise of the natural scientific world view was liberating intellectually. Moreover, Marcuse radically truncated his dialectic. If science and technology, the theory of and praxis upon nature were repressive, they were, by the same token, potentially liberating as he had pointed out in *Eros and Civilization*. The higher synthesis, in which science and technology would presumably be liberating, was mentioned, but not developed.

Ironically Peter Sedgewick has taken Marcuse's views of science and technology to task for being "misleading in gross and detail . . . a thoroughly moth-eaten proposition."[102] In attacking Marcuse's idea of the scientific world view, Sedgewick asserts that in contemporary philosophy of science, man is not seen as overcoming and dominating nature; rather man and nature are engaged in a type of dialogue with one another. This is close to what one imagines Marcuse had in mind when he called for a rethinking of the relationship of man and nature. Marcuse may be objecting to a philosophy of science which no longer holds sway among the most contemporary of scientific thinkers.

Marcuse's attack upon linguistic analysis has also been challenged, most vehemently by Alasdair MacIntyre. MacIntyre claims that Marcuse has misinterpreted, indeed misunderstood linguistic philosophy. MacIntyre's case is convincing up to a certain point,[103] yet he fails to deal with the larger issue that Marcuse raises. From a "social" point of view Marcuse's claim is that linguistic analysis has abdicated the duty of philosophy to not only describe and clarify the world, but also to criticize it. Along with the existentialists from the other end of the spectrum, Marcuse's charge is that in the hands of the linguistic analysts, the latter-day empiricists and positivists, philosophy has become a trivial enterprise, by leaving to others the task of judging existing reality. Philosophy "fiddles" while the society "burns." It has become a narrow academic speciality and one-dimensional. And if Marcuse is guilty of trying to fit philosophy into an ideological straitjacket, he is no more guilty than the linguistic analysts and the logical positivists who have done the same thing in the name of "objectivity."

Finally there were Marcuse's criteria for judging the rationality of "the transcendent project." As in earlier work, Marcuse's most crucial terms were left undefined even in the most rudimentary fashion. What, for example, were "the productive achievements to be preserved and protected?" What were vital needs and faculties? Who decided these questions as a matter of practice? These problems were not elaborated upon. Nor were Marcuse's specific suggestions so revolutionary that a moderate radical could not subscribe to them.

As most observers have recognized, *One-Dimensional Man* represented a backing away from Marcuse's radical Freudianism.[104] In a sense the book was a critique of his own *Eros and Civilization* in that Marcuse's conclusion, shorn of all its complexities, was that the erotic was not potent enough by itself to provide the basis for a radical alternative to existing society. Thus the nonrepressive order became the goal and not the presupposition of radical change. As Freud had recognized long before, the dialectical relationship between sexuality and culture works both ways; sexuality opposes and supports, is an agent of alienation and accommodation. *One-Dimensional Man* was a consolidation of much post-World War II social analysis with a radically pessimistic interpretation imposed upon it. As Haug noted, the book was generally descriptive rather than analytical.[105] Marcuse had worked himself into a "corner" and it was difficult to see how he could extricate himself.

Marcuse's writings since *One-Dimensional Man* have represented an attempt to break out of the theoretical box he had placed himself in with that book. More specifically his subsequent works have focused on the possibility of political action, indeed "liberation" in advanced industrial society. As early as

1961 Marcuse had asserted that instinctual liberation had become a "political matter" and then later in his essay on Weber that "technical reason thus reveals itself as political reason."[106] The political question—where is power located and how should it be gained—rather than the "cultural question" assumed an ever-increasing importance in his work. This shift to politics was only a reflection of Marcuse's belief that in the totally administered world every human thought and action, both private and public, were subject to external manipulation. As a result the transformation of thought and behavior had perforce to involve a radical transformation of the political structures and the instruments of social control and ideology. Opposition was, however, doubly difficult; first, because the individual in the period of the decline of the patriarchal family "appears as a rather weak thing" since he is not required to form a "strong" personality over against the influence of a strong father;[107] and second, because the locus of oppression is so diffuse and subtle in the advanced industrial society. The media, educational systems, industrial and bureaucratic organizations all exert their influence by covert manipulation, not overt and crass coercion. Simply locating political responsibility had become a quite difficult matter.

One of the most pressing questions for Marcuse was the justification of revolution in a social order where, in traditional radical terms, there was no need or desire for revolution. In an address "Ethik und Revolution" given in 1964, Marcuse expanded on the ethical and philosophical problems bound up with the use of force and violence in revolutionary action. Granting that revolution involved violence (*Gewalt*) Marcuse asked whether "there exists a moral justification for repression and violence in a revolution"?[108] Marcuse's initial response to the query was a sensitive one. He granted that revolutionary ethics conflict with commonly accepted values and that this conflict is a genuinely tragic one, not merely an illusory conflict: "The ethic of revolution bears witness to the collision and conflict of two historical 'rights' . . . what is . . . and what can and perhaps should be."[109] There was clearly no easy resolution of the conflict.

Not surprisingly Marcuse did advance a justification for revolutionary force. First he excluded the sanction of absolute morality to either position,[110] and in doing so revealed his distance from a natural rights justification of revolution—or a justification based on the "movement" of history. Second, he ruled out "forms of force and suppression . . . [which] negate precisely the goal for which the revolution is a means . . . arbitrary violence, cruelty and undifferentiated Terror."[111] With these two caveats, Marcuse's basic position was that the revolutionary standard must be historical and rational. That is, a revolution must lead to "a demonstrable extension of the space of freedom."[112] Furthermore the rational decision was finally (and one senses Marcuse's reluctance to admit it) to be based on a calculation whose "inhuman quantifying character is apparent."[113] The goal was in Benthamite terms "greater freedom for a greater number of people."[114]

Nevertheless violence had to be used, but violence which was "rational"; it should not contradict the end-goal, or have a negative relationship to the goal of the revolution. Not violence per se, but inappropriate violence was unjustifiable. The goals of the revolution—freedom and happiness—remained constant and absolute.

Marcuse's "Ethik und Revolution" essay was a prologue to his less abstract and more polemical essay "Repressive Tolerance" (1966). Perhaps this essay more than any other of Marcuse's writings brought him to general public notice in the late 1960s, a fact which was rather unfortunate since it was seized upon by friends and foes as the essence of Marcuse's thought. In reality, the essay was one of Marcuse's less impressive intellectual efforts. More than most of Marcuse's works it was characterized by a mixture of valid and sensible points, banal half-truths, and frankly antidemocratic sentiments. Abandoning his often subtle dialectical mode of procedure, Marcuse alternated between bald assertion and weak qualification. At whatever level—analysis or prescription—the essay was confused and, by Marcuse's own criteria, irrational.

Marcuse's argument was as follows. Because American society is characterized by "total administration," the positive exercise of civil and political rights and the negative tolerance of reactionary views and actions serve only to strengthen an emerging totalitarian democracy rather than to undermine or change it. This thesis was based on the prior assumption that "it is the whole which determines the truth"[115] and thus any action or idea which did not represent a total refusal of the "rules of the game" was in fact supportive of the system. As a result tolerance should be withdrawn from those groups and ideas which were inimical to freedom and humanity; it should be extended to the actions, violent or not, of the oppressed minorities who have a "natural right" of resistance.[116] As Marcuse quite openly admitted, this would involve the use of undemocratic means by a minority "in the maturity of [their] faculties,"[117] justified by rational and objective standards. Only in this way could the monolithic totalitarian democracy be broken, the manipulation of the majority's consciousness be halted, and "progress in the consciousness of freedom" be furthered.[118]

Marcuse's position can be attacked on several levels. Taking his holistic position at face value, one might ask why Marcuse himself did not fall under the sway of the totalitarian structure, or why the very publication of his work did not strengthen rather than undermine the system. Marcuse's position illustrated an elitist voluntarism joined with the belief that the masses were locked into a deterministic situation. Somehow he and other "progressive" forces had escaped the totalitarian nexus. Either the nexus was not so total and others had as well escaped manipulation of consciousness—or his "project" was a vain one. One could also turn Marcuse's argument around. Was it any more true that selective tolerance, denial to reactionaries of speech and action, led to an undermining of repressive social forces, or would not intolerance, just as tolerance, lead to a strengthening of the system? If in theory the whole is all-determining, any particular action, regardless of its source or purpose, should lead to the bolstering up of the system.

Indeed there was a vagueness in Marcuse's analysis as to exactly who should withdraw tolerance. Individuals and isolated groups? The governing political structure? Obviously the latter established forces would not take action leading to their own demise. If it was the former, then because of minority status, the action would either be ineffectual or lead to a strengthening of the forces of repression. And the action of "a dictatorship of intellectuals" would almost by definition fail to gain wider support. In the essay Marcuse made use of a quote by John Stuart Mill, which advocated weighted suffrage favoring the educated class, to support his point. This was passing strange for a Marxist since Mill's argument had been addressed to the issue of voting, not free speech, and was directed against the working class. In short, Marcuse ripped Mill's quote totally out of the historical context and used it to support a position which Mill would probably have found indefensible.

Marcuse was similarly vague concerning who and what should not be tolerated. Nowhere did he really distinguish thought and action, the private and public entertainment of ideas and their implementation. At one point "that which was radically evil" was to be suppressed. Yet this concept of radical evil covered a host of phenomena ranging from "systematic moronization of children and adults . . . [to] release of destructiveness . . . to planned obsolescence" and was certainly too vague to be very helpful.[119] At another point he linked the "Right . . . movements of aggression . . . the party of hate" and contrasted it with "the Left . . . movements of peace . . . humanity."[120] Such phrase-mongering was demonology rather than political analysis, not to mention the empty nature of the concepts, Left (Right), peace (aggression), humanity (hate), or their sheer banality. To establish such equations was ahistorical and an abdication of critical reason. Likewise Marcuse's use of threadbare Marxian terms such as "progress" and "regression" served to obfuscate rather than to clarify. Despite Marcuse's assertion that such distinctions could be made "rationally on empirical grounds,"[121] it was not at all clear which policies led to which goals.

In his 1968 "Postscript" Marcuse elaborated upon his demonology by advocating intolerance toward "movements of a demonstrably aggressive or destructive character" and those "opposing the extension of social legislation to the poor, weak and disabled."[122] Yet Marcuse's point in *One-Dimensional Man* and implicitly in "Repressive Tolerance" was that the welfare state, presumably the perpetrator of such "social legislation," was an integral part of the developing total system. Marcuse's support for humanitarian legislation may be valid, but it hardly represented a "Great Refusal," and indeed sounded like a call for selective support of the given order. At present, it is not all that clear which type of social legislation—increased welfare benefits, a guaranteed annual income, or an abolition of the entire system of government support to poor people—would be most desirable. The rubric "extension of social legislation" was of little or no help in categorizing friends and enemies.

Finally, in the context of American historical and political development, Marcuse's position was irrational, and betrayed an insensitivity to the American situation. If one could pinpoint an area in which the American political structure has been in the balance formally "progressive," it would be in the area of civil liberties and free speech. To negate this historical given would seem to contradict Marcuse's assertion that revolutionary action must preserve the "productive achievements of civilization."

At present, the conditions for revolution do not seem to be present in American society, and thus Marcuse's call for selective tolerance is a call for minority action. Marcuse's plea that "the educator and intellectual [have no] right to preach them [oppressed minorities] abstention"[123] from violence was morally quite sound. But as a blanket political judgment, it signaled an abdication of political reason and seemed to contradict Marcuse's own "calculus of revolution." For, as Jürgen Habermas wrote in his introduction to *Antworten auf Herbert Marcuse*: "Violence can become legitimate and have an emancipating effect to the extent that it is called forth by the oppressive force in a situation where that oppressive force is seen as *generally* unbearable. It is only such force that is revolutionary. . . ."[124]

Likewise it could be argued that violence may be used by a group to gain access to those rights and privileges which are morally and legally theirs, but to turn around and deny those rights to others is reactionary and repressive. To make force and denial of free speech programmatic runs the danger of making a tactical necessity a philosophically desirable part of revolutionary thought and practice. In sum it may make no difference to the victim, but it does to the executioner and to those who live with and under him, whether violence is positively sanctioned, or seen merely as a necessary evil.

Thus Marcuse's "Repressive Tolerance" seems both irrational on Marcuse's own grounds and the result of a serious misreading of the nature of American politics and society. It was frankly and openly elitist. Like so much of his other work, the structure of Marcuse's argument was dictated by and reflected the structure of the social and political system he claimed to be describing. Total control implied total refusal; totalitarian manipulation implied subversive manipulation. The lack of "spaces of freedom" implied the denial of such to opponents. The circle remained closed.

An Essay on Liberation was published in the wake of four years of sporadic student rebellions in the United States, ghetto uprisings, dogged Vietcong resistance to American military might in Vietnam, and the May-June, 1968, student-worker rebellion in France. All these apparently forced Marcuse out of his deeply pessimistic mood concerning the possibility of radical change in advanced industrial society toward a position of measured optimism.

Marcuse's basic thesis was that a restructuring of human needs was necessary in advanced industrial society. To the radical intelligentsia would fall the theoretical work and to the students and oppressed minorities the exemplification of the new lifestyle. This position was in turn based on the belief that biological needs were socially and culturally formed and that to change them was the goal (and proper province) of radical political action. Thus there was an explicit identification of the political and the cultural, public with private, politics and sex. Due to the all-determining nature of advanced industrial society, the means of production, the cultural patterns, the language, sexual habits, patterns of consumption—in sum the life-style—had to be transformed.

Portions of *An Essay on Liberation* were a reply to some of the previous criticisms of his work. Marcuse apparently altered his view that technology and science were repressive per se; he now felt they should be turned to new ends.[125] Though granting that the working class was "objectively in itself . . . the potential revolutionary class,"[126] Marcuse remained by his contention that "subjectively" it was not, and would hence "depend on catalysts outside its ranks."[127] Likewise Marcuse maintained his political elitism in saying that liberation would imply "subversion against the will and against the prevailing interests of the great majority of people."[128]

The bulk of *An Essay on Liberation* consisted of a description of the radical consciousness, "the new sensibility," of those who would serve as the goads for social change and as paradigms of a new type of man. The thrust of Marcuse's message was that this new sensibility was posited on "the ascent of the life instincts over aggressiveness and guilt."[129] The goal of the new sensibility would be an aesthetic ethos in which society would essentially become "a work of art."[130] Both sensibility as response to experience and reason as interpretative mastery of that experience would be subsumed under the imagination. The imagination would in turn work in the service of Eros toward the goal of reshaping social reality and consciousness. Technology would become an art form and art would emerge from its isolation and be joined with reality. Thus the "aesthetic principle" would become the dominating "Form of the Reality Principle."[131]

Though more hopeful than before, Marcuse did not underplay the ambiguities and difficulties in the emergence of such a reality. He pointed to the divisions between the white intelligentsia and the white working class and between whites and blacks generally. Nor did he ignore the dilemma of those forces which had to resort to antidemocratic means to bring about the truly democratic society. Marcuse also noted that "the precondition for the liberation and development of the Third World must emerge in the advanced capitalist countries."[132] Thus though a link was established, the exact connection, the relationship of liberation of one world to the other, was not taken up in any detail. Nevertheless the tone of the book tended toward optimism. The "moral fiber" or consensual framework of advanced industrial society gave signs of collapsing or at least weakening. If and when the collapse occurred, Marcuse's work would serve to indicate one possibility for the shape of the new man and the contours of a new reality.

Marcuse's final vision of "society as a work of art" was the culmination of his emphasis on the "aesthetic" as a political and social category beginning with *Eros and Civilization*. As such it was both appealing and frightening. It appealed insofar as it recognized the real possibility, due to technological development and mastery of nature, of man's shaping his world according to a human and humane vision of freedom, happiness, and plenty. As Marcuse noted at the beginning of *An Essay on Liberation*, utopias were no longer utopian; they had become real possibilities.

And yet the vision was also a frightening one. Unlike Goodman's focus on small-scale experiments and decentralized planning, Marcuse's emphasis was on society as a whole. Furthermore the application of the category "aesthetic" to political action brought to mind Walter Benjamin's observation that "Fascism sees its salvation in giving these masses not their rights, but instead a chance to express themselves . . . the logical result of Fascism is the introduction of aesthetics into political life."[133] To be sure Benjamin was referring to a social order in which the economic structure remained unaltered while the people were "bought off" with spurious self-expression. And Marcuse might reply that contemporary American society was precisely approaching the condition that Benjamin described, and that his own work has been devoted to altering property relations and social structures so as to obviate a quasi-Fascist order. Nevertheless the elevation of the aesthetic to the principle governing social reality gave one pause.

The problem with the aesthetic as a social and political category resided in the fact that, as a concept, it points toward an end and neglects means. In modernist aesthetics, the artist has usually been conceived of as a Godlike master over his material, willing to use imaginative and "real" characters and themes for a desired end-effect. The end becomes all, and toward the ingredients themselves, the artist assumes a detached indifference. They are of concern only as means to an end—the creation of the beautiful and the pleasing—at whatever cost to the materials themselves. The aesthetic contains within itself as a concept the justification for its realization. Other external "moral" judgments are irrelevant or at best secondary.

The frightening possibility is that this individual mode of perception and "behavior" would be applied on a collective social scale. A society as a work of art would seem to need an "artist" (dictator) or artists (minority consciousness) working, regardless of means, toward society as an aesthetic product. To realize the "aesthetic," private consciousness, individual needs and wants, tastes, and habits, as well as economic and political structures, public actions and laws would need to be manipulated and transformed. The result would be a system of total domination and control, an order every bit as one-dimensional, if not more so, than that of existing society. "Subjective" and "objective" existence would be subject to external domination. As such this vision of an aesthetic order transcends fascism or communism or totalitarian democracy. It is highly reminiscent of the most prescient anticipation in modern western culture of the totalitarian spirit—the tale of the Grand Inquisitor in Dostoevsky's *The Brothers Karamazov*.

5. NORMAN O. BROWN

Norman Brown's relationship to radical Freudian social thought is somewhat tenuous and problematic. Though as a student in the 1930s Brown was involved in leftist politics, his training and intellectual efforts prior to the 1950s were neither very "political" nor very Freudian. He has most often been grouped with Marcuse on the basis of the similarities in terminology and conclusions of his *Life Against Death* and Marcuse's *Eros and Civilization*. (Brown reports that he met Marcuse in the early fifties and was taken by Marcuse's discussion of a nonrepressive society.)[1] Though the parallels are striking, a close examination of Brown's work reveals radical differences between the two. Furthermore an examination of the two men's intellectual development subsequent to the above-mentioned works reveals quite clearly the divergent tendencies present in their thought.

Common to both the Freudian and Marxian approaches to reality is a thoroughgoing reductionism; that is, "superficial" phenomena are seen in terms of something more fundamental and basic. In this reductionist tendency Brown is much more "radical" than either Goodman or Marcuse, and in "tone" reminds one most of Wilhelm Reich. It is perhaps no accident that both Reich and Brown, in pushing their analyses to the most radical conclusion, emerged finally as religious rather than political or social thinkers. It is as if their use of modern, secular, and ostensibly antireligious ideas led them to positions fundamentally at odds with the entire post-Enlightenment corpus of western thought. Though Reich arrived at a cosmic religiosity, mixed with quasi-scientific terminology, and Brown arrives at a body mysticism undergirded by literacy and religious concepts, both transcended and undermined the intellectual tradition from which they began.

Thus Brown's work is finally not so much a critique of "the organized system" or "advanced industrial society" or a plea for "mental health" or freer sexual expression as it is a radical questioning of the very assumptions about man and culture upon which individual and social existence have hitherto been based.

Brown's only published work prior to *Life Against Death* was a monograph in classical studies entitled *Hermes the Thief* (1947), a work which displayed impressive erudition brought to bear on a fairly limited subject. Aside from an occasional mention of Bronislaw Malinowski, Brown's study contained no references to psychoanalytically trained anthropologists or psychoanalytic interpretations of mythic structures. (This was ironic in that the god Hermes had often been associated with various phallic cults of classical antiquity.) Brown charted the evolution of the role of Hermes in Greek life as it related to economic and social developments in Greek society. In particular Brown demonstrated that by the sixth century B.C., Hermes had become the patron deity of the emerging acquisitive craftsmen and merchant class in Athens. As a by-product of this effort, Brown reversed a standard interpretation by fixing the composition of the *Homeric Hymn to Hermes* at a late date (520-511 B.C.) rather than much earlier, and demonstrated that it emerged in an urban rather than a rural context.[2] Though Brown referred to Hermes in *Life Against Death* as an early example of the "Trickster," and hence a forerunner of the Christian concept of Satan, *Hermes the Thief* had remarkably little relevance to Brown's later work.

Death and Sexuality

Brown took as his central concern in *Life Against Death* the problem of human happiness. It was Brown's notion that man, because he "refuses to recognize the realities of human nature,"[3] is repressed and represses himself. Man, Brown maintained, must accept the reality that he is and has a body and hence will die.

Because man cannot accept the latter "given" of human existence, he is unable to accept the former either. The result has been a collective and individual attempt by man to protect himself from this awareness of death, coupled with an attempt to reach (or regain) a dimly recalled state of happiness. In various ways cultural and technological achievements, individual character and personality, and human sexual organization all give testimony to man's fear of death and his attempt to avoid this awareness. Hence, fear of death is likewise a fear of life; and to be open to life and Eros is to accept the fact of one's death. Life and death are bound up together in and through the body, which is the source of life and whose end is death.

Behind this problem of happiness and the answer Brown arrived at loomed Freud's psychoanalytic teachings, in relation to which Brown functioned as a rebellious Hermes. Brown served as a messenger from Freud to contemporary man, while in transit reshaping, extending, and transforming the original Freudian teachings. Along with Freud, Brown looked to Nietzsche, Hegel, and the Christian mystic, Boehme, as the teachers of modern man who, if attended to, might help man regain his health and achieve "salvation." Unlike Marcuse, Brown located the origin of repression in man, not in society: man was "the slave . . . in love with his own chains."[4] Oppressive and repressive society and culture were epiphenomena, projections onto a collective historical plane of man's self-repression. Thus not a revolution in social and economic structures but a revolution in human consciousness was of first priority. Abolition of repression was an individual rather than a social task. Man must by his own efforts conquer his fear of death. Then the rest would follow.

As to how this situation came (and comes) about, Brown was not clear. For Brown, early childhood proceeded under the aegis of the pleasure principle rather than the reality principle. The child originally experiences pleasure at all parts of the body and is thus "polymorphously perverse."[5] The culmination of a "fall" from this state of erotic grace is the triumph of genital sexuality, an indication that human sexuality has been "perverted" by the reality principle for purposes of procreation, rather than remaining under the sway of the pleasure principle. This fall into genital sexuality is not, as with Marcuse, the result of socioeconomic domination, but due to man's underlying fear of death. Brown did stand with Marcuse against Freud and Reich in identifying genuine health and nonrepressive existence with polymorphous perversity rather than with the capacity for a satisfactory orgasm. The paradigm for all erotic, indeed all human relationships, was "being-one-with-the-world,"[6] a condition in which self and other, subject and object, pleasure and pain dualisms were overcome. And Brown, like Marcuse, identified this state with the child at the mother's breast, the condition marked by primary narcissism.[7] At this point there was an "instinctual fusion," desire for pleasure and for rest, life and death.

Thus Brown, like Marcuse, posited a primary fusion of instincts in contrast to Freud's instinctual dualism. If, Brown argued, there was a time when the instincts were fused, the opposition between Eros and Thanatos was "not an innate datum of human nature."[8] The death instinct was originally at one with Eros and only "the incapacity to accept death turns the death instinct into its distinctly human . . . morbid form."[9] The assumption of a key role in human existence by the death instinct represented in reality "a flight from death."[10] Technological efforts to "conquer" nature and the exploitation of man by man were both projections of the death instinct, in the form of aggression directed outward upon the external world. The two archetypal figures of western consciousness—Faust and Don Juan—thus perfectly illustrate two alternate modes of escaping the anxiety of death.[11]

As Brown saw it, the death-separation anxiety arose at the moment of birth, was reenforced by separation from the mother's breast and finally by separation from the family: "Anxiety is a response to experiences of separateness, individuality and death."[12] Thus to a degree Brown adopted the position that the birth trauma was the prime cause of neurosis and repression. If this were true, however, it is hard to see how the fear of death and its consequences—the desire to be reunited with the mother through copulation, genital not polymorphous sexuality—could ever be overcome. Man would seem to be by birth the anxious animal.[13] No matter what happened later, his fate would be sealed.

For Brown the prime example of the flight from death and individuality emerged most clearly in the Oedipus complex, which was in reality based on an earlier formed castration complex. What took place in the Oedipal situation, Brown held, was an attempt on the part of the child to become the father of himself and simultaneously be reunited with the mother. The instrument of this union—the phallus—was cathected with libidinal energy withdrawn from other parts of the body. Because of the fear of castration and the "bad" reunion desire, polymorphous perversity becomes an individual and then cultural taboo. In this way human culture, as we know it, emerges since "the castration complex represses infantile sexuality and inaugurates sublimation and sexual differentiation."[14] The desire to be one's own creator, expressed by desire for the mother, betrays the desire for power and domination at the root of genital sexuality and by implication human culture.

Crucial to Brown's entire thesis was the concept of sublimation. Unlike Marcuse, Brown held that sublimation "does not really avoid the curse of repression."[15] That is, culture, which is the product of sublimated libidinal energy, develops at the expense of true body sexuality and is essentially a flight from life—and death. Nonrepressive sublimation was a contradiction in terms, and surplus repression a redundancy. Only insofar as art contradicted the reality principle and attempted "to regain the lost laughter of infancy,"[16] could it be seen as subversive to civilization and in the service of Eros. But Brown did not make clear in what way art escaped the influence of sublimation.

Brown ended the first part of *Life Against Death* by calling for the construction of a Dionysian or body ego, as an alternative to sublimated existence. This new mode of consciousness would embrace and affirm instinctual reality. It would seek to unify not separate, affirm not negate, overflow limits rather than erect boundaries, and would draw no distinction between soul and body, self and other, life and death. Alienation would be abolished. Rather than a dualistic view of reality, there would be a dialectical one in which concepts and things would be dependent on one another and unified in opposition. This new move of existence would not be regressive, but rather would represent a new level of consciousness.[17]

It would be impossible to do justice to the wide range of topics Brown covered in the second half of *Life Against Death*. In this section, titled "Studies in Anality," Brown sought to establish the connection between sublimation, anality, and human culture. He devoted a chapter each to examinations of Jonathan Swift and Martin Luther, the main point being that both men were precursors of Freud in having, through literature and theology, grasped the relationship of the spiritual and the material, specifically the fecal, in the sublimation process. To Luther, especially, Brown attributed the insight that Satan (in psychoanalytic terms the death instinct) dominated life. As a result, human vice and virtue, reason, good works—activities according to the reality principle—all were done in his service. "Things" were ultimately fecal, no matter how transmuted or etherealized. As Luther had suggested in his doctrine of salvation by faith not good works, "worldly" activities are by nature corrupted and hence for naught.

Particularly important was Brown's rejection of the view that changes in thought and behavior, e.g., the Reformation or Industrial Revolution or rise of Capitalism, were related mechanically to changes in toilet training, and larger social forces as such. Rather there occurred periodically in human experience "an irruption of fresh material from deeper strata of the unconscious."[18] The source of this unconscious material was a "fantasy of guilt perpetually reproduced by the ego so that the organism can repress itself."[19] This fitted with Brown's fundamental contention that the problem of man was man himself. As long as man lived under the reality principle, which was empowered by the death instinct, the "daimonic" would periodically reemerge: "The dynamic of history is the slow return of the repressed."[20] All social and economic reforms, any attempts to "loosen" sexual and instinctual practices, were useless if man's fundamental attitude toward his own death was not changed. And this change was up to man himself.

In a long chapter entitled "Filthy Lucre" Brown linked together a critique of money, quantifying rationality, the scientific method, and the spirit of capitalism and saw behind them all the impulse of "possessive mastery over nature" and the "economizing in the means," both expressions of anal-sadistic impulses.[21] Along the way Brown suggested the need, as Marcuse had, for a new philosophy of nature and technology which would aim at "union with nature"[22] rather than seeking to exploit it and a new "science of use values" or economics in which consumption and satisfaction rather than production and economizing would be the goal.[23]

Most ingenious was Brown's thesis that the original value of money arose from the realm of the sacred not the secular, that money was inseparable from symbolism, i.e., sublimation, and that sublimation "is the drive to produce an economic surplus."[24] Irrational production is production of the superfluous or sacred. The drive for surplus production is not based on a psychology of enjoyment but a psychology of guilt: giving gifts to gods or to others means getting rid of guilt which, in turn, means, of course, getting rid of feces. Brown contended that as long as man failed to transcend the syndrome of guilt-production-money-sacred, which implied the ethics of self-repression, nonenjoyment, work— in short the Protestant Ethic—he would never be happy. Again parting company with Marcuse, Brown did not ascribe this "surplus repression" to any one social and economic system: "neurotic perversion of needs is not a child of civilization or class domination, but begins in archaic man."[25] We are all guilty and thus condemned to confuse necessity (food—oral) with superfluity (surplus—anal). Not only, Brown suggested, does man not know what he needs, he does not really know what he wants. He does not strictly need most of what he wants and once he has it, he proceeds to give it away to assuage his guilt.

Brown also subjected the phenomenon of time to scrutiny. It (time) was "like money, neurotic and correlative with instinctual repression."[26] A time sense emerged in man when he first realized that he was unhappy (repressed), remembered a time of former happiness, and dreamt of a future happiness. Thus all revolutions projected into the future are really attempts to return to the past. Dialectically "time is a schema necessary for expiation of guilt."[27] To have a time sense is to be both guilty and nostalgic. The end of repression would imply the end of time as we know it. And, Brown pointed out, the chief physical embodiment of sublimation, the locus of man's chief efforts to conquer death, the place where money rules is "that fundamental institution of civilization, the city."[28] The city was originally a sacred place where the superfluous was disposed of. Its vertical structures symbolize a defiance of nature and an aggressive phallicity. The city is the center of finance, "of accumulated sublimation . . . a deposit of accumulated guilt"[29] and finally stands for the reification of time and an attempt to conquer death through lasting and enduring monuments.

The goal was finally to transcend sublimation, the death instinct and the excremental vision of the human body. Only, Brown maintained, could a man "strong enough to live and therefore strong enough to die . . . and strong enough to set aside guilt"[30] be in a position to abandon the reality principle which worked in the service of Thanatos. The task was to abolish repression and sublimation, thereby returning all values to bodily values and fulfilling, as it were, the ancient Christian hope of the resurrection of the body. The resurrection of the body would mean the end of time as men had previously known it. No longer would men yearn for a golden age past or hope for a utopia in the future. Happiness would be eternally present. Bodies with bodies, polymorphous contact rather than genital penetration, mutuality rather than dominance—these were Brown's hopes.

As with Marcuse a strict comparison of Brown's use of Freud with Freud's thought itself is not at issue. Brown "took off" from Freud toward the construction of a new vision of human reality and, like Reich, assumed the tone and urgency of a prophet in expounding his ideas. In effect what Brown did was to radically simplify certain crucial concepts in psychoanalytic doctrine; the result was, for all of Brown's self-proclaimed dialectical mode of procedure, a work much more. dualistic, i.e., simplistic, and certainly more moralistic, to the point of Manicheanism, than Freud's. As we have noted, sublimation, work, culture, all became effectively synonymous with repression. The reality principle was subsumed under the death instinct. And genital sexuality became aggressiveness and dominance and then, finally, Thanatos. Contrarily, libido, polymorphous perversity, and Eros all were subsumed under the life-force. Other than the basic distinction between the forces of life and death, there were few other distinctions made.

In a similar way, despite a nod toward a distinction between primitive and civilized men and societies, Brown's purview was man in general. This ahistorical framework fitted quite well with Brown's thesis that man's problem was himself and not particular economic or social or cultural structures, and with his contention that changes *within* the present mode of consciousness were ineffectual.

Even though one might accept Brown's "ahistoric" approach, there was a major problem with Brown's essentially "religious" vision of man's condition. In the Christian framework, salvation was seen as the result of God's action or the product of divine-human interaction through good works, ecclesiastically sanctioned rituals, and faith. It is obvious, however, that there was, in Brown's theology, no "God" who is involved in man's return from his fallen condition to a state of grace. Man must quite literally save himself through a willing into being of the Dionysian consciousness, a process which dialectectically involves losing oneself. Thus one might agree with Brown's admiration for the Dionysian consciousness without having much of a notion as to how it was to emerge. It was the strength of the Christian position as well as the Marxian one that a mechanism—God's grace or man's action with the movement of history—existed for ushering in the new age.[31] In Brown's schema no such supraindividual force existed.

Another puzzling aspect of Brown's thought as presented in *Life Against Death* was his discussions of the essentially human as contrasted with the animal and the biological. It was Brown's contention that the distinction between man and animal lay in the former's propensity to repression, and that "Life and Death coexist in some undifferentiated unity at the animal level."[32] That which is living and yet nonhuman has no fear of death and hence is unrepressed. Yet Brown failed to deal with the fact that animals, at least mammals, are sexually organized for reproduction, that any foreplay seems to be in the service of the reproduction function, and that though animals have a sexual life, they do not have an erotic life. (Erotic being sexuality in the service of pleasure rather than propagation.)[33] It is difficult, therefore, to see the necessary connection in humans between genital sexuality, the fear of death and repression, on the one hand, and polymorphous perversity, acceptance of death and nonrepressive existence, on the other. Because most human interaction is characterized by the drive for dominance and power due to a fear of death does not necessarily mean that the "normal" mode of heterosexual sexuality is inherently connected with the drive for power. As a metaphor showing the possibility of an alternative mode of sexual expression and human interaction, the vision of polymorphous perversity was useful. But as more than a metaphor, it was not very convincing.

Finally the goal of *Life Against Death* was a new man. Brown would seem to stand with philosophers such as Heidegger and Sartre who see man as the being who is aware of his mortality, and argue that to live authentically this fact must be accepted. (Marcuse, it should be remembered, felt that death should be rendered as painless as possible.) Brown parted company, however, with the existentialists, as well as with anthropological and historical testimony, by asserting that man must not only accept his own death, but he can also transcend his fear of death. What Brown in fact evoked was a conscious animal or an incarnate God. This brings us to *Love's Body*.

Behind Brown's *Life Against Death* and *Love's Body* stands Nietzsche's dictum that man is the being who must overcome himself. Indeed the biographical parallels between Neitzsche and Brown are striking. Both began as professors of classics and used their classical learning to transcend not only that discipline but also contemporary thought. Both not accidentally were Protestant heretics, rebels against worldly asceticism, who attempted to forge a new religion, the focus of which was to be man, not God. Both sought to move from a Christian morality of good and evil to a man-made morality of health and sickness. One stood as the precursor of Freud; the other as a radical interpreter of Freud. Brown along with Nietzsche and Freud started with the assumption that "mind was at the end of its tether" and it was up to man himself to find a "way out."[34]

The way out for Brown was not the life of the mind and rationality as it had been for Freud. Appealing to Emerson for support Brown held that men were in bondage "to the authority of books . . . the authority of the past."[35] The way out for Brown lay, rather, in the rediscovery of mystery, the infusion of the spirit into man. The result was to be a "Dionysian Christian," answering to the "power of enthusiasm."[36] It was this enthusiast spirit, the bête noire of Enlightenment thinking, which marked most explicitly Brown's distance from Freud. Brown's intellectual ancestors had become Emerson, Whitman, and the Quaker, George Fox. This vision of the immanent divinity of each man led as well to belief in the essential "oneness" of all men, in that all participated in the power of the spirit. Thus by *Love's Body* Brown had moved toward a position partaking of eastern mysticism and, strangely enough, an antinomian tradition of American cultural radicalism which has vacillated between extreme individualism and a mystic oneness that negates individuality.

Love's Body is a strange "book." In it, Brown paraded the authority of books and the past in the name of their negation. His own thoughts were grouped and even confused with citations from many other sources—eastern and western, ancient and modern. In dialectical fashion these past authorities were acknowledged and transcended by partial incorporation. The work vacillated between poetry and pedantry and finally came to rest nowhere and everywhere.[37]

In *Love's Body* the medium was certainly the message. A linear-progressive, causal-genetic approach was eschewed; rather the procedure was contrapuntal and circular. A theme was introduced, elucidated, dropped, and then returned to later. The "argument" was constructed of overlapping yet connecting circles and was spiralic. Argument was by analogy rather than cause and effect. Indeed several sections of the book were themselves glosses upon the structure and procedure of the book. Rather than being presented with a "clear" argument, the reader was forced to make his own connections and participate in the book's development. Hence one way of understanding *what* Brown was saying in *Love's Body* was to note *how* he was saying it.

Early in *Love's Body* Brown writes that "the fall is the Fall into Division of the one universal man."[38] The goal of the Dionysian consciousness is to perceive the unity behind the separation and to heal the divisions within and among men. Pluralism is the condition and wholeness is the goal, the true reality to be achieved. According to Brown it is an illusion, productive of much unhappiness, that men have or are discrete personalities, egos, and characters. Brown rejects the concern of ego psychology for individual identity; the goal should be the discovery that we have no definite self—"the ego . . . a piece of illusion."[39] To maintain the contrary is a refusal to face reality that we are one with others and ourselves. It was Freud who discovered that we were unhappily and incompletely others through introjection, repression, and identification. The task, as Brown sees it, is to become happily and completely at one with others and ourselves. To do this requires that we go beyond a division of the psychic apparatus into id, ego, and superego. In thought and in fact they must become one and reenter the body and the world. As Brown says: "To give up boundaries is to give up the reality principle;"[40] in this way will man and the world be transformed.

According to Brown the crucial fact of existence to be recognized is not that we live, but that we are "lived" by Reality which is "not things (dead matter, heavy stuff), in simple location. Reality is energy or instinct . . . One Substance, the id or it."[41] Nor is a body a thing but a "continuous creation . . . never static."[42] Thus, for Brown, underlying what we commonsensically take to be matter and mental "processes" is a field of energy or instinct. In a formulation highly reminiscent of Reich's cosmic orgone energy, Brown describes this energy field as one within which "action at a distance . . . psychic streams, projects, in direction"[43] would suffuse the body and space around bodies bringing them in contact with one another and restoring the false gaps between the bodies. (One assumes "bodies" are concentrations within this energy field.) To realize that "reality" is so is to overcome dualism and division and "to arise from the dead."[44] The nearest example we have of such a state of being is "schizophrenia [in which] the false boundaries are disintegrating."[45] Thus the Dionysian sense of reality "abolishes the *principium individuationis.*"[46] In Schopenhauerian fashion the world, as we know, is Idea; the goal is the insight into the underlying unifying Will. To die to the old reality is to be reborn and resurrected.

In *Love's Body* Brown calls this new consciousness a "symbolic" consciousness. Whereas in *Life Against Death* Brown had seen symbolism as the outcome of sublimation, the attempt to escape the reality of the body by projecting a spiritual world, in *Love's Body* symbolic consciousness becomes that which reestablishes connections and overcomes divisions, much in the manner of Freud's Eros: "[symbolic consciousness] . . . terminates in the body, remains faithful to the earth. The dreamer awakens not from a body but to a body. Not an ascent from body to spirit, but the descent of spirit into body; incarnation not sublimation."[47] Thus symbolic consciousness unites spirit to body, the word to the flesh and makes them one. It is antiliteral, playful, and the analogue of polymorphous perversity. To be born anew is to recover the body and the spirit. The spirit is "not the ghost but life itself."

As Brown notes repeatedly, the force which makes distinctions is Thanatos and it must be displayed by a new erotic sense, a Dionysian consciousness. Just as the self, the individualized ego, is illusion and in the service of Thanatos, so are genital organization of the body, social and economic divisions, and political institutions in general. To have a "representative" is to have a disembodied self who becomes distinctly other. All exercise of power is under the reality principle which must be overthrown. Thus all boundaries between public and private, sex and politics are illusory: "Psychoanalysis is that revolving stage which completes the revolution, disclosing the bedroom and bathroom behind the bourgeois facade . . . abolishing the reality principle and its unreal distinction between public and private, between head and genital."[48] So long as men hold to the distinctions instead of making connections, they are dead to the "real" world of the body and the spirit. Once the "common sense" world is recognized for the illusion it is, then men will first begin to live. Thus Brown's Dionysian or symbolic consciousness, mind and body as one and polymorphously perverse, becomes the final stage of the unmasking process which Marx and Freud began.

The publication of *Love's Body* provided the first direct public "confrontation" between Brown and Marcuse.[49] As might be expected Marcuse was highly critical of *Love's Body*, though the criticism was tempered with praise for Brown's intellectual daring. In essence Marcuse's objection to *Love's Body* lay in what Marcuse considered the inadequacy of Brown's dialectic, his substitution of mystery for politics, and his concept of symbolism.

Marcuse held that Brown had been mesmerized by the unconscious, the contents of the repressed, and made them "normative values, as ends."[50] Brown's dialectical analysis was incomplete in that he had recognized, comprehended but had not "conquered," the material.[51] As a result, though Brown had quite rightly pointed to the symbolic nature, the latent content, of human history, both individual and collective, he had neglected the "real" effect history had upon man: "Radical destruction of history terminates in the religious tale, in which history is, not *aufgehoben*, but simply negated, abolished."[52] Indeed Brown had spiritualized history and failed to "return from the symbolic to the literal."[53] The point was, according to Marcuse, not so much that all boundaries, divisions, and distinctions should be abolished, for upon these pleasure and happiness were dependent. Rather the imperative was that men should have the right to determine them "instead of leaving their determination to our fathers and leaders and representatives."[54] Such was the object of political action in contrast with Brown's political "quietism" and spiritual "radicalism."

Finally Marcuse pointed out that in Brown's *Love's Body*: "Revolution, freedom, fulfillment become in turn symbolic . . . [but] symbolic of what?"[55] Though he did not develop this further, Marcuse was noting the crucial weakness in Brown's religious vision and his idea of symbolic consciousness. The nature of the symbol is in essence dialectical and/or intentional. It is something concrete and specific yet pointing beyond itself to a wider meaning or reference. The literalness of the symbol must be respected and acknowledged at the same time its reference is recognized. What Brown tended to do in *Love's Body* as well as *Life Against Death* was "dissolve" the specificity of the symbol into its general meaning and thus neglect the "power" of the literal object. For example, the empty cross is a powerful Christian symbol because it refers not only to the death and resurrection of the Christ, but also to a specific instrument of torture and death used by Romans at a certain time in history to crucify men, particularly a man named Jesus. Or an example from Brown which Marcuse refers to: the king was a symbolic father and phallus, but also a powerful human being who proposed and disposed in the affairs of men. What Brown had done in *Life Against Death* in telescoping Freudian concepts into one of two all-encompassing forces—Eros and Thanatos—exemplified an allegorical rather than a symbolic or dialectic one. Individual and collective existence becomes the locus of "a cosmic melodrama."[56] And if, according to Brown in *Love's Body*, there are no distinctions in thought and reality among concepts and things, then there is likewise no symbolism. Reality becomes one-dimensional and etherealized. And politically crucial, the procedure that makes no distinctions in thought or fact is potentially totalitarian.

By *Love's Body* Brown had moved beyond his initial assertion that men's attitudes toward their bodies were crucial to their attitude toward existence in general. Instead of incorporating and transcending given reality, Brown, as Marcuse quite perceptively notes, had simply abolished reality. The implication was that life under the reality principle was of secondary importance and that political action was vain and of little importance.

Love's Body was finally a calvary of the mind pointing to a resurrection of the body. For Brown, death referred to the liberation of the mind and body from the reality principle, rather than an actual end to existence. The resurrection of the body meant a revitalization of the body rather than literally living again after physical death. But as mentioned before, Brown's was a religious project without a transcendent reference. The reference, if one existed, was to "life." Though no Jungian, Brown's efforts were reminiscent of Jung's (and Reich's) attempt to point the way for a new resurgence of spiritual vitality, a new religiosity; or in Brown's case, as Frederick Crews has noted, "an inverted Transcendentalism."[57]

Brown's work so far has represented an effort to transcend human existence, the burden of rational consciousness, and forge a new "whole" and nonalienated version of life. In reality Brown's is another attempt in modern western culture to connect a personal with a collective myth, indeed create a new mythos, for a culture which has lost its traditional religious and ideological underpinnings. But because of its very personal, rather arcane and finally academic origins, Brown's vision is more than likely to remain a gnostic curiosity—or like Nietzsche's efforts, the source, albeit perverted, for some collective madness.

Brown has clearly moved away from a concern with social analysis and theory as such. There is undoubtedly a profound truth in Brown's contention that the way we confront our death determines the way we consider our bodies and that this in turn influences the way we individually and collectively relate to other men. Consciousness and social reality are related dialectically, and to transform one requires a transformation of the other. But by focusing exclusively on a change in consciousness, Brown's thought is in reality the clearest example of the "Great Refusal."

6. *THE NEW TRANSCENDENTALISM*

Specialists without spirit, sensualists without heart;
this nullity imagines that it has attained a level of
civilization never before achieved.

MAX WEBER

If one thing is clear, it is that ideologies have not disappeared. No sooner had Daniel Bell made his pronouncement than there emerged "New Left" movements in England and America seeking to revivify radical theory and practice in the vacuum left by the demise of the "Old Left." In America, the 1960s saw the emergence of a movement for Negro civil rights which by the end of the decade had developed into black cultural and political nationalism; student uprisings that fed a growing sense of generational solidarity against the dominant institutional and cultural structures; and an American involvement in a quasi-colonial war which touched off a debate over the foundations of American foreign policy and ultimately the very nature of the American experience. It was in such a context of political and cultural ferment that the work of Goodman, Marcuse, and Brown found resonance.

Yet even as these thinkers addressed themselves to pressing contemporary problems, they also worked within an intellectual tradition some 150 years old. In the context of American intellectual history (though Marcuse remained a resolutely "European" thinker) one might classify these three thinkers as the theorists of a second transcendentalist revolt; or as Frederick Crews has noted in connection with Norman Brown, "an inverted Transcendentalism." Just as the first transcendentalist movement had its utopian political and religious wings, so this time around we have Paul Goodman as a representative of the former category and Norman Brown of the latter, with Herbert Marcuse providing a link with continental Idealism and a mode of romantic cultural criticism. For the transcendentalists of the 1830s Nature had been the vehicle, the mediating term, for the moral and spiritual; for the new transcendentalists, Nature, as the sexual and erotic, becomes the touchstone of individual and collective virtue and health.

There are other parallels as well. In both instances there has been a questioning of institutional and cultural legitimacy, a challenge to established "liberal" rationality in the name of a "higher" spirituality or "lower" erotic rationality, and a vacillation between a radical individualism and the yearning for the "spiritual" (or erotic) community. Where the first transcendentalist revolt was "a religious demonstration . . . religious radicalism in revolt against rational conservatism"[1] with sexual radicalism hovering at the fringes, the contemporary transcendentalist movement attempts to re-eroticize individual and social existence and the religious impulse threatens to break into the open at any time.

Perhaps the best way of characterizing Goodman, Marcuse, and Brown is to adopt the terminology of Philip Reiff and call them "secular antinomians." The first transcendentalist revolt represented a way station between the religious antinomians, who based their stance upon the belief that they were infused with the divine spirit and thus beyond the law, and contemporary secular antinomianism. Just as the religious antinomians rejected the legitimacy of human institutions and earthly guidance and elevated the promptings of the heart (and the body) to divine truth, so the secular antinomians, Reiff notes, became "anti-political" radicals (or I would say political in a different way) and insisted that "whatever is is right," basing their positions on "an ethic as old as the classical mystery cults: the worship of Life."[2] In the way of all radical positions, extremes soon converge: spiritual antinomianism leads to sexual antinomianism and vice versa. Eros and Agape are reunited.

It is also significant that the two transcendentalist movements stand at the beginning and end of western industrialization. In America the transcendentalists (and in Europe the Fourierists and "Young Germans") came onto the scene at the beginning of the transformation of a largely agrarian, relatively stable order into a society characterized by the growth of industries and cities and the fragmentation of the traditional institutional and cultural order. Whether the alternative advanced was a "utopian" or "reactionary" one, the goal was the reestablishment of purposive and organic bonds among isolated individuals. Standing at the end of the process of modernization, Goodman, Marcuse, and Brown all voiced the desire to move from the bureaucratic Gesellschaft held together by artificial and impersonal bonds to some sort of more "natural" and intimate Gemeinschaft given cohesion by erotic and emotional bonds.

To them the large-scale governmental, corporate, and educational structures were inimical to and stifled that which was natural in and among men. Where, as Daniel Bell noted in his "Work and Its Discontents," early industrial enterprises had been characterized by obvious and often cruel oppression, advanced industrial society had learned to manipulate rather than brutalize, persuade rather than force, and offer the illusion of freedom while all the time maintaining control. By the 1960s it appeared that the characteristic form of rule in the society was neither tyranny nor aristocracy nor democracy, but, as Hannah Arendt has put it, "rule by Nobody," a situation in which "there is not one left who could even be asked to answer for what is being done."[3]

To be more positive, the efforts of Goodman, Marcuse, and Brown can best be seen as probings into the nature of life in a society which has gone beyond the industrialization stage. Once beyond this stage of development, its cultural superego—the Protestant Ethic—has come to seem irrelevant or positively damaging to individual and social well-being.

Related to this rejection of the Protestant Ethic as the inform-
ing standard for behavior is a reaction against what Max Weber
called the "de-mystification of the world." It is at this point that
one can begin to understand the religious undertones found in
the writings of these three men; these undertones in turn reflect a
more general search in the society for a sense of wholeness and a
dimension of existence beyond a rationalized sense of self and
society. As Weber suggested in the quotation prefacing this
chapter, the potential fate of industrial society was the "achievement" of a mode of existence in which specialization and
compartmentalization had destroyed a sense of wholeness of the
spirit and in which sensuality had become cold and mechanical.
One need only recall the most recent efforts of Americans to gain
a sense of competence and "workmanship" through "do it yourself" hobbying and a mania for "roughing it" to realize that what
Weber feared has been partially realized. Nor is it accidental that
an ersatz religion, sensitivity training, which combines the religious confessional, group therapy, and open sensuality among
strangers, has become something of a fad. The proliferation of
manuals on how to increase sexual performance, institutes for
learning what were once considered natural "techniques" of
lovemaking, the fad of psychological and physical disrobing in
public as with groups such as the Living Theater, all point to a
society populated with sensualists desperately in search of a
meaning for their sensuality.

It is also significant that all three—Goodman, Marcuse, and
Brown—call for a new view of man's relationship with the natural
world in which man and nature are part of the same continuum
of life. In such a view man should not seek to "subdue" and
exploit either the natural world or his own natural instincts.
Between man and man as well as between man and nature there
should be a mutuality; neither other men nor nature is wholly
other, foreign and dangerous, but part of oneself and alive.

Up to now it seems clear that the writings of Goodman,
Marcuse, and Brown have found the most resonance and acceptance among the children, usually college students, of the affluent,
educated, professional middle class, for it is precisely this class in

advanced industrial society that has incorporated and transcended the Protestant Ethic. The result has been the emergence of a youth culture and beyond that an "alternative" or "counter" culture. It is to the ideology of the counter culture that we will now turn.

The Counter Culture: Last Best Hope or New Barbarianism?

In recent years America has drawn its "unacknowledged legislators" from the ranks of sociology. Despite the oft-heralded (or bemoaned) hegemony of "value-free" sociology, there has been no dearth of social critics ready to speculate upon the future of American society and culture. A first wave of popular, speculative sociology broke in the 1950s with David Riesman's *The Lonely Crowd* (1953), William Whyte's *The Organization Man* (1956), and, on a more popular level, the many books of Vance Packard. In a somewhat similar fashion the late sixties and early seventies have witnessed another burst of popular social analysis. In contrast with the fifties' sociologists who concentrated upon the adult middle-class world and a "new" character type emerging from the older society, the "new" sociology has taken youth as its focus and has speculated upon the possible emergence of still another "new" culture. Where the sociologists of the 1950s often hinted at nostalgia for the "inner directed" man and life under the aegis of the Protestant Ethic, the latest wave of social prophets are almost unanimous in rejecting past social and cultural configurations and give themselves over unreservedly to the future.

There are also similarities. Both came at a time when political radicalism was quiescent or in disarray and searching for new goals and fresh tactics. Both thus tended to concern themselves with social and cultural developments rather than with programs for political or economic change. Moreover, the ideologists of the counter culture give explicit voice to the unease which Riesman, Whyte, and others experienced when faced with the new man and new society they saw emerging. Life among the "lonely crowd" has indeed proven to be sterile and alienating; the "organization man," in all his incarnations from conservative to

Kennedy liberal, businessman to university professor, has revealed himself a personal, social, and political disaster. What had been a nagging doubt in the fifties became a conventional wisdom by 1970—the society and the culture were in peril and had to change.

The works which have sought to define the counter culture—Theodore Roszak's *The Making of a Counter Culture* (1969), Philip Slater's *The Pursuit of Loneliness* (1970), and Charles Reich's *The Greening of America* (1970)—could scarcely have been written without the theoretical foundations laid by Goodman, Marcuse, and Brown. It was the conceptual framework defined by these men and others such as Erik Erikson, Edgar Friedenberg, and Kenneth Kenniston, the vocabulary of "growing up absurd," "identity crisis," "one-dimensionality," "life-style," the search for a new way of looking at the world, that made possible the ideology of the counter culture.

The first and perhaps most critical advocate of the counter culture was Theodore Roszak. For Roszak the choice facing the society was clear: we could continue a morally discredited order, "the technocracy," managed by experts, adhering to what Roszak called "the myth of objective consciousness," and seeking to rationalize all existence; or we could work for the emergence of a new consciousness embodied in the counter culture which stood for an openness to the nonrational and the visionary, a desire for cooperative and communal forms of social existence, and a decentralization of power.

Roszak was candid about the faults of the counter culture: it was primarily a youth phenomenon; it displayed a disturbing weakness for commercialization and exploitation by the media; and it was a sucker for bogus prophets of chemical transcendence such as Timothy Leary. Nor did Roszak slight the fact that the vision of the counterculturites had little to offer to workers and minorities who, as yet, existed precariously on the edges of the affluent society or were excluded from its material benefits altogether. Finally, however, Roszak came down on the side of the new culture as the only alternative worthy of critical support. Given an admixture of eastern religion and philosophy which would join intellect with contemplation and openness to the nonrational dimensions of experience, Roszak hoped for the development of a "gentle, tranquil, and thoroughly civilized contemplativeness."[4]

Though historical perspective was not Roszak's strong suit, he did devote several chapters to the ideological progenitors of the movement. Roszak gave Norman O. Brown higher marks than Herbert Marcuse, since Brown's radical Freudianism was more resolutely utopian in its call for the abolishing of repression and a view of man which added the religious dimension to contemporary man's one-dimensional existence; Roszak scored Marcuse for philistinism in rejecting religious consciousness as a desirable possibility. The problem was that Roszak, like Brown, continually plumped for the religious without giving any indication as to its form or content.[5] Thus religiosity, not religion, became the goal. Unlike the revival of interest in religion among intellectuals after World War II, Roszak's concept of the religious was generally non-Christian and thus had no use for the idea of original sin or the related notion of the tragic as a fundamental fact of human existence. It was optimistic and utopian. As specific as Roszak became was when he made the obligatory references to William Blake, "the curative powers of the visionary imagination," and spoke favorably of eastern modes of thought in discussing Alan Watts and Alan Ginsberg. Roszak devoted a rather uncritical chapter to Paul Goodman in which Goodman was treated primarily as an artist with his Gestalt view of reality given an "eastern" gloss. Beyond that Goodman's main service consisted in his willingness to back his words with action and his advocacy of communitarian living experiments.

In the last third of the book Roszak moved from a measured and perceptive discussion of the counter culture to a bit of philosophizing of his own. The result was a visionary humanism straining for religious significance, but seldom rising above the banal. Drawing upon the analyses of Marcuse and Ellul, Roszak took aim at what he named "objective consciousness." He objected to the "psychology" of rational scientific-technological consciousness and its obsession with discovering or imposing order upon the external world, its denigration of the personal and the subjective, and its impiety before man and nature. In its place Roszak plumped for an imaginative, artistic, even magical view of the world.

Though Roszak did strike several telling blows at "objective consciousness," it was difficult to know just where it might be found or who was guilty of it. He took the worst elements of second-level scientific and technocratic impulses and identified them with all scientific endeavor. The result was another superficially attractive, but unconvincing, one-sided diatribe against "objectivity." He all but denied that scientists saw any but a derivative type of beauty in nature; for them order not inspiration, information not awe was of the highest priority. Roszak quoted Michael Polanyi at several points, yet failed to note that the essential message of Polanyi's *Personal Knowledge* dealt with the scientist's personal involvement in the process and outcome of his activity, a view that more and more scientists were coming to accept and that philosophers of science have held for quite some time. All Roszak seemed to grant was that when scientists marveled at the beauty and order of nature, their admiration was a spurious narcissism.

Roszak also *seemed* to imply that awe and wonder before nature were somehow life-enhancing and value-giving in themselves. Yet the example of J. Robert Oppenheimer and the atomic scientists at Los Alamos should suffice to cast doubt upon this assertion. Oppenheimer was a man deeply read in literature, particularly and ironically in oriental languages and thought. Yet he and his colleagues were so engrossed by the sheer intellectual and aesthetic beauty involved in unraveling the secrets of nature, that they became all but blind to the ethical and political considerations involved in their activities.[6] Without belaboring the point, it is safe to say that awe and aesthetic awareness do not necessarily lead to humane feeling or action; for as George Steiner has pointed out, the aesthetic may blind us to ethical considerations and the suffering of other people.[7] Roszak contrasted the artist with the scientist and held that we should shape our lives as the sculptor does his materials in producing a piece of sculpture. The example was telling, but not in the way Roszak intended, since everything he charged the "objective consciousness" with being guilty of could as well have been laid at the feet of the artist.

This critique may be somewhat unfair to Roszak since he granted that more humanities courses or an appreciation of Aristotle will not make a man more sensitive to his fellow man. Nevertheless, there was a tendency in Roszak, following Marcuse and Brown, to elevate the aesthetic-erotic to primacy and subtly identify it with the moral. Insofar as Roszak tried to correct an imbalance in dominant contemporary modes of consciousness and behavior he performed a service, though one that was hardly novel in this century or the last. Polemics, however, are not sufficient basis for a new world view and it is at the polemical level, for all its particular insights, that Roszak's book remained. When all was said and done, Roszak's positive vision boiled down to a hope and a prayer that a change in consciousness (or culture) would somehow change the social, political, and economic structures.

There has been a perennial tension in the counter culture, and in the thought of its apologists, between the search for individuality ("doing your own thing") and the search for community. It was to a resolution of this problem that Philip Slater addressed himself in his provocative little book *The Pursuit of Loneliness* (1970). Slater, as did Roszak and Charles Reich, vacillated between the darkest pessimism and the most callow optimism though Slater was not completely blind to the problems inherent in what he called the "new culture." Echoing Tocqueville and Riesman, Slater traced America's social, cultural, and political problems back to the pervasive individualism at the center of the American experience. By individualism Slater referred to geographical and social mobility in combination with a weak sense of communal ties. Thus not Thoreau's retreat to the woods, but the experiments in utopian communalism were the sources of guidance for the problems that ailed America.

In the mandatory apocalyptic vein, Slater saw a conflict shaping up between an "old" and a "new" culture, with the middle ground occupied by a "swing" group, which the new culture had to ally with in order to be victorious. Wrote Slater: "The old culture, when forced to choose, tends to give preference to property rights over personal rights, technological requirements over human needs, competition over cooperation, violence over sexuality, concentration over distribution, the producer over the consumer, means over ends, secrecy over openness, social forms over personal expression, striving over gratification, Oedipal love over communal love, and so on. The new counterculture tends to reverse all these priorities."[8] At the core of the old culture, according to Slater, lay the "scarcity" assumption; its particular cultural expression was individualism; and its conduit, the traditional nuclear family.

Slater linked these together in the following manner. Due to the cultural assumption of scarcity, individuals learn that competition is necessary (to get a share of the fixed pie), that sexuality must be repressed (energy must be husbanded), inequality is inevitable, and thus the race goes to the swiftest. In the family, the mother, who has been assigned to her station in the home by Dr. Spock (a theme which Slater felt was far more significant than Spock's much trumpeted permissiveness), exploits her child to fulfill her own thwarted dreams and blocked talents. It is impressed upon the child that he must be the "best" and thus he enters the world an ambitious individual.

Slater's analysis was more convincing than Roszak's, since he pointed to social institutions which needed changing if the new culture was to emerge. A questionable aspect of the "scarcity" assumption (which came directly from Marcuse) was that Slater seemed to be saying that it had no actual grounding in reality at any time in history. Slater could only posit some vague conspiracy to explain its occurrence. So far, Marcuse was not prepared to go. Moreover, it would also seem that Slater neglected what Marcuse, Brown, and an assortment of critics of advertising had called attention to—what we imagine our needs and wants to be changes and the level of our expectations is constantly being raised. What is scarcity for us is plenty for another and vice versa. Though plausible as a mechanism to explain our individualistic striving and ambitions, the scarcity thesis needed much more development to be persuasive.

The recent concern with ecology—the pollution of the environment, the exhaustion of natural resources, the population problem—suggests that scarcity may be no figment of the imagination. The assumption that we have an economy of potential abundance and thus the inhibitions and restraints of the old culture are outmoded may be as shortsighted a view as it is claimed the scarcity assumption is. That is, the alternatives may be affluence for a few and poverty for most; or, if we are serious about achieving some general level of equality, a "standard of living" which will be well below the present one. Again the problem was definitional—what is scarcity and to what extent is it a psychological and cultural concept and not a biological one?

In focusing upon the family as the main institution of social and emotional control and the breeding ground for destructive individualism, Slater returned to a favorite theme of Wilhelm Reich and European Freudians. Yet there was a problem. On the political level, one could well argue that America's problems arose from a paucity of individualism and unwillingness to go against the wishes of the society or the state (Tocqueville's "tyranny of the majority"). How would the dissenting impulse be preserved while moving toward communal child-rearing and liberation, particularly of women, from the bonds of the nuclear family? How could the cultural imperatives of competition and ambition be abolished, how could concern for the group be elevated over private concerns, and at the same time civil disobedience be cherished? The cultural imperative and the political imperative seemed in conflict. Our retreat to the suburbs may be a disastrous application of Thoreau's retreat to the woods, but how can Thoreau's civil courage be preserved? Somehow the term "individualism" seemed too worn-out to be of much use.

Slater was forthright in his admission that life in the new culture would seem almost totalitarian in its disregard for privacy and individuality and its emphasis upon social cooperation. He granted as well that it would be bland and rather flat once the competitive ethos and cultural phenomena such as romantic love were no longer operative. Nevertheless such was the only answer for the society as a whole and the individuals in it. The alienation and affectlessness of life in the lonely crowd were but expressions of an individualism embodied in sprawling suburbs, extensive highway nets, environmental destruction, and the hegemony of technology. For Slater, the choice was clear.

Slater's provocative work anticipated and discussed more cogently many of the ideas Charles Reich was to voice in his publishing sensation *The Greening of America*, which appeared at the end of 1970. Reich's "cri de coeur" bordered upon the fatuous in its breathless admiration for the young and the youth culture. Most astonishing, however, was that Reich could have written the book when he did. Paul Goodman's *Growing Up Absurd*, published in 1960, had expressed more of a hope than anything else that youth would be the cutting edge of change. Perhaps a book so optimistic and admiring as *Greening* could have been written during the middle sixties with the first flowering of the "hippie" movement and before it succumbed to what Roszak had warned of—drugs, commercial exploitation, and a life-style of not so quiet desperation. But in 1970 the appearance of Reich's book was hard to comprehend. Masquerading as a prospectus for the future, it was in reality an exercise in nostalgia for a past, which had probably never existed. Taken to be some sort of definitive statement by its defenders, it was nearer to being a trite and often self-congratulatory collection of the clichés and half-truths of two decades of social criticism.

Reich's thesis was essentially that of Roszak and Slater: American society was increasingly dominated by a new Leviathan, the "Corporate State" (Roszak's technocracy), given its philosophical underpinnings by what Reich named "Consciousness I" (Slater's old culture, Riesman's inner-direction, Whyte's Protestant Ethic), but more crucially by "Consciousness II" (New Deal or Corporate Liberalism, Riesman's outer-direction, Whyte's Organization Ethic) which had replaced Con I in the corridors of power. For all their differences, both levels of consciousness were characterized by a skepticism concerning man's innate goodness, expressed in Con I's reliance upon market mechanisms or by Con II's emphasis upon institutions to curb man's rapacious tendencies. The result was a tottering system which stifled individual fulfillment, usurped civil rights and liberties, devoured lives in a foreign war, and organized lives at home to keep the Corporate State grinding away.

If the Corporate State was the principle of evil in Reich's conceptual schema, his "deus ex machina" was Consciousness III (Slater's new culture, Roszak's counter culture). This mode of consciousness, reflected most clearly in the life style of the affluent young, was, according to Reich, so clearly superior to Con I and Con II that its ultimate triumph was all but inevitable. Unmasked by the Vietnam War and domestic repression, flawed at its core by the contradictory imperatives to produce and to consume, the Corporate State would collapse of its own accord, all the while being nudged in that direction by the gospel according to Con III, since Con III embodied the secret values of even those still chained in the cave of illusions. The "heart of the heartless world," Con III took "the individual self as the only true reality"[9] and valued above all else personal authenticity, adherence to nonmaterial values and an openness to experience in all its fullness. (Interestingly enough, Reich and Slater part company on the individualism issue. For Reich, Thoreau was a forerunner of Con III; for Slater, the Thoreauvian impulse lay at the core of America's problems.) Change consciousness and the system would crumble; any other way only insured that man's bonds would be tightened and his slavery confirmed.

Despite Reich's lyric celebration of Con III, *Greening* was a monotonous and heavy-handed book. In particular, Reich's use of literary references to support his points was often flat-footed and unilluminating. For example, Philip Roth's *Portnoy's Complaint* turned out to be "the finest portrayal in America of the struggle to adjust to the organizational world,"[10] an interpretaion about as enlightening as the judgment that *Hamlet* is about a man who can't make up his mind. Wallace Stevens's painfully ambivalent "Sunday Morning" became for Reich "the doctrine of the new generation, the doctrine of present happiness,"[11] an interpretation which, though partially true, missed the underlying pathos and threat of meaninglessness in the poem. Most outrageously: "Not even the turbulent fury of Beethoven's Ninth Symphony can compete for sheer energy with the Rolling Stones . . . classical music seems dainty and mushy . . . the new music rocks the whole body and penetrates the soul."[12] A man who believed that, and had such aesthetic standards, could believe anything.

Reich was unreservedly smug and condescending to the lesser breeds still enthralled by Con I and Con II. In a statement which might have come as a shock to Wallace Stevens, Reich noted: "No person with a strongly developed aesthetic sense, a love of nature, a passion for music, a desire for reflection, or a strongly marked independence, could possibly be happy or contented in a factory or a white collar job."[13] Elsewhere: "Anyone who can function efficiently in an airport or large hotel is uptight because he has to be."[14] And finally: "The majority of adults in this country *hate their work*."[15] How did Reich know all this? Empirical research? Personal experience? Such were samples of Reich's irritating habit of clumsily disguising value judgments as statements of fact. All of the above statements might be the case, but Reich gave us no reason to believe so.

On the conceptual level Reich's book was also unsatisfactory. *Greening* was a glaring example of the type of work which, by establishing all-inclusive categories, forestalls adverse judgments by locating such judgments in one of the categories that the book itself establishes; e.g., if you object to Con III, then you are still a Con I or Con II. By such logic, the book was unassailable. Nor was it exactly clear whether Reich's Corporate State and his modes of consciousness were analytical or empirical concepts. Did they represent reality or mere potentialities? Was there any way to prove that the Corporate State was as Reich said it was or did the positing of the concept prove its reality?

Reich's book exhibited an unbelievable optimism. Assuming that man was, by nature, good, its psychology was incredibly naïve. Wrote Reich: "Nobody wants inadequate housing and medical care—only the machine. Nobody wants war except the machine. And even businessmen, once liberated, would like to roll in the grass and lie in the sun."[16] To say that "nobody wants war" ignored much of what we know about human psychology. Granted that no one would defend inadequate housing, the problem was that, according to Con I or Con II, other desiderata take precedence for the individual or "the machine." Businessmen, one assumes, can "roll in the grass" right now. Nor is it clear why some could not both "lie in the sun" and make war.

Behind Reich's sequential development of consciousness lay an assumption of automatic progress which was thoroughly American, and even highly reminiscent of Con I: out of individual fulfillment will come social good; Con II, which had proven a disaster, would produce children who would somehow shake free of their past. Like Slater, Reich loaded the dice in his schema: Con I and Con II displayed few virtues, since they were based upon a false view of man. Conversely, Con III displayed absolutely no shortcomings or vices. Reich, for example, was irresponsibly complacent about the use of drugs and their place in Con III. Instead of Marx's revolutionary proletariat, the mechanism for historical change in Reich's schema consisted of sweet and good-natured young people, a type of cultural Peace Corps. Yet in other parts of his book Reich located a type of ideal America in the past when political decisions were made by the "people" and civil rights and liberties were exercised freely. Leaving aside the experience of black people and Indians, even a cursory glance at the American past reveals that various individuals and groups have been denied all sorts of what we now take to be fundamental rights, hounded into the wilderness, or even lynched. There is thus little evidence to support Reich's historical optimism, in reference to the past or to the future.

Nor was Con III without internal contradictions and vagueness. What exactly did adherence to nonmaterial values mean? What world view would not claim the same? Was a life guided by nonmaterial values any guarantee of individual or social well-being? Like the idea that human nature is basically "good" or "bad," the concept of nonmaterial values was banal and empty. Reich denied that openness to experience might include experimentation with murder and rape. But why not? Is it really possible to have a society which reconciles personal identity with an extremely fluid social and cultural structure? Is the "protean man" also an authentic one or is he merely a role player unhappy in his world of infinite possibility, a modern version of Kierkegaard's "aesthetic" man, an aficionado of experience, but in despair?[17]

For Reich we were finally "two nations." No longer, however, was the division between rich and poor, white and black. America's unresolved racial conflict, a conflict which is psychocultural as well as political and social, had faded into near oblivion. Out of Woodstock and the commons-rooms at Yale would emerge Reich's third Consciousness. Thus the greening of America.

The New Kulturkampf

Despite the claim that the virtues of the counter culture were self-evident and their triumph either inevitable or absolutely necessary, the "new transcendentalism" was not without its critics. Many older intellectuals, who had traditionally seen themselves as men of the Left and defenders of cultural modernism, mounted a counterattack which generally took three forms: political, psychosocial, and cultural.

The political argument was directed against what was identified as the political expression of the new culture, the "New Left." For many critics, the New Left had early adopted to use Irving Howe's phrase, "Kamikaze" tactics which, in demanding the impossible, only encouraged a backlash from the Right and alienated elements in the left-liberal coalition. Support for community control of the schools in New York and the generally affluent origins of many New Leftists led some to accuse the New Left of antiunionism and snobbishness toward the (white) working class; critiques of the Welfare State and bureaucracy as well as the anarchist ethos of the new culture boded ill for traditional social democratic and liberal programs. Moreover, older social democrats and liberals were disturbed by Marcuse's call for a withdrawal of tolerance from "repressive" elements in the society and a general disregard for civil liberties. Finally the New Left, but centrally the counter culture, was scored for the quietistic implications of its radical demands; a philosophy of all or nothing meant, in effect, nothing. Thus the doors were open to a conservative control of the nation's politics.

The problem with this political critique was precisely the fact that it was political. If Charles Reich's book is at all indicative, the counter culture has become less and less interested in politics of any sort. Its concern up to now has been with changing consciousness and as such is nonpolitical. The history of attempts to abolish alienation and satisfy spiritual longings through politics is not a happy one. Only if a largely apolitical counter culture were transformed into a genuine mass political movement would it present a positive political danger.

The psychosocial line critique also failed to join the argument with the counter culture. It was a variety of the ad hominem approach which seeks to discredit *what* is said by an examination of its sources. Its most forceful advocate was Bruno Bettelheim, who charged that young protesters and devotees of the counter culture are less concerned with specific political and social issues than they were with acting out psychosocial tensions. Thus the mode of protest, the tone of the slogans, and expression of demands were seen by Bettelheim as a plea for authority by and through which identities could be discovered by neurotic young people. Action was essentially therapeutic, an attempt to prove and test masculinity and resolve Oedipal conflicts. Indulged in their childhoods, yet subject to the most subtly extreme demands for achievement by their parents, young people needed a firm hand and little more in order for the whole problem to the solved.[18] The weakness of this approach lay in its penchant for psychologizing and explaining away and an unwillingness to grant that the conditions reacted against might be serious in their own right. Form not content was stressed and thus the counter culture became a neurotic phenomenon, a failure of adjustment.

Bettelheim also expressed another concern which is widespread among older intellectuals and leads into the cultural argument. A survivor of Nazi concentration camps and a witness to the rise of Nazism, a movement which received significant support from German youth, Bettelheim and others quite clearly feared the emergence of a cult of irrationality, an atavistic tribalism, which could become a mass movement, challenging the very structures of civilized existence. For these men, the Weimar analogy functioned as a paradigmatic warning in much the same way as the Munich analogy has for shapers of postwar American foreign policy. In a situation of cultural and social disintegration, it was feared that the antinomian impulses, the deep-seated distaste for institutional restraints, the anti-intellectualism of the counter culture would seriously undermine liberal-democratic values, traditions of civility and tolerance, and High Culture in general. In the brutally explicit phrase of Daniel Boorstin, the new radicals and counterculturites were the "New Barbarians," who, not just by provoking the forces of the Right or by retreating into quietism, but by their own values and action shook the foundations of civilization.[19]

The most incisive and stimulating critique of the counter culture was John Passmore's "Paradise Now," *Encounter* (November 1970). In his essay Passmore went beyond sterile name-calling and located the basically religious impulse behind the ideology, such as it was, of the counter culture. Using Norman Brown as a reference, Passmore described and then analyzed what he called the "new mysticism," which sought to abolish repression, destroy the restrictions of time, and establish an order of playfulness and immediate gratification. He noted that it was another in a long tradition of "perfectabilism," a view by which man is basically good, and salvation lies in communal not institutional forms, gratification not inhibition. Passmore cited as examples the new mysticism's search for community, the ideals of unisexuality and nudity, the use of drugs, the attempts in drama and the "happening" to abolish the distinctions of time and space.

Though granting that the new mysticism was responding to genuine problems—the tyranny of time and postponement of pleasure, a sense of loneliness and atomization, growing specialization and organization—Passmore nevertheless held that "play is not enough."[20] In contrast to a society dominated by the impulse to "toil" or one dominated by the "play" impulse, Passmore wrote that a society could best be judged by the quality of its "loves."[21] Love, as defined by Passmore, was "enjoyment with care [which] cherishes its object."[22] Emphasis was placed upon care in a double sense: care denoted concern for and interest in the object, but also kept its connotations of worry, distress, and effort. Passmore also stressed the independent existence of the object; one loved or cared for a "something else" which was distinct from and not a narcissistic reflection of oneself. There was in the unity of subject and object (whether in art, science, or interpersonal relationships) a maintenance of independence. For Passmore the new mysticism was finally a reactionary and regressive movement. Its dominant impulse was "play" and its triumph would mean the end of culture and individuality as we have known it.

While Passmore's rubric of "mysticism" may be a bit extreme and smooths over diversity within the ideology of the counter culture, it nevertheless points to the particularly religious quest at the core of the counter culture. This is historically ironic since the origin of modern radical ideology was a revolt against Christianity and its philosophical expression, German idealism. Now over a century later a crucial segment of the affluent western world is rejecting the demystification carried through by Feurbach and Marx, the disenchantment of the world which Weber recognized as a main component of western rationality and the antireligious vision which Freud himself bequeathed us. In strange form the emphasis upon sexuality and the erotic since Wilhelm Reich through Goodman, Marcuse, and Brown and then on into the counter culture has come, via the aesthetic, to assume a strangely religious aura.

Perhaps better than anyone else, Philip Rieff has diagnosed our condition in his *Triumph of the Therapeutic*, a work which suggests that Freud and Max Weber (not Marx) provide the best analytic framework for understanding our present situation. For Rieff, Freud was the true father of modern consciousness in that he denied once and for all the possibility of a communal faith or a culture which could offer final consolation. He suggests that Freud's vision in turn has found so much resonance in America because ours is a "waning ascetic culture"[23] which, deprived of its Protestant religion framework, embraced Freud's message as a way of coping with loneliness rather than searching for salvation, a means of tolerating ambiguities rather than grasping for security.[24] In the 1830s Tocqueville had already noted the atomized individualism and emotional privation which characterized the egalitarian American ethos of his day. And one might add that it was precisely during the decade of Tocqueville's visit that America saw an explosion of secular and religious utopian communitarian experiments, and the emergence of the transcendentalist movement, both of which expressed the dialectic of individualism and search for community which has been one of the central themes of the American experiment, a development recapitulated today. Thus America became truly the first and oldest modern western nation; its "spiritual" development becomes paradigmatic for western societies in general. With traditional bonds broken and religious institutions fragmented, America indeed became the "new world" where the "new Adam" would emerge. The "new transcendentalism" is thus an example of "the return of the repressed," another religious reaction to secular society.

In turn Max Weber's personal as well as scholarly concerns become profoundly relevant to modern society, and particularly in America, since America was, as Weber implied in his *Protestant Ethic and the Spirit of Capitalism,* the place where the dynamic of the Protestant Ethic (inner worldly asceticism) would provide the motive force for development of capitalism and more importantly the eventual rationalization of existence in a highly bureaucratized society. What happened was that Weber's "iron cage" became the prison of individuality in which one was emotionally isolated from others and able to sustain no commitment to God or to community. Honest and illusionless, sober and detached, "psychological man" confronts a life bereft of enriching symbolic structures, that, larger than himself and "given" rather than solipsistically created, would enclose him in a community of faith and the faithful. Where Weber and Freud were intellectual and emotional titans, profoundly divided and at war with themselves, modern man has become a "virtuoso of the self"[25] in a "democracy of the sick."[26] In this post-Christian society one finds that "where family and nation once stood, or Church or Party, there will be the hospital and theater too, the normative institutions of the next culture. . . ."[27]

Yet Rieff points to a next stage, which represents the attempt to transcend Freud's negative faith and analytic view of reality and Weber's heroic individualism in the face of a meaningless world. He suggests that C. G. Jung, Wilhelm Reich, and D. H. Lawrence all attempted to go beyond Freud's position and, as prophets of the new, reinstate belief and a positive community as possibilities. It is quite clear that the ideologists of the counter culture, as well as Norman Brown, Herbert Marcuse, and Paul Goodman, belong in this group. However, Rieff suggests that the attempt to advance a new "therapeutic" ideal based upon the "gospel of self-fulfillment," which has as its goal a nonrepressive society is rendered impossible precisely because it is a conscious construct, the use of intellect in the service of its opposite. There is no Archimedean point, no way to both project a new symbolic and still believe in it. Max Weber was painfully aware of this dilemma when he wrote in 1919: "Never as yet has a new prophecy emerged . . . by way of the need of some modern intellectuals to furnish their souls with, so to speak, guaranteed genuine antiques . . . they play at decorating a sort of domestic chapel with small sacred images from all over the world, or they produce surrogates . . . to which they ascribe the dignity of mystic holiness, which they peddle in the book. . . . An academy prophecy, finally, will create only fanatical sects but never a genuine community."[28] Thus in Weber's analysis the search for meaning, for religious belief becomes mere intellectual preciosity and aesthetic-cerebration.

In another essay "Religious Rejections of the World and Their Directions" (1915), Weber suggested that the "erotic" was the last refuge of the intellectual classes from the forces of rationalization and demystification. Such has certainly been the case with the thinkers and ideologies that we have examined. Indeed the erotic-aesthetic seems to have become the pervading principle of the counter culture. Ironically it was a renegade Hegelian, Soren Kierkegaard, who suggested the intimate connection between the erotic and what he named the "aesthetic" mode of existence.

It is instructive, however, to remember what Kierkegaard had to say about the aesthetic and its relationship to the self since the thinkers we have discussed here fail to come to terms with Kierkegaard's critique. Where Charles Reich, for example, praises Con III as an openness to experience and experimentation and Marcuse calls for a new aesthetic sensibility, Kierkegaard wrote that in the aesthetic stage: "Your life resolves itself . . . into interesting particulars . . . everything is possible for you . . . enjoyment is the chief thing in life, . . . Life is a masquerade . . . In fact you are nothing; you are merely a relation to others and what you are, you are by virtue of this relation."[29] Kierkegaard took this mode of existence to be fundamentally unserious; it did not in Passmore's terms take "care." In a world of infinite possibility and by virtue of the possibility, one could paradoxically never finally choose and thus commitment remains provisional. One was continually dissatisfied and on the move to another source of pleasure. In contemporary form this is the search for self-fulfillment. And because one can never *finally* choose, one never has a self. The fact that one can constantly assume a new identity means that he does not have one. "Life becomes life-style";[30] not happiness and self-fulfillment, but discontent and an ongoing search come to characterize one's life.

What all this suggests is that the religious impulse, denied the intermediary stage of the ethical or the demand of the transcendent, collapses back into the erotic-aesthetic. Religiosity, which is the aesthetic masquerading as the religious, is the result. Thus the religious eclecticism bordering on the ludicrous of the counter culture. The counter culture is, undoubtedly, a convulsive gasp of a culture which cries out for transcendence and meaning. The impulses it represents—the desire for meaning and for happiness—are not to be scorned; the ways in which it has so far expressed itself, however, are symptoms of, not solutions for, the dilemma.

NOTES

Introduction

1. I have taken the liberty of using Robinson's terms: "Freudian Left," "sexual radicalism," and "radical Freudianism," where they seemed appropriate.

2. I exclude Frantz Fanon since his theoretical efforts did not arise from or focus upon the racial situation in America. As of yet I have seen little discussion of the relevance of Fanon's analysis of the psychosocial dynamic of colonizer and colonized or his revolutionary therapeutic to the American context.

Chapter 1

1. Richard Hofstadter, *The American Political Tradition* (New York: Random House, Vintage Books, 1948), p. viii.

2. Richard Hofstadter, *The Age of Reform* (New York: Random House, Vintage Books, 1955), p. 318.

3. Morton White, *Social Thought in America*, p. xii.

4. Daniel Bell, *The End of Ideology*, p. 400.

5. Ibid., p. 404.

6. Ibid., p. 406.

7. See, for example, Henry David Aiken's "The Revolt Against Ideology," *Commentary* 37 (April 1964): 29-39.

8. Bell, *The End of Ideology*, p. 406.

9. Ibid., p. 402.

10. T. B. Bottomore, *Critics of Society*, p. 37.

11. See Stephan Thernstrom's "Urbanization, Migration, and Social Mobility in Late Nineteenth Century America," in *Towards a New Past*, ed. Barton J. Bernstein (New York: Pantheon Books, 1968), pp. 158-75.

12. There are a number of excellent works dealing with this type of "conservative" cultural criticism. See Raymond Williams, *Culture and Society: Seventeen Eighty to Nineteen Fifty* (New York: Harper & Row, Harper Torchbooks, 1966); Fritz Stern, *The Politics of Cultural Despair: A Study in the Rise of Germanic Ideology* (Berkeley, Calif.: University of California Press, 1961); George Mosse, *The Crisis of German Ideology: Intellectual Origins of the Third Reich* (New York: Grosset & Dunlap, 1964); Erich Heller, *The Disinherited Mind* (New York: World Publishing Co., Meridian Books, 1959); and H. Stuart Hughes, *Consciousness and*

Society: The Reorientation of European Social Thought, 1890-1930 (New York: Random House, Vintage Books, 1958).

13. See John Higham, *Strangers in the Land* (New York: Atheneum Publishers, 1963); Barbara Solomon, *Ancestors and Immigrants: A Changing New England Tradition* (Cambridge, Mass.: Harvard University Press, 1956); and C. Vann Woodward, *The Strange Career of Jim Crow* (Oxford, Eng.: Oxford University Press, 1966) for discussions of racism and nativism during this period.

14. Robert Wiebe, *The Search for Order: 1877-1920* (New York: Hill & Wang, 1967), p. viii.

15. See Richard Hofstadter's *Anti-Intellectualism in American Life* and C. Wright Mills' *Sociology and Pragmatism: The Higher Learning in America*, ed. Irving L. Horowitz (Oxford, Eng.: Oxford University Press, 1966), for a discussion of the emergence of graduate education, philosophical pragmatism, and academic involvement in reform movements around 1900.

16. Hofstadter, *Anti-Intellectualism*, p. 39.

17. I have taken the term "social control" from Lasch's *New Radicalism in America: 1889-1963* and applied it in a manner generally consistent with Lasch's apparent intentions.

18. Lester Frank Ward, "Dynamic Sociology," in *Lester Frank Ward and the Welfare State*, ed. by Henry Steele Commager, p. 46.

19. "Art is the Antithesis of Nature," ibid., p. 81; "Psychic Factors of Civilization," ibid., p. 147.

20. "Scientific Lawmaking," ibid., p. 19.

21. "Some Social and Economic Paradoxes," ibid., p. 121.

22. "Collective Telesis," ibid., pp. 234-35.

23. Thorstein Veblen, "The Theory of the Leisure Class," in *The Portable Veblen*, ed. Max Lerner, p. 67.

24. "The Instinct of Workmanship," ibid., p. 321. Veblen's instinct of workmanship, his emphasis upon efficient as opposed to mystical and anthropomorphic thinking, remind one of Max Weber's emphasis upon "rationalization" as the central principle of modern Western society. The main difference is that while Weber was profoundly ambivalent concerning this ever increasing "rationality," Veblen endorsed it wholeheartedly.

25. "Ownership and the Industrial Arts," ibid., p. 330.

26. "The Discipline of the Machine," ibid., pp. 336-37.

27. Ibid., pp. 344, 348.

28. "The Technicians and Revolution," ibid., p. 441.

29. Ibid., p. 439.

30. Ibid., p. 461.

31. Ibid., p. 462.

32. Ibid., pp. 463, 464.

33. See, for example, Jacques Ellul's *The Technological Society* (1954) for an extended exposition of the ideology of "technique."

34. Besides the "technocracy" fad and slogans such as "production for use, not for profit" which were prevalent in the 1930s, the Veblenian tradition was at work in James Burnham's *The Managerial Revolution* (1941) and the writings of John Kenneth Galbraith, particularly his *The New Industrial State* (1967).

35. See Lasch's *New Radicalism in America* and Daniel Aaron's *Writers*

on the Left (New York: Avon Books, 1969).

36. Lawrence Cremin, *The Transformation of the Schools*, p. viii.
37. Hofstadter, *Anti-Intellectualism*, p. 47.
38. Ibid., p. 305.
39. Lasch, *The New Radicalism*, p. 71.
40. Randolph Bourne, *Youth and Life*, p. 27.
41. Ibid., p. 37.
42. Ibid., p. 48.
43. Ibid., p. 55.
44. Lasch, *The New Radicalism*, p. 81.
45. Bourne, *Youth and Life*, p. 58.
46. Ibid., pp. 90, 91.
47. Ibid., pp. 232, 241.
48. Ibid., p. 298.
49. Bourne, *The Gary Schools*, p. 35.
50. Ibid., p. 39.
51. Ibid., p. 130.
52. Ibid., p. 59.
53. Ibid., pp. 171-72.
54. Lewis Feuer, *Marx and Engels: Basic Writings in Politics and Philosophy* (Garden City, N.Y.: Doubleday & Co., Anchor Books, 1959), p. 245.
55. See Dewey's *Reconstruction in Philosophy* (New York: Henry Holt & Co., 1920) for a particularly clear expression of this view.
56. John Dewey as quoted in Hofstadter's *Anti-Intellectualism*, from Dewey's *My Pedagogic Creed*, p. 367.
57. John Dewey, *Democracy and Education*, p. 2.
58. Ibid., p. 6.
59. Ibid., p. 59.
60. See particularly Hofstadter's *Anti-Intellectualism*.
61. T. B. Bottomore, *Critics of Society*, p. 77.
62. Dwight Macdonald, "Why Politics," *Politics* 1, no. 1 (February 1944): 6.
63. Ibid., p. 7.
64. So scornful was Macdonald of "fifth columnists" and "liblabs" that his attacks on them, from today's perspective, seem frighteningly similar to anticommunist invectives used by Joseph McCarthy and his ilk only a few years later. One can understand how easy it must have been for anticommunist conservatives and "Cold War" liberals to pick up such rhetoric for purposes of red-baiting; and conversely how easy it might have been for anti-Stalinist intellectuals to be relatively complacent, at least for a time, concerning the dangers of such rhetorical attacks. Indeed Macdonald so much as admitted that he had overindulged his own anti-Stalinist attacks and that he had much more in common with certain "fellow travelers" than he did with the anticommunists on the Right. See his report on the conference at the Waldorf Hotel in New York in *Politics* 6, no. 1 (Winter 1949): 32A-32D.
65. Macdonald, "Henry Wallace (Part II)," *Politics* 4, no. 3 (March 1947): 116.
66. Macdonald, "Notes on the Truman Doctrine," *Politics* 4, no. 3 (March 1947): 87.

67. Ibid.
68. Macdonald, "Here Lies Our Road Said Writer to Reader," *Politics* 1, no. 8 (August 1948): 251.
69. Macdonald, "The Root Is Man (Part I)," *Politics* 3, no. 4 (April 1946): 109-10.
70. Macdonald, "Ancestors," *Politics* 2, no. 10 (October 1945): 297.
71. J. H. Jackson, "The Relevance of Proudhon," ibid., p. 297.
72. A fascinating study could be done on the revival of interest in Tocqueville among American intellectuals and academics after World War II. Among the reasons might be the concern with the problems of mass society, a disenchantment with radical and populist ideologies, and a preoccupation with America's uniqueness as a nation and as a culture. See, for example, David Riesman's *The Lonely Crowd: A Study of the Changing American Character* (New Haven: Yale University Press, 1950).
73. Sebastian Frank, "DeTocqueville," *Politics* 3, no. 4 (April 1946): 127.
74. Ibid., p. 217.
75. Ibid., p. 128.
76. Leo Tolstoy, "Modern Science," *Politics* 3, no. 5 (May 1946): 162.
77. Ibid., p. 163.
78. Tolstoy, "Stop and Think," ibid., p. 166.
79. George Woodcock, "Godwin," *Politics* 3, no. 9 (September 1946): 260.
80. Ibid., p. 261.
81. Ibid.
82. This sketch appeared in the winter of 1948 by which time *Politics* was appearing quarterly.
83. Macdonald, "Alexander Herzen," *Politics* 5, no. 1 (Winter 1948): 40.
84. Hans Sahl, "Kurt Tucholsky," *Politics* 5, no. 3 (Summer 1948): 171.
85. Macdonald, *Politics* 1, no. 9 (September 1944): 244.
86. Paul Goodman, "The Political Meaning of Recent Revisions of Freud," *Politics* 2, no. 7 (July 1945): 198-201. See chapter 3 on Paul Goodman for a more extensive discussion of this article.
87. Helen Costas, "A Critique of Marxian Ideology," *Politics* 3, no. 1 (January 1946): 12.
88. Ibid., p. 15.
89. Albert Votaw, "Toward a Personalist Social Philosophy," *Politics* 3, no. 1 (January 1946): 15.
90. Ibid., p. 17.
91. Nicola Chiaromonte, "One the Kind of Socialism Called Scientific," *Politics* 3, no. 2 (February 1946): 36.
92. Philip Spratt, "Marxism and Ethics," *Politics* 3, no. 3 (March 1946): 80.
93. Dwight Macdonald, "The Root Is Man: Part I," *Politics* 3, no. 4 (April 1946): 100. Macdonald's extended essay belongs with a whole tradition of antihistoricist social and philosophical analysis that sprung up in the 1940s and 1950s and includes Karl Popper's *The Open Society and Its Enemies*, Albert Camus's *The Rebel*, and Hannah Arendt's *The Origins of Totalitarianism*.

94. Ibid., p. 100.
95. Ibid., p. 105.
96. Ibid., p. 109.
97. Ibid., p. 112.
98. Ibid., p. 110.
99. Ibid., p. 107.
100. George Elliott in a letter to *Politics* 3, no. 5 (May 1946): 138.
101. Macdonald, "Reply by the Editor," *Politics* 3, no. 5 (May 1946): 141.
102. Macdonald, "Root: Part II," *Politics* 3, no. 6 (July 1946): 198.
103. Ibid., p. 199.
104. Ibid., p. 208.
105. Ibid., p. 209.
106. Ibid.
107. Ibid., pp. 209-10.
108. Louis Clair, "Digging at the Roots or Striking at the Branches," *Politics* 3, no. 10 (October 1946): 326.
109. Irving Howe, "The Thirteenth Disciple," ibid., p. 331.
110. Ibid., p. 329.
111. Ibid., p. 330.
112. See, for example, Irving Howe's "The New York Intellectuals," *Commentary* 46, no. 4 (October 1968): 29-51. I am not maintaining that it was Macdonald's conscious intention to formulate an ideology for the New York intellectuals; rather, that his proposals in "The Root Is Man" were symptomatic of his and other "radical" intellectuals' withdrawal from active radical and political involvement after World War II. (Nor am I saying that anarchism is in itself an ineffectual and "elitist" position. We have Paul Goodman to show us the contrary; but not, I think, Dwight Macdonald.)
113. Dwight Macdonald, *Memoirs of a Revolutionist* (Cleveland and New York: World Publishing Co., Meridian Books, 1963), p. 26. Macdonald also noted in this work the strange fact that anarchism had never enjoyed significant and widespread support in America.
114. Milton Klonsky, "Greenwich Village: Decline and Fall," *Commentary* 6, no. 5 (November 1948): 461. To make the war the dividing line may be a bit misleading. Actually it was the concentration upon economic and social issues during the Depression as expressed by the rhetoric of Marxism that forestalled the impact of Freud and the widespread use of Freudian terminology: Freud and psychoanalysis were considered hopelessly bourgeois and reactionary. Once the Marxist hegemony was established, very few American intellectuals made serious use of Freud in social analyses. For example, James Gilbert notes in *Writers and Partisans* (New York: John Wiley and Sons, 1968) that Philip Rahv and William Phillips, coeditors of *Partisan Review* and champions on the Left of literary modernism, did not begin seriously reading Freud until the late thirties.
115. See Philip Rieff's *The Triumph of the Therapeutic* and John Seeley's *The Americanization of the Unconscious* for further discussions of this point.
116. See Donald Fleming and Bernard Bailyn, eds., *Perspectives in American History, vol. 2, The Intellectual Migration: Europe and America, 1930-1960;* and *Salmagundi,* no. 10-11 (Fall 1969-Winter 1970), entitled

"The Legacy of the German Refugee Intellectuals" for a discussion of the intellectual diaspora from Europe to America in the 1930s.

117. See Donald Meyer's *The Positive Thinkers* for a discussion of the uses made of Freud and depth psychology in post-World War II religious thought.

118. A. M. Schlesinger, Jr., *The Vital Center* (Cambridge, Mass.: Riverside Press, 1962).

119. Trilling has remained concerned with this problem both from an intellectual and pedagogic point of view. See his *Beyond Culture*. In essence this was the same controversy that the radicals, associated with *Partisan Review*, faced in the 1930s—how could radical social and political ideologies be reconciled with modernist literature which was often avowedly aristocratic, difficult to read, non-"realistic," and the product of "reactionaries"? See Gilbert's *Writers and Partisans* plus John R. Harrison's *The Reactionaries: A Study of the Anti-Democratic Intelligensia* (New York: Schocken Books, 1969).

120. Lionel Trilling, *The Liberal Imagination*, p. 94.

121. Ibid., p. 95.

122. Ibid., pp. 53-54.

123. Ibid., pp. 254-55. Trilling's reference here was to the revisionist work of Erich Fromm.

124. Lionel Trilling, *Freud and the Crisis of Our Culture*, p. 50. This essay was later shortened and appeared in Trilling's *Beyond Culture* as "Freud: Within and Beyond Culture."

125. Will Herberg, "Freud, The Revisionists, and Social Reality," *Freud and the Twentieth Century*, ed. by Benjamin Nelson (Cleveland and New York: World Publishing Co., Meridian Books, 1957), p. 157.

126. Reinhold Niebuhr, "Human Creativity and Self Concern in Freud's Thought," ibid., p. 260.

127. See Morton White's *Social Thought in America* for a thorough discussion of the philosophical differences between Dewey and Niebuhr along with White's skepticism concerning the differences thus entailed for politics.

128. David Riesman, "Authority and Liberty in the Structure of Freud's Thought," in *Individualism Reconsidered*, p. 228.

129. Reisman, "The Themes of Work and Play in the Structure of Freud's Thought," ibid., p. 176.

130. Riesman "Authority and Liberty," ibid., p. 214.

131. Ibid., p. 239.

132. Riesman, "Freud, Religion and Science," ibid., p. 283.

133. Ibid., p. 285.

134. Ibid., p. 286.

135. Ibid., p. 296.

136. Riesman, "Some Observations on Community Plans and Utopias," ibid., p. 67.

137. Ibid., p. 68.

138. Riesman, "The Themes of Heroism and Weakness in Freud's Thought," ibid., p. 268.

Chapter 2

1. Philip Rieff, *The Triumph of the Therapeutic*, p. 143.
2. See Martin Birnbach's very thorough *Neo-Freudian Social Philosophy* and John Schaar's *Escape from Authority*.
3. See William Leuchtenberg's *Perils of Prosperity* (Chicago: University of Chicago Press, 1958) for a quick overview of the Freud craze in the 1920s and also Hendrik Ruitenbeek's *Freud and America*.
4. Culture refers to that group of values and assumptions, not always harmonious with each other but relatively permanent, which governs and explains thought and behavior. Philip Rieff in *Triumph of the Therapeutic* defines culture as "the system of significances attached to behavior by which a society explains itself to itself" (p. 69). From Marx on, Western radical thought has generally held, as expressed by the concept of ideology, that values are related to economic and social arrangements and that if the latter are changed, the former will change also. While generally true, the problem with the concept of ideology is that it is too general and inadequate to explain "cultural" and even institutional lags. To jump ahead, Reich believed that the correlation between socioeconomic and cultural change was not as "automatic" as most Marxists had assumed. In short Marxism needed a cultural and individual psychology.
5. Sigmund Freud, "Three Contributions to a Theory of Sexuality," in *The Basic Writings of Sigmund Freud*, p. 576.
6. Freud, "Instincts and Their Vicissitudes," in *A General Selection*, p. 75.
7. Freud, "Three Contributions," *The Basic Writings*, p. 573.
8. Ibid., p. 569.
9. Ibid.
10. Freud, "On Narcissism," *A General Selection*, p. 112.
11. Ibid., p. 107.
12. Freud, "Thoughts for a Time of War and Death," *Standard Edition, XIV* (London: Hogarth Press, 1953), p. 273.
13. Ibid., p. 286.
14. Ernest Jones, *The Life and Work of Sigmund Freud*, ed. Lionel Trilling and Steven Marcus, p. 386.
15. Freud, *Beyond the Pleasure Principle*, pp. 46, 60-61.
16. Ibid., p. 67.
17. Ibid., p. 68.
18. Ibid., p. 72.
19. Ibid., p. 93. That Freud was so obviously concerned that his theories not be read as explaining everything by sexuality is revealing, and may perhaps support Reich's later observation in *Reich Speaks of Freud* that Freud's hypothesis of the death instinct was an expression of Freud's own psychological state at the time he advanced it.
20. Ibid., pp. 94-95.
21. Ibid., p. 109.
22. Freud, *Civilization and Its Discontents*, p. 38.
23. Ibid., p. 33.
24. Ibid., p. 25.
25. Ibid., p. 50.
26. Ibid.

27. Ibid., p. 51.

28. Ibid., p. 74.

29. Ibid., p. 77.

30. Freud, *New Introductory Lectures on Psychoanalysis*, p. 64.

31. Freud, *Civilization*, p. 88.

32. Freud, *The Ego and the Id*, p. 32.

33. J. A. C. Brown, *Freud and the Post-Freudians*, p. 28.

34. Philip Rieff, *Freud: The Mind of the Moralist*, pp. 223, 237.

35. It would be well at this point to note the general neglect of Reich in discussions of post-World War II American intellectual life. In his chapter on Reich in *The Triumph of the Therapeutic*, Rieff claims that Reich's sexual radicalism and antipolitical bias had a peculiar appeal to many American intellectuals after the Second War. (See my section on "Politics" and chapter on Paul Goodman). While true in its descriptive claim, Rieff scores these intellectuals as "anti-intellectual radicals" and "defeated men of the left" and thus I think does many of them an injustice. In 1947 an article on Reich appeared in *Harper's*. The author, Mildred K. Brody, noted the appeal of Reich's teachings—"offering sex as the source of individual salvation in a collective world that's going to hell"—to proto-Beat communities in the Big Sur area, along with the works of Henry Miller and D. H. Lawrence. Later, in the 1950s, Allen Ginsberg, Jack Kerouac, and William Burroughs would mention Reich in their writings. And of course Reich was also one of the intellectual progenitors of Norman Mailer's work, particularly in the 1950s. For Mailer the orgasm became the last realm of authenticity and feeling against the encroaching totalitarianism of modern life.

In 1960 Paul Goodman wrote an article entitled "Dr. Reich's Banned Books" for *Kulchur* (later included in *Utopian Essays and Practical Proposals*) in which he protested the ridiculous decision of the government to ban Reich's works. Yet other than this article and Goodman's earlier one in *Politics*, which has never been reprinted, there exist only three discussions of Reich—Rieff's, a chapter in Paul Robinson's *The Freudian Left*, and David Elkind's "Wilhelm Reich—The Psychoanalyst as Revolutionary." As Robinson notes, Reich's writings are in a chaotic state and need organization and editing. Though Reich's last wife Ilse Ollendorff Reich has written *Wilhelm Reich: A Personal Biography*, a more complete biography is needed.

36. *Reich Speaks of Freud*, pp. 5-6, 20.

37. Ibid., p. 21.

38. Ibid., p. 33.

39. Ibid., p. 43.

40. I. O. Reich, *A Personal Biography*, pp. 13-19.

41. *Reich Speaks of Freud*, p. 44.

42. Reich, *The Sexual Revolution*, p. 4.

43. Ibid., p. 5.

44. Ibid., p. 9.

45. Ibid., p. 14.

46. Ibid., p. 19.

47. Ibid., p. 28.

48. Ibid., p. 19.

49. Ibid., pp. 71-72.

50. Ibid., pp. 73, 74.

51. Ibid., p. 79.

52. Reich's assumption about the state was a Marxist one; that is, the state operates in the interests of the ruling class and hence has no independence or power against the dominant social and economic interests.

53. Reich, *The Sexual Revolution,* p. 119. Current ideologies of women's liberation might with some profit turn to Reich as an antidote for Freud's more traditional views.

54. Reich, *Character Analysis* ("Preface to First Edition," 1933), pp. xx-xxi.

55. Ibid., p. 15.

56. Ibid., p. xxv.

57. Ibid., p. 150.

58. Ibid., p. 174.

59. Ibid., p. 147.

60. Ibid., p. 169.

61. Ibid., p. 222.

62. Reich, *Die Massenpsychologie des Faschismus,* p. 16.

63. Ibid., p. 35 (my translation).

64. Ibid., p. 82.

65. Ibid., p. 48 (my translation).

66. Ibid., p. 50 (my translation).

67. Ibid., p. 110.

68. Ibid., p. 99.

69. Ibid., p. 102.

70. Ibid., p. 101.

71. Ibid., p. 105 (my translation).

72. Ibid., p. 247 (my translation).

73. Ibid., p. 250 (my translation).

74. Reich, *The Sexual Revolution* (Part II, "The Struggle for the 'New Life' in the Soviet Union" was published in 1935), p. 181.

75. Ibid., pp. 191-92.

76. Ibid., p. 157.

77. It would be interesting to know if Reich was aware of the kibbutzim being established in Palestine in the 1930s. The structure and goals of these communities were to a surprising degree similar to Reich's communal clan democracy in which men and women were socially and economically independent of each other, the conventional family did not exist, and the rearing of children was a community function.

78. Erich Fromm, "Über Methode und Aufgabe einer analytischen Sozialpsychologie," *Die Zeitschrift fur Sozialforschung* 1, no. 1 (1932): 28-54.

79. Karl Landauer, Review of Reich's *Massenpsychologie* and *Character-Analyse,* ibid., 3, no. 2 (1934): 106-7.

80. The idea of a work democracy is obviously a prototype for Paul Goodman's concept of community as well as A. S. Neill's educational experiments. Neill and Reich were fast friends from 1937 on, with Neill being one of the few people that Reich had not alienated by the time of Reich's death. See I. O. Reich's *A Personal Biography.*

81. Reich, *The Sexual Revolution,* p. 234.

82. Ilse Ollendorff Reich notes that Reich was very strongly opposed to homosexuality.

83. According to George Woodcock, anarchism has tended to be ascetic and antisexual, at least in its classical formulations. The natural for most anarchists has been equated with simplicity and the antiurban since the city is where luxuries, of all sorts, present a constant temptation. See his study *Anarchism* (Cleveland: World Publishing Co., Meridian Books, 1962).

84. See, for instance, Kenneth Keniston, *Young Radicals*, for a discussion of the way young people involved in the anti-Vietnam war movement often acted out of values learned from their parents which were in opposition to those of the society and national government.

85. Reich, *The Discovery of the Orgone: The Function of the Orgasm*, 1:24.

86. Ibid., p. 245.

87. Reich, *Character Analysis* ("From Psychoanalysis to Orgone Biophysics," 1935), p. 358.

88. Ibid., Preface to Second Edition, 1945, p. xviii.

89. Ibid., "From Psychoanalysis to Orgone Biophysics," p. 359.

90. Ibid., "The Emotional Plague," 1945, pp. 248-49.

91. Reich, *Reich Speaks of Freud*, p. 6.

92. Ibid., p. 271.

93. Rieff, *Triumph of the Therapeutic*, p. 144.

94. Reich, *The Sexual Revolution* (Preface to Third Edition, 1944), p. xxi.

95. See Rieff's *Triumph of the Therapeutic*.

96. I. O. Reich, *A Personal Biography*, pp. 115-28.

Chapter 3

1. Norman Mailer, "The Steps of the Pentagon," *Harper's* 236, no. 144 (March 1968): 55-58.

2. Lewis Feuer, *The Conflict of Generations*, pp. 525-27.

3. Alfred Kazin, "The Girl from the Village," *Atlantic Monthly* 227, no. 2 (February 1971): 62-63.

4. Paul Goodman, "Diary of Makapuu," *Oatmeal of Homespun Gray*, p. 71.

5. Goodman, "For a Young Widow," *Oatmeal*, p. 92.

6. Goodman, "For My Birthday: 1967," *Oatmeal*, p. 94.

7. Because of the reasons given above, I am not going to deal with Goodman's fiction or poetry at any greater length. I am aware that Goodman's fiction has its admirers. George Dennison has written that Goodman's prose "especially in the last two volumes of *Empire City*—. . . is an absolutely dazzling creation" and holds that *Adam and His Works* is "the best [collection of short stories] in my opinion, our country has seen in many years." *New American Review* #9 ed. by Theodore Solotaroff (New York: Signet Books, 1970), p. 96. Though Dennison's critical opinion must command respect, I simply do not understand it. Not only do I not find *Empire City* dazzling stylistically, I find the book nearly impossible to read. The world which Goodman creates, whatever its particular structures, fails to compel my attention.

8. Goodman, *Making Do*, p. 274. This novel is interesting only as a sort

of *roman à clef,* and as usual the figure scrutinized through the "clef" is Goodman.

9. Paul Goodman, "The Political Meaning of Recent Revisions of Freud," *Politics* 2, no. 7 (July 1945): 198. Thus, Goodman anticipated Marcuse's attack on Fromm and the Revisionists by a good ten years.

10. Ibid., p. 199.

11. Ibid., p. 201.

12. Ibid.

13. See Lionel Trilling's *Freud and the Crisis of Our Culture* for a similar discussion of Freud's instinct theory and an implicit rejection of the Revisionists.

14. Goodman, "Political Meaning," p. 202.

15. C. Wright Mills and P. J. Salter, "The Barricades and the Bedroom," *Politics* 2, no. 10 (October 1945): 315.

16. Goodman, "Political Meaning," p. 202.

17. Goodman, "The Barricades and the Bedroom: A Rejoinder," *Politics* 2, no. 10 (October 1945): 315.

18. See my chapter "Freud and Reich."

19. Goodman, "Revolution, Sociolatry and War," *Politics* 2, no. 12 (December 1945): 378.

20. Ibid., p. 379.

21. Ibid., p. 340.

22. Paul Goodman, *Drawing the Line,* p. 4.

23. Ibid., p. 11.

24. Ibid.

25. Ibid., p. 22.

26. Ibid., p. 26. Obviously Goodman's concept of community closely resembled Wilhelm Reich's idea of work democracies.

27. Ibid., p. 26.

28. Ibid., p. 36.

29. Ibid., p. 47.

30. Ibid., p. 33.

31. Ibid., p. 48

32. Ibid., p. 31.

33. Paul and Percival Goodman, *Communitas,* pp. 19-20.

34. Ibid., p. 119.

35. Ibid., p. 148.

36. Ibid., pp. 155-56.

37. Ibid., p. 157.

38. Ibid., p. 160.

39. Ibid., p. 172.

40. See Bruno Bettelheim's *The Children of the Dream* (New York: Macmillan Co., 1969) for a critique of life in the kibbutzim along these lines.

41. See the ensuing pages of this chapter for a more detailed treatment of Goodman's psychology.

42. Paul Goodman, Frederick Perls, Ralph Hefferline, *Gestalt Therapy,* p. x.

43. F. S. Perls, *Ego, Hunger and Aggression* (New York: Random House, Vintage Books, 1947, 1969), pp. 69-71. From internal evidence it appears

that Perls wrote *Ego* during World War II. Gestalt therapy and many variations thereupon have of course come into their own in the 1960s through the Esalen Institute where Perls was active until his death.

44. Ibid., p. 185.

45. Goodman, *Gestalt Therapy*, p. 228.

46. I agree with Theodore Roszak's contention in *The Making of a Counter Culture*, pp. 186-90, that *Gestalt Therapy* is absolutely central to Goodman's thought. Though Roszak's characterization of Gestalt ideas as similar to "oriental mysticism" is an interesting one, it is, at least in connection with Goodman's thought, wide of the mark. As Goodman describes him, man is primarily an active being, not a passive and contemplative one. Perls, however, did stress the goal of restoring "organismic balance" and perhaps would better fit Roszak's tendency to "orientalize" the Gestaltist approach.

47. The general bias in *Gestalt Therapy* upon the "here and now," a relatively easy "solution" to problems, and its generally "do it yourself" attitude may explain its recent popularity in an America which has apparently outgrown its Puritan introspection.

48. Ibid., p. 392. Strictly speaking this was a misinterpretation of Reich who held that the culture was built upon sublimated, pregenital sexual energy.

49. Ibid., p. 396. Goodman as well parts company from Norman Brown and to an extent Herbert Marcuse in his idea of the relationship of creativity and culture to "normality."

50. Ibid., p. 350.

51. Ibid., p. 340.

52. Ibid., pp. 347-48.

53. Ibid., p. 349. This interpretation of the repetition compulsion obviously derived from Reich's interpretation of masochism.

54. Ibid., p. 350.

55. Ibid., p. 293.

56. Marcuse's *Eros and Civilization* and Brown's *Life Against Death* were both done in the early fifties, but it was only in the early sixties that they really began to attract underground and then academic attention.

57. Norman Podhoretz, *Making It* (New York: Bantam Books, 1969), pp. 219-20.

58. Paul Goodman, *Growing Up Absurd*, p. 7.

59. Ibid., pp. 139-42.

60. Ibid., p. 160.

61. Podhoretz, *Making It*, p. 218.

62. Goodman, *Growing Up Absurd*, p. 170.

63. Ibid., p. 171.

64. Paul Goodman, *5 Years*, p. 218.

65. Goodman, *Growing Up Absurd*, p. 217.

66. Ibid., p. 219.

67. Goodman, *Compulsory Mis-Education and the Community of Scholars*, p. 44.

68. See Goodman's "Education Now," *New York Review of Books* 12, no. 7 (10 April 1969). Perhaps the best example of neo-Progressivism in

education is George Dennison's *Lives of Children,* a book which owed much to Dewey, Neill, Goodman, and Gestalt psychology. In fact Goodman and Dennison are friends and Dennison had once trained as a Gestalt therapist under Goodman.

69. Goodman, *Compulsory Mis-Education,* p. 8.

70. Goodman, *Community of Scholars,* pp. 216-17.

71. Ibid., p. 215.

72. Ibid., p. 167.

73. Ibid., p. 309.

74. Ibid., p. 153.

75. Goodman claims that the free universities missed his point insofar as their curricula were often a hodgepodge of the occult, the political, and the trivial. Goodman had hoped that the free universities would provide an alternate education in the professions, the humanities, and the sciences, which would be viable in the "real" world.

76. Goodman, "The Devolution of Democracy," reprinted in *Drawing the Line,* pp. 55-75.

77. Goodman, "Berkeley in February," *Dissent* 12 (Spring 1965): 162.

78. Goodman, *People or Personnel* and *Like a Conquered Province,* p. 16.

79. Ibid., pp. 9-10.

80. Ibid., p. 134.

81. Ibid., p. 157.

82. Paul Goodman, "The Psychology of Being Powerless," ibid., pp. 336-52.

83. Ibid., p. 279.

84. Ibid., pp. 283-84.

85. Paul Goodman, *New Reformation: Notes of a Neolithic Conservative,* p. 49.

86. Ibid., p. 48.

87. Ibid., p. 178.

88. Ibid., p. 145.

89. Ibid., p. 192-93.

90. Ibid., p. 197.

91. Ibid., p. 7.

Chapter 4

1. Most of the essays from *Die Zeitschrift für Sozialforschung* have been collected in *Kultur und Gesellschaft* 1 and 2 (Frankfurt-am-Main: Suhrkamp Verlag, 1965). In turn several of these same essays have been published in English in *Negations.*

2. Herbert Marcuse, "Über die philosophischen Grundlagen des wirtschaftswissenschaftlichen Arbeitsbegriff," *Kultur und Gesellschaft* 1:10 (my translation).

3. Ibid., p. 13.

4. Ibid., p. 20.

5. Ibid., p. 31.

6. Ibid.

7. Ibid., p. 34.
8. Ibid., p. 32.
9. Ibid., p. 39.
10. Ibid., p. 44.
11. Ibid., p. 46.
12. Ibid., pp. 47-48.
13. Marcuse, "The Concept of Essence," *Negations,* pp. 71, 69.
14. Marcuse, "Philosophy and Critical Theory," ibid., pp. 134-35.
15. Ibid., p. 135.
16. Ibid., p. 143.
17. Ibid., p. 144.
18. Marcuse, "The Affirmative Character of Culture," ibid., p. 89.
19. Ibid., p. 93.
20. Ibid., p. 97. (See Raymond Williams's *Culture and Society* for a similar discussion of the concept of culture in nineteenth-century English social thought.)
21. Ibid., p. 99.
22. Ibid., p. 103.
23. Marcuse, "On Hedonism," ibid., p. 169.
24. Ibid., p. 159.
25. Ibid., p. 180.
26. Ibid., pp. 186-87.
27. Ibid., p. 189.
28. Herbert Marcuse, *Reason and Revolution,* pp. 218-19.
29. Ibid., p. 19.
30. Ibid., p. 256.
31. Ibid., p. 283.
32. Ibid., p. 293.
33. Ibid., p. 315.
34. Ibid., p. 319.
35. Ibid., p. 322.
36. Thus long before the emergence of the "affluent society" and the incorporation of the working class into the structure and ideology of the advanced industrial society, Marcuse had all but abandoned the proletariat as an active revolutionary force.
37. In his highly critical polemic against Marcuse, Alasdair MacIntyre makes much the same point, though giving it a highly pejorative gloss. For MacIntyre, Marcuse becomes a pre- rather than post-Marxian social theorist, more Feuerbachian than Marxian. See MacIntyre's *Herbert Marcuse.* I agree with many of MacIntyre's ideas, but find his animus against Marcuse excessive.
38. Defenders of Marcuse and the enterprise of "critical theory" point out that critical theory grants this point in seeing itself as bound up with "concrete social reality" at any given time. See William Leiss, "The Critical Theory of Society: Present Situation and Future Tasks," *Critical Interruptions* (New York: Herder and Herder, 1970), p. 77. Be that as it may, critical theory, for all practical purposes, assumes a point of view transcending social reality.
39. Herbert Marcuse, *Eros and Civilization,* p. 32. As presented by Marcuse the performance principle is roughly synonomous with Weber's

"Protestant Ethic." Although Marcuse sees the performance principle as extending over most of "civilized existence," the implication is that its fullest expression has been the period of modern industrial development in the West. The performance principle thus by implication is a "cultural super-ego" that must be transcended, now that it has done its work.

40. Ibid., p. 33.

41. Ibid., p. 32.

42. Ibid., p. 43n.

43. Ibid., p. 22.

44. Ibid., p. 47.

45. Ibid., p. 75.

46. Ibid., p. 74.

47. Ibid., p. 94.

48. Ibid., p. 95.

49. Ibid., pp. 120-22.

50. Ibid., p. 101.

51. Ibid., p. 104.

52. Ibid., p. 111.

53. Ibid., p. 113.

54. Ibid., p. 168.

55. Ibid., p. 184.

56. Ibid., p. 211.

57. Ibid., p. 216.

58. Ibid., p. 205.

59. Ibid., p. 222.

60. Ibid., p. 257.

61. Ibid., p. 242.

62. Erich Fromm, "The Human Implications of Instinctivistic Radicalism," *Dissent* 2, no. 4 (Autumn 1955): 342-49.

63. Ibid., pp. 345-56.

64. Herbert Marcuse, "A Reply to Erich Fromm," *Dissent* 3, no. 1 (Winter 1956): 79-81.

65. Ibid., p. 80.

66. Ibid., p. 81.

67. See Norman Brown's *Life Against Death* and my chapter on Brown for a diametrically opposed attitude toward death and the possibility of a nonrepressive existence.

68. Marcuse, *Eros and Civilization*, p. 212.

69. Marcuse, "Das Veralten der Psychoanalyse," *Kultur* 2, p. 105.

70. Herbert Marcuse, *One-Dimensional Man*, p. xv.

71. Paul Robinson notes in his *The Freudian Left* that Marx was the unmentioned "hero" of *Eros and Civilization*. In similar fashion Max Weber dominates *One-Dimensional Man*, though he is never mentioned throughout the book. In fact, Weber as much as Marx dominates *Eros and Civilization*. Weber is never mentioned there either.

72. Marcuse, "Industrialization and Capitalism in the Work of Max Weber," *Negations*, p. 207.

73. Marcuse, *One-Dimensional Man*, p. 23.

74. Ibid., p. 31.

75. Ibid., p. 32. Marcuse's discussion of the "cooptation" of the working

class is remarkably similar to Goodman's in *Drawing the Line*.

76. Ibid., pp. 65, 70.

77. Ibid., p. 75.

78. Ibid., p. 78. A prime example of this is most pornography in which sexuality becomes identical with exploitation of and sadism toward the "other."

79. Ibid., p. 98.

80. Ibid., p. 137.

81. Ibid., p. 132.

82. Ibid., p. 142. Quite obviously much of the philosophical discussion in *One-Dimensional Man* was a repetition of the themes first elucidated in the thirties' essays.

83. Ibid., p. 164.

84. Ibid., p. 153.

85. Ibid., p. 157.

86. Ibid., p. 171.

87. The classic statement of analytical philosophy's unabashed championing of science is to be found in A. J. Ayer's *Language, Truth, and Logic* (New York: Dover Publications, 1936).

88. Ibid., pp. 187, 191.

89. Ibid., p. 209.

90. Ibid., p. 212.

91. Ibid., p. 213.

92. Ibid., p. 220.

93. Ibid., p. 221.

94. Ibid., p. 253.

95. Ibid., pp. 237-44.

96. Ibid., pp. 251-52.

97. Ibid., p. 257.

98. Wolfgang Fritz Haug, "Das Ganze und das ganz Andere: Zur Kritik der reinen revolutionären Transcendenz," *Antworten auf Herbert Marcuse*, ed. Jürgen Habermas (Frankfurt-am-Main: Suhrkamp Verlag, 1968), p. 63 (my translation).

99. Ibid., p. 54.

100. Claus Offe, "Technik und Eindimensionalität: Eine Version der Technokratiethese?" ibid., p. 87.

101. See, for example, Allen Graubard, "Herbert Marcuse—One Dimensional Pessimism," *Dissent* 15, no. 3 (May-June 1968): 216-28; and George Kateb, "The Political Thought of Herbert Marcuse," *Commentary* 49, no. 1 (January 1970): 48-63, for liberal-left critiques of Marcuse.

102. Peter Sedgewick, "National Science and Human Theory: A Critique of Herbert Marcuse," *Socialist Register*, pp. 174, 184.

103. Alasdair MacIntyre, *Herbert Marcuse*, pp. 83-97.

104. See Robinson's *The Freudian Left* and Roszak's *The Making of a Counter Culture*.

105. Haug, *Antworten*, p. 54.

106. Marcuse, *Eros and Civilization*, p. xi; and "Max Weber," *Negations*, p. 225.

107. Marcuse, "Das Veralten," *Negations*, p. 93. Marcuse has expanded on this idea in two essays originally written in 1956, "Freedom and Freud's

Theory of Instincts" and "Progress and Freud's Theory of Instincts." These latter two essays were included in *Five Lectures*.

108. Herbert Marcuse, "Ethik und Revolution," *Kultur und Gesellschaft* 2:136 (my translation).

109. Ibid., p. 137.

110. Ibid., p. 143.

111. Ibid., pp. 138-39.

112. Ibid., p. 142.

113. Ibid., p. 137.

114. Ibid., p. 140.

115. Marcuse, "Repressive Tolerance," *A Critique of Pure Tolerance*, p. 83. Thus civil liberties become the analogous phenomena in the political sphere to "repressive desublimation" in the sexual sphere.

116. Ibid., p. 116.

117. Ibid., p. 106.

118. Ibid., p. 112.

119. Ibid., p. 83.

120. Ibid., p. 85.

121. Ibid., p. 105.

122. Ibid., p. 120.

123. Ibid., pp. 117, 116.

124. Jürgen Habermas, "Zum Geleit," *Antworten*, p. 16 (my translation).

125. Marcuse, *An Essay on Liberation*, p. 12.

126. Ibid., p. 16.

127. Ibid., p. 54.

128. Ibid., p. 17.

129. Ibid., p. 23.

130. Ibid., p. 45.

131. Ibid., p. 90.

132. Ibid., p. 81.

133. Walter Benjamin, "The Work of Art in the Age of Mechanical Reproduction," in *Illuminations* (New York: Schocken Books, 1969), p. 241.

Chapter 5

1. Thomas Morgan, "How Hieronymus Bosch (XVth C) and Norman Brown (XXth C) Would Change the World," *Esquire*, p. 105. See also an interview with Brown in *Psychology Today* 4, no. 3 (August 1970) 42-47. Brown was apparently led to read Freud in the early fifties when his leftist political, enlightenment intellectual framework no longer seemed adequate to reality. Though *Life Against Death* was finished in 1956, it went unpublished until 1959.

2. Norman O. Brown, *Hermes the Thief*.

3. Norman Brown, *Life Against Death*, p. 4.

4. Ibid., p. 242.

5. Though both Marcuse and Brown point to polymorphous perversity as an alternative to genital sexuality, Paul Robinson's judgment—that Brown takes the idea much more seriously—is, I think, correct. One is usually hard put to conceive what is meant by the phrase. The best example of the contrast between the "healthiness" of polymorphous perversity and the

"sickness" of genital sexuality occurs in Jerzy Kosinski's *The Painted Bird* (New York: Pocket Books, 1966), pp. 147-48. Another example of the relationship of compulsive genitality to violence and domination would certainly be Norman Mailer's essay, "The White Negro."

6. Brown, *Life Against Death*, p. 43.

7. Ibid.

8. Ibid., p. 54.

9. Ibid., p. 284.

10. Ibid., p. 101.

11. Strangely enough neither Brown nor Marcuse make much use of Don Juan as an archetypal figure of the Christian West. Don Juan's compulsive sexuality, his keeping count of the number of women he has seduced, would seem to be perfect examples of aggressive genitality and the quantification of sexual feelings.

12. Ibid., p. 115.

13. Brown does not ask himself if any evidence indicates that mammals suffer from birth trauma. *Life Against Death* depends so much on the distinction between animals and man that Brown would have done well to have at least tried to support his contentions with ethological data.

14. Ibid., p. 130. Reich would have agreed basically with this idea but valued it positively since for him the energy for cultural achievement came from repressed pregenital sexuality.

15. Ibid., p. 141.

16. Ibid., p. 60.

17. Ibid., pp. 157-76.

18. Ibid., p. 230.

19. Ibid., p. 167.

20. Ibid., p. 230.

21. Ibid., p. 236.

22. Ibid.

23. Ibid., p. 253.

24. Ibid., p. 259.

25. Ibid., p. 257.

26. Ibid., p. 274.

27. Ibid., p. 277.

28. Ibid., p. 281.

29. Ibid., p. 283.

30. Ibid., p. 292.

31. In the 1960s one mechanism for aiding the emergence of the new man would be hallucinogenics, particularly LSD. For instance, in Jane Kramer's *Allen Ginsberg in America* (New York: Random House, Vintage Books, 1970), Miss Kramer notes that psychiatrists reported that what "Ginsberg had accomplished through drugs was, in their terms, a complete disintegration of the ego structure, a descent into the id, and then a recreation and integration of the ego structure, slightly changed." This "mind blowing" process may resemble what Brown had in mind.

32. Brown, *Life Against Death*, p. 77.

33. See George Bataille's *Death and Sensuality* (New York: Ballantine Books, 1962).

34. Norman O. Brown, "Apocalypse: The Place of Mystery in the Life of the Mind," *Harper's* 222 (May 1961): 47.

35. Ibid., p. 49.

36. Ibid.

37. Theodore Roszak has suggested "Professor Dionysos" as an apt title for Brown.

38. Norman O. Brown, *Love's Body*, p. 21.

39. Ibid., p. 105.

40. Ibid., p. 149.

41. Ibid., p. 155.

42. Ibid.

43. Ibid., p. 157.

44. Ibid., p. 159.

45. Ibid. See also R. D. Laing's *The Divided Self* (Baltimore, Md.: Pelican Books, 1966) and *The Politics of Experience* (Harmondsworth, Middlesex, England: Penguin Books, 1967).

46. Ibid., p. 161.

47. Ibid., p. 222.

48. Ibid., p. 236.

49. Herbert Marcuse, "Love Mystified: A Critique of Norman O. Brown," in *Negations*.

50. Ibid., p. 229.

51. Ibid.

52. Ibid., p. 232.

53. Ibid., p. 235.

54. Ibid., p. 236.

55. Ibid., p. 241.

56. Frederick Crews, "Love in the Western World," *Partisan Review,* p. 278. The modernist post-Freudian counterpart of allegory is reductionism, allegory stood on its head.

57. Ibid., p. 279. See also Rieff's *Triumph of the Therapeutic* for a discussion of the "religious" nature of the thought of Jung, Reich, and D. H. Lawrence.

Chapter 6

1. Perry Miller, ed., *The Transcendentalists* (Cambridge, Mass.: Harvard University Press, 1950), p. 8.

2. Philip Rieff, *The Triumph of the Therapeutic*, pp. 148-49. See also Norman Cohn's *The Pursuit of the Millennium*, rev. ed. (New York: Oxford University Press, 1970) for a history of religious antinomian movements during the Middle Ages.

3. Hannah Arendt, *On Violence* (New York: Harcourt Brace Jovanovich, Harvest Books, 1970), pp. 38-39.

4. Theodore Roszak, *The Making of a Counter Culture*, p. 82.

5. The "religious" is obviously a vague concept. In general the religious impulse involves a faith (or a search for a faith) which explains the world and man's place in it, usually by appeal to a transcendent source. The "religious" becomes a "religion" when the will to faith is common to fairly

large numbers of people, is embodied in certain institutions and rituals, and receives dogmatic and intellectual elaboration.

6. See Nuel Pharr Davis's *Lawrence and Oppenheimer* (Greenwich, Conn: Fawcett World Library, 1968). Davis records that soon after Enrico Fermi arrived at Los Alamos, he said in amazement to Oppenheimer: "I believe your people actually *want* to make the bomb," p. 181.

7. See George Steiner's *Language and Silence* (New York: Atheneum Publishers, 1967).

8. Philip E. Slater, *The Pursuit of Loneliness,* p. 100.

9. Charles Reich, *The Greening of America,* p. 225.

10. Ibid., p. 65.

11. Ibid., p. 346.

12. Ibid., p. 245-46.

13. Ibid., p. 135.

14. Ibid., p. 145.

15. Ibid., p. 274.

16. Ibid., p. 348.

17. See the following pages for discussion of this point.

18. See William Braden's *The Age of Aquarius* (Chicago: Quadrangle Books, 1970), pp. 43-65, for a discussion with Bettelheim on this and related points.

19. This cultural counterattack has been essentially defensive and, perhaps for that reason, peculiarly carping and devoid of humor. At its worst, as in Saul Bellow's "Culture Now: Some Animadversions, Some Laughs," *Modern Occasions* (Winter 1971), it becomes mere ranting and scolding. *Commentary* magazine has been the leader in the counterattack. In late 1970 and on into 1971 it gave signs of increasing editorial rigidity. Paul Goodman no longer contributed. Where a few years before *Commentary* had printed Marcuse's review of Brown's *Love's Body* and Brown's reply, both Brown and Marcuse came to be pilloried with regularity. Norman Mailer, who was once a regular columnist, seldom if ever graced *Commentary's* pages. Indeed *Commentary* seemed to be uninterested in any new thinkers or ideas. Worthy though the democratic-socialist tradition, a commitment to rational and humane values, a belief in civility and tolerance are, one begins to suspect that they have become an excuse for not thinking rather than the spur to fresh insights.

20. John Passmore "Paradise Now" *Encounter* 35, no. 5 (November 1971): 17.

21. Ibid., p. 19.

22. Ibid., p. 7.

23. Philip Rieff, *Triumph of the Therapeutic,* p. 50.

24. Ibid., p. 57.

25. Ibid., p. 32.

26. Rieff, *Freud: The Mind of the Moralist,* p. 391.

27. Rieff, *Triumph of the Therapeutic,* p. 24. For a fictional account of the post-Christian world, haunted by a search for meaning yet informed by a psychoanalytic consciousness, see Walker Percy's novels, *The Moviegoer* (1962), *The Last Gentleman* (1966), and particularly *Love in the Ruins* (1971). In *The Last Gentleman* the diary of one character suggests that the

only way "abstracted" modern man can "re-enter" the world is through the orgasm, yet the orgasm by definition is not lasting and thus man is once more left in despair. If Rieff is the chief sociologist of the post-Christian, postideological world, Percy is its poet.

28. Max Weber, "Science as a Vocation," *From Max Weber*, ed. Hans Gerth and C. Wright Mills, pp. 154-55. Arthur Mitzman's *The Iron Cage: An Historical Interpretation of Max Weber* (New York: Alfred A. Knopf, 1970) is a brilliant analysis of the relationship between Weber's psychological problems and intellectual concerns.

29. Soren Kierkegaard, *Either/Or* (Garden City, N.Y.: Doubleday & Co., Anchor Books, 1959), 2:15, 25, 163.

30. Shierry M. Weber, "Individuation as Praxis," *Critical Interruptions*, ed. Paul Breines (New York: Herder and Herder, 1970), p. 40.

SELECTED BIBLIOGRAPHY

Abel, Lionel. "Important Nonsense: Norman O. Brown." *Dissent* 15 (March-April 1968): 147-57.
——. "A Reply to Arthur Efron." *Dissent* 15 (September-October 1968): 455-58.
Bell, Daniel. *The End of Ideology.* New York: Macmillan Co., Collier Books, 1962.
Bennis, Warren. "Norman O. Brown's Body." *Psychology Today* 4 (August 1970):42-47.
Berman, Ronald. *America in the Sixties.* New York: The Free Press, 1968.
Birnbach, Martin. *Neo-Freudian Social Philosophy.* Stanford: Stanford University Press, 1961.
Boorstin, Daniel. *The Decline of Radicalism.* New York: Random House, Vintage Books, 1969.
——. *The Genius of American Politics.* Chicago: University of Chicago Press, 1953.
Bottomore, T. B. *Critics of Society.* New York: Random House, Vintage Books, 1969.
Bourne, Randolph. *The Gary Schools.* Boston, New York, and Cleveland: Houghton Mifflin Co., 1916.
——. *War and the Intellectuals.* Edited by Carl Resek. New York: Harper & Row, Harper Torchbooks, 1964.
——. *Youth and Life.* Freeport, N.Y.: Books for Libraries Press, 1913.
Braden, William. *The Age of Aquarius.* Chicago: Quadrangle Books, 1970.
Breines, Paul. *Critical Interruptions.* New York: Herder & Herder, 1970.
Brown, J. A. C. *Freud and the Post-Freudians.* Baltimore, Md.: Penguin Books, 1966.
Brown, Norman O. "Apocalypse: The Place of Mystery in the Life of the Mind." *Harper's* 222 (May 1961): 46-49.
——. "A Reply to Herbert Marcuse." In *Negations* by Herbert Marcuse. Boston: Beacon Press, 1969. Pp. 243-47.

——. *Hermes the Thief*. New York: Random House, Vintage Books, 1969.

——. *Life Against Death*. New York: Random House, Vintage Books, 1959.

——. *Love's Body*. New York: Random House, Vintage Books, 1966.

Commentary (1945-).

Cremin, Lawrence. *The Transformation of the Schools*. New York: Random House, Vintage Books, 1961.

Crews, Frederick. "Love in the Western World." *Partisan Review* 34 (Spring 1967):272-87.

Dewey, John. *The Child and the Curriculum: School and Society*. Chicago: University of Chicago Press, 1956.

——. *Democracy and Education*. New York: Macmillan Co., 1924.

Dissent (1954-).

Efron, Arthur. "In Defense of Norman O. Brown." *Dissent* 15 (September-October 1968):451-55.

Elkind, David. "Wilhelm Reich—The Psychoanalyst as Revolutionary." *New York Times Magazine*, 18 April 1971.

Ellul, Jacques. *The Technological Society*. New York: Random House, Vintage Books, 1967.

Feuer, Lewis. *The Conflict of Generations*. New York: Basic Books, 1969.

Fleming, Donald, and Bailyn, Bernard, eds. *The Intellectual Migration: Europe and America, 1939-1960*. Vol. 2 of *Perspectives in American History*. Cambridge, Mass.: Charles Warren Center, 1968.

Freud, Sigmund. *The Basic Writings of Sigmund Freud*. New York: Random House, Modern Library, 1938.

——. *Beyond the Pleasure Principle*. New York: Bantam Books, 1959.

——. *Civilization and Its Discontents*. Garden City, N.Y.: Doubleday Co., Anchor Books, 1931.

——. *The Ego and the Id*. New York: W. W. Norton & Co., 1962.

——. *New Introductory Lectures on Psychoanalysis*. New York: W. W Norton & Co., 1964.

——. *Sigmund Freud: A General Selection*. Garden City, N.Y.: Doubleday & Co., Anchor Books, 1957.

Friedenberg, Edgar. "The Thought of Norman O. Brown." *TriQuarterly* 12 (Spring 1968):43-66.

Fromm, Erich. "The Human Implications of Instinctivistic Radicalism." *Dissent* 2 (Autumn 1955):342-49.

Gerth, Hans, and Mills, C. W. *From Max Weber*. New York: Oxford University Press, 1958.

Goodman, Paul. *Adam and His Works: Collected Stories*. New York: Random House, Vintage Books, 1968.

———. *Compulsory Mis-Education and the Community of Scholars.* New York: Random House, Vintage Books, 1966.

———. *Drawing the Line.* New York: Random House, 1946, 1962.

———. *The Empire City.* New York: Macmillan Co., 1959, 1964.

———. *5 Years.* New York: Brussel & Brussel, 1966.

———. *Growing Up Absurd.* New York: Random House, Vintage Books, 1960.

———. *Hawkweed.* New York: Random House, Vintage Books, 1967.

———. *Homespun of Oatmeal Gray.* New York: Random House, Vintage Books, 1970.

———. *Making Do.* New York: Macmillan Co., 1963.

———. *New Reformation: Notes of a Neolithic Conservative.* New York: Alfred A. Knopf, 1970.

———. *People or Personnel* and *Like a Conquered Province.* New York: Random House, Vintage Books, 1968.

———. *The Society I Live in Is Mine.* New York: American Heritage Publishing Co., Horizon Books, 1962.

———. *Utopian Essays and Practical Proposals.* New York: Random House, Vintage Books, 1964.

———, and Goodman, Percival. *Communitas.* New York: Random House, Vintage Books, 1947, 1960.

———, with Perls, Frederick, and Hefferline, Ralph. *Gestalt Therapy.* New York: Dell Publishing Co., Delta Books, 1951.

Graubard, Allen. "Herbert Marcuse—One Dimensional Pessimism." *Dissent* 15 (May-June 1968):216-28.

Habermas, Jürgen, ed. *Antworten auf Herbert Marcuse.* Frankfurt-am-Main: Suhrkamp, 1968.

Hofstadter, Richard. *Anti-Intellectualism in American Life.* New York: Alfred A. Knopf, 1964.

Johnston, Thomas. *Freud and Political Thought.* New York: Citadel Press, 1965.

Jones, Ernest. *The Life and Work of Sigmund Freud.* Edited by Steven Marcus and Lionel Trilling. Garden City, N.Y.: Doubleday & Co., Anchor Books, 1963.

Kateb, George. "The Political Thought of Herbert Marcuse." *Commentary* 49 (January 1970):48-63.

Keniston, Kenneth. *The Uncommitted.* New York: Dell Publishing Co., Delta Books, 1967.

———. *Young Radicals.* New York: Harcourt, Brace & World, Harvest Books, 1968.

Kettler, David. "The Vocation of Radical Intellectuals." *Politics and Society* 1 (November 1970):23-50.

Lasch, Christopher. *The New Radicalism in America, 1889-1963.* New York: Alfred A. Knopf, 1965.

Lichtheim, George. "Forward to Utopia." *The Concept of Ideology.* New York: Random House, Vintage Books, 1967. Pp. 177-89.

——. "From Marx to Hegel: Reflections on Georg Lukacs, T. W. Adorno and Herbert Marcuse." *Tri-Quarterly* 12 (Spring 1968):5-42.

Lifton, Robert Jay. "Protean Man." *Partisan Review* 35 (Winter 1968):13-27.

MacIntyre, Alasdair. *Herbert Marcuse.* New York: Viking Press, 1970.

Manuel, Frank, ed. *Utopias and Utopian Thought.* Boston: Beacon Press, 1967.

Marcuse, Herbert. *Eros and Civilization.* New York: Random House, Vintage Books, 1962.

——. *An Essay on Liberation.* Boston: Beacon Press, 1969.

——. *Five Lectures.* Boston: Beacon Press, 1970.

——. *Kultur und Gesellschaft.* I and II. Frankfurt-am-Main: Suhrkamp, 1965.

——. *Negations.* Boston: Beacon Press, 1969.

——. *One-Dimensional Man.* Boston: Beacon Press, 1964.

——. *Reason and Revolution.* Boston: Beacon Press, 1960.

——. "Remarks on a Redefinition of Culture." *Science and Culture.* Edited by Gerald Holton. Boston: Beacon Press, 1967. Pp. 218-35.

——. "Repressive Tolerance." In *A Critique of Pure Tolerance.* Boston: Beacon Press, 1969.

——. "Socialism in the Developed Countries." *International Socialist Journal* 2 (April 1965):139-52.

——. *Soviet Marxism.* New York: Random House, Vintage Books, 1961.

Morgan, Thomas. "How Hieronymous Bosch (XVth C) and Norman O. Brown (XXth C) Would Change the World." *Esquire* 59, no. 3 (March 1963): 42-47, 105.

Myer, Donald. *The Positive Thinkers.* Garden City, N.Y.: Doubleday & Co., Anchor Books, 1966.

Nelson, Benjamin. *Freud and the Twentieth Century.* Cleveland and New York: World Publishing Co., Meridian Books, 1957.

New York Review of Books (1963-).

Partisan Review (1945-).

Passmore, John. "Paradise Now." *Encounter* 35 (November 1970): 3-21.

Politics (1944-49).

Reich, Charles. *The Greening of America.* New York: Random House, 1970.

Reich, Ilse Ollendorff. *Wilhelm Reich: A Personal Biography.* With an introduction by Paul Goodman. New York: St. Martin's Press, 1969.

Reich, Wilhelm. *Character Analysis*. New York: Farrar, Straus & Giroux, Noonday Press, 1967.

——. *The Discovery of the Orgone: The Function of the Orgasm*. New York: Farrar, Straus & Giroux, Noonday Press, 1961.

——. *Listen, Little Man*. New York: Orgone Institute Press, 1948.

——. *Die Massenpsychologie de Faschismus*. Kopenhagen-Prag-Zürich: Verlag für Sexualpolitik, 1933.

——. *Reich Speaks of Freud*. New York: Farrar, Straus & Giroux, Noonday Press, 1967.

——. *Selected Writings*. New York: Farrar, Straus & Giroux, Noonday Press, 1961.

——. *The Sexual Revolution*. New York: Farrar, Straus & Giroux, Noonday Press, 1962.

Rieff, Philip. *Freud: The Mind of the Moralist*. Garden City, N.Y.: Doubleday & Co., Anchor Books, 1961.

——. *The Triumph of the Therapeutic*. New York: Harper & Row, Harper Torchbooks, 1968.

Riesman, David. *Individualism Reconsidered*. Garden City, N.Y.: Doubleday & Co., Anchor Books, 1955.

Roazen, Paul. *Freud: Political and Social Thought*. New York: Alfred A. Knopf, 1968.

Robinson, Paul. *The Freudian Left*. New York: Harper & Row, Harper Torchbooks, 1969.

Roszak, Theodore. *The Making of a Counter Culture*. Garden City, N.Y.: Doubleday & Co., Anchor Books, 1969.

Ruitenbeek, Hendrik. *Freud and America*. New York: Macmillan Co., 1966.

Salmagundi. No. 10-11. Fall, 1969 and Winter, 1970.

Schaar, John. *Escape from Authority*. New York: Harper & Row, Harper Torchbooks, 1961.

Sedgewick, Peter. "Natural Science and Human Theory." *The Socialist Register*. 1965.

Seeley, John. *The Americanization of the Unconscious*. New York: International Science Press, 1967.

Slater, Philip. *The Pursuit of Loneliness*. Boston: Beacon Press, 1970.

Spitz, David. "On Pure Tolerance: A Critique of Criticism." *Dissent* 13 (September-October 1966):510-25.

Therborn, Goran. "The Frankfurt School." *New Left Review* 63 (September-October 1970):65-96.

Trilling, Lionel. *Beyond Culture*. New York: Viking Press, Compass Books, 1968.

——. *Freud and the Crisis of Our Culture*. Boston: Beacon Press, 1955.

——. *The Liberal Imagination*. Garden City, N.Y.: Doubleday & Co., Anchor Books, 1957.

Veblen, Thorstein. *The Portable Veblen.* Edited by Max Lerner. New York: Viking Press, 1948.

Ward, Lester Frank. *Lester Frank Ward and the Welfare State.* Edited by Henry Steele Commager. New York: Bobbs-Merrill Co., 1966.

Weber, Max. *The Protestant Ethic and the Spirit of Capitalism.* New York: Charles Scribner's Sons, 1958.

White, Morton. *Social Thought in America.* Boston: Beacon Press, 1957.

Why-Resistance (1943-49).

Wiebe, Robert. *The Search for Order: 1877-1920.* New York: Hill & Wang, 1967.

Die Zeitschrift für Sozialforschung (1932-39).

INDEX

A

Adams, Henry, 15, 16
Advanced industrial society, 4, 13, 80, 117, 145, 147, 148, 153, 155, 158, 175; Marcuse's critique of, 131, 138-44; and the Protestant Ethic, 177
Age of Reform, The (Hofstadter), 10
Anarchism, 34, 35, 37, 39, 41, 42, 43, 72, 78, 80, 86, 87, 113
Arendt, Hannah, 175
Aristotle, 141, 181
Armies of the Night (Mailer), 79

B

Barth, Karl, 48
Beats, the, 101, 102, 104
Bell, Daniel, 139, 173, 175; and the end of ideology, 11-13
Benjamin, Walter, 155
Bettelheim, Bruno, 189-90
Beyond the Pleasure Principle (Freud), 54-55
Boorstin, Daniel, 190; as consensus historian, 11, 12
Bottomore, T. B., 13, 30
Bourne, Randolph, 4, 40, 43, 106; and ethic of youth, 24-25; and educational reform, 25; as critic of social engineering, 27; and Veblen, 27; and the generational struggle, 27
Brown, J. A. C., 59
Brown, Norman O., 5, 6, 7, 8, 50, 72, 173, 174, 175, 176, 179, 182, 191, 193; and Marcuse, 157, 161, 163; and Wilhelm Reich, 157, 169; as a religious thinker, 157, 172; acceptance of body and death, 158-59; on polymorphous perversity, 159; on repression, 159-61; on sublimation, 161; the Dionysian ego, 161; critique of science and technology, 163; critique of time, 163-64; and Nietzsche, 166-67, 172; as enthusiast, 167; on Man's fall, 168; reality as energy, 168-69; symbolic consciousness, 169; Marcuse on, 170-71; abandonment of social thought, 172
Burnham, James, 33

C

Capitalism, 14, 162, 192
Character Analysis (W. Reich), 65-67, 70
Chiaromonte, Nicola, 38, 39
Civilization and Its Discontents (Freud), 55-59, 63, 64
Clair, Louis, 41-42
Cleaver, Eldridge, 6, 113
Commentary, 79, 100, 102
Communitas (Paul and Percival Goodman), 49, 88-91, 105, 114, 115, 141, 144
Community of Scholars, The (Goodman), 109
Conant, James Bryant, 100, 107